FATHER McBRIDE'S

COLLEGE CATECHISM

Books by Father McBride

*The Kingdom and the Glory: Commentary on Matthew
*To Love and Be Loved by Jesus: Commentary on Mark
*The Human Face of Jesus: A Commentary on Luke
*The Divine Presence of Jesus: A Commentary on John
*The Gospel of the Holy Spirit: A Commentary on Acts
*The Second Coming of Jesus: A Commentary on Apocalypse
* Essentials of the Faith
* Father McBride's Teen Catechism
*Father McBride's Family Catechism
*Millennium: End of Time or a Jubilee?
Invitation: A Catholic Learning Guide
The Seven Last Words of Jesus
A Retreat with Pope John XXIII
The Story of the Church
Catholic Evangelization
Images of Jesus
Images of Mary
Saints Are People

Other books by Father McBride

Homilies for the New Liturgy
Catechetics: A Theology of Proclamation
A Short Course on the Bible
The Human Dimensions of Catechetics
The Pearl and the Seed
Heschel: Religious Educator Growing in Grace: Bible History
Christian Formation of Catholic Education
Year of the Lord: Cycles A,B,C
Father McBride's Homily Reflections: Cycles A,B,C
Death Shall Have No Dominion
Creative Teaching in Christian Education
The Quest For Content in Christian Education
Catechists Never Stop Learning
The Ten Commandments: Sounds of Love From Sinai
Staying Faithful

*Published by Our Sunday Visitor, Inc.

FATHER McBRIDE'S

COLLEGE CATECHISM

Alfred McBride, O. Praem.

Our Sunday Visitor Publishing Division
Our Sunday Visitor, Inc.
Huntington, Indiana 46750

Nihil Obstat
Rev. Romanus Cessario, O.P.

Imprimatur
✠ Bernard Cardinal Law
July 19, 2000

Scripture quotations and references are reproduced from *The New American Bible,* copyright © 1970 by the Confraternity of Christian Doctrine, Washington, D.C. All rights reserved.
Psalm texts are taken from *The Psalms: A New Translation,* copyright *The Grail,* England, 1963.
Excerpts from the English translation of the *Catechism of the Catholic Church* for use in the United States of America, copyright © 1994, United States Catholic Conference, Inc. — Libreria Editrice Vaticana. Used with permission.
If any copyrighted materials have been inadvertently used in this work without proper credit being given in one form or another, please notify Our Sunday Visitor in writing so that future printings may be corrected accordingly.
Copyright © 2000 by Our Sunday Visitor
Publishing Division,
Our Sunday Visitor, Inc.

ISBN: 0-87973-346-2
LCCCN: 00-130465
Cover design by Rebecca Heaston
Illustrations by Steve Erspamer
PRINTED IN THE UNITED STATES OF AMERICA

Contents

INTRODUCTION

"I declare [the **Catechism of the Catholic Church]** *to be a sure norm for teaching the Faith."*

Fidei Depositum, Pope John Paul II[1]

Over ten million people have purchased and begun to study and pray over the *Catechism of the Catholic Church* since its publication in 1992. This phenomenal outpouring of interest in the *Catechism* illustrates the widespread hunger for a comprehensive and systematic presentation of the Catholic faith.

At the same time there also seems to be a need for a guidebook to walk people through the *Catechism*. That is the purpose of this College Catechism. It is not a substitute for the real thing. Users of this book are encouraged to go directly to the *Catechism* and explore its thorough presentation of Catholic teaching.

As the title implies, this book is directed to college and university students. It will be most useful in Catholic campus ministry programs both in Catholic colleges and universities as well as in secular ones.

This text will be of value for RCIA programs, inquiry classes, catechetical study groups, and evangelization outreach by campus ministries. It will be helpful, of course, for individual faith searching as well.

Today's college students present a diverse religious situation. Some students are baptized, practicing Catholics. Others are not baptized, but are searching for meaning and purpose in life. Some are experiencing serious crises of faith, while others are coming to faith and are ready to make a decision.

It is understood here that the best catechesis occurs in the context of a wider pastoral care of young people, especially when this care deals with the problems affecting their lives. A good catechesis also deals with the beliefs, attitudes, and practices of people — and not just with intellectual content alone.

Spiritual direction will make the use of this book more effective. The leaders of the catechesis should be open to the sensibilities and problems of the contemporary college student.

This catechesis deals with the four major thrusts of the *Catechism*: (1) Creed — The Faith Teachings of the Church; (2) Liturgy — Celebration of the Sacraments; (3) Morality — Life in Christ through Covenant and Commandments; (4) Prayer — Growth in Spirituality and the Model of the Our Father.

It is hoped that today's young adults can be brought to appreciate the reality of truth and authentic freedom as taught in the Gospel. Along with this, they need conscience formation and an education in love. This should prepare them for a Christian involvement in society and a missionary responsibility to the world.

How To Use This College Catechism

The major elements in each chapter are as follows:
1. Introductory faith story
2. Question followed by three replies:
   A. Some say . . . A wrong or inadequate reply
   B. The *Catechism* teaches. . . A short summary of the *Catechism's* reply to the question, along with three questions followed by answers taken from the *Catechism* itself.
   C. Response to objections. . . A brief reply to the objections raised in part A, along with some further clarification of Catholic teaching on the issue.
3. For Dialog: Open-ended questions designed to help the user probe the teaching more deeply and make applications to one's personal and social life.
4. Prayer
5. Glossary: Definitions of some Catholic vocabulary terms that need clarification.

The best way to use this guidebook is in some group setting, whether that be a study session, a preparation for a sacrament, a deepening of the faith of committed Catholics, an inquiry group, a method for stirring up greater societal involvement or missionary spirit.

Opening Story. The opening story is meant to engage the user's imagination by attaching the faith teaching to an experience from the life of a saint or other outstanding witness from Scripture or the history of the Church. The more we can help our young adults to see gospel teachings enacted in real life the better. The participants can be invited to give their reactions to this story or tell personal stories, which are stimulated by the narrative provided.

The Question and Three Responses. Since college and university students usually function in a world of questions, it seemed suitable to offer them a catechesis framed around a question. Each question flows from one aspect of the catechetical teaching proposed. Three responses to the question are provided:

Some say. . . This is a wrong or inadequate response. It is taken from various objections to a Catholic teaching either arising from the culture or from people of other religious persuasions. This approach is not meant to be divisive or to stir up any kind of militancy. Generally, it is hoped that the objection is presented fairly. We often come to understand our own positions more clearly when we hear an opposing position. A contradictory teaching frequently wakes us up to reflect on our own beliefs and serves to make us think more deeply about them.

The Catechism teaches. . . The *Catechism* offers us a sure norm of faith. This does not mean it presents us with every imaginable question about the faith. But it does give us a comprehensive, systematic presentation of the faith in such a way that we have a set of principles, teachings, and norms from which we can confidently respond to numerous other questions and discover ways to apply the faith to our lives.

This section always begins with a short summary of what the *Catechism* has to say about the objection as well as what the teaching is all about. For example, chapter three is about the gift of faith. The objection claims that faith isn't necessary and that many people of good will seem to get along very well without it. The reply from the *Catechism* first notes that faith is just as much a way of knowing as reason, that there is no contradiction between the proper use of reason and faith, and that faith would enrich the person of good will. The section then proceeds to outline the many dimensions of faith.

Finally, there are always three questions followed by answers taken directly from the *Catechism*. The main reason for doing this is to open the user to direct contact with the *Catechism's* own words in the hope that it will invite the reader to go to the source itself for further study and reflection.

Response to objections. . . This section directly addresses the shortcomings in the objections. It does not try to deal with every aspect of the objection, but rather offers a general reason why the position is unacceptable to Catholics. At the same time, this section frequently includes further clarification of the Catholic teaching under consideration.

Every effort has been made to present this process in a tone that avoids polemics. A civil discourse is desirable despite dealing with obvious disagreements. Dialogue produces more light than heat, without relativizing the issues. In this matter we follow the example of one of the Church's greatest catechists, St. Robert Bellarmine, who dealt frequently with controversy during the Reformation, yet found a way to present the opposition fairly and the Church's teachings accurately.

For Dialog. After the question and the three responses, there are sets of questions which are designed to involve the participants in the conversation in such a way that they are drawn to see what the Catholic teaching means for them and how they could apply it to their personal lives and social and societal situations.

Ideally, the participants will be prompted to raise a host of their own questions. No one leader can reasonably expect to be able to answer all such questions that may arise in a lively exchange. It is advisable for the participants to bring a copy of the *Catechism* along for the meeting in order to look up responses. It will also help to keep a Bible on hand, with several commentaries such as the *Jerome Biblical Commentaries*, both old and new, and other useful resources.

Gatherings, however, should be more than parry and thrust of intellectual ideas and questions. These meetings are meant to be invitations to faith and community, called by the Father, around the Son, and brooded over by the Spirit. These should be events of faith growth and not just opportunities for one-upmanship. Spiritual cooperation more than rivalry-inspired competition is more desirable.

The goal is salvation from sin, the gift of divine life, obtained by Jesus Christ, a hoped-for involvement in the Church's sacramental and moral life, and an outcome that improves the social order as well as an evangelizing energy toward others.

A word needs to be said about evangelization. Catholics are normally uncomfortable with this, partly because it is identified with the hard-sell preachers found on radio and television and on street corners in busy cities. This is an evangelization that seems to force itself on people. This is not Catholic evangelizing.

Catholic evangelization *proposes but does not impose* the faith on anyone. Our evangelizing is an invitation to faith, not a burdening of the others' conscience nor a threatening and pushy manner of presenting the gospel. In its simplest form it is a loving, sharing of our faith with others. It works best when the presenter is also a vivid witness of the faith that is offered.

Love in action is the most attractive evangelizing possible. But, of course, we must also be ready to explain the gospel and bear oral witness to Jesus as well.

The *General Directory for Catechesis* notes that evangelizing is an essential part of catechesis, not just for prospective converts but even for cradle Catholics. Within the core of every catechesis lies the call to believe in Jesus more deeply and love him more fervently. This is the evangelizing moment in any catechesis.

Finally there is a small glossary at the end of each chapter. Catholicism, like any other institution or community has an official vocabulary. Many of

these terms were hard-won words bred in the heat of religious controversies in centuries past. Now they have become code words, short cuts to the meaning of many central teachings of the Church. They are provided here as a little dictionary of terms to enable the users to communicate more easily with one another.

In conclusion, it must be said again that this guidebook is meant to open the participants to the *Catechism of the Catholic Church* itself. It would seem that campus ministries on college and university campuses of all kinds would be the proper setting for using this guidebook. Group usage seems more valuable, but certainly individual use is also encouraged.

If faith in Jesus Christ and active membership in the Church and the spiritual and moral improvement of our culture and society are the outcome, then the effort to produce this book will have been worthwhile.

Praised be Jesus Christ now and forever.
Ave Maria.

Endnote

1. Apostolic Constitution *Fidei Depositum*, the Deposit of Faith, October 11, 1992, John Paul II, *Catechism of the Catholic Church* (Citta del Vaticano: Libreria Editrice Vaticana, 1997), paragraph 3.

Chapter 1

THE LONGING FOR GOD
IS A GIFT OF LOVE

CCC 26-49

"Wounded by love, they longed to look upon God with their bodily eyes. It is intolerable for love not to see the object of its longing."

St. Peter Chrysologus

Beauty Opened Him to God

Thomas Merton recalls the following scene from his childhood. "The sound of the churchbells came to us across the bright fields. I was playing in front of the house and stopped to listen. Suddenly all the birds began to sing in the trees above my head, and the sound of the birds singing and the churchbells ringing lifted up my heart with joy. I said to my father, 'All the birds are in their church. Why don't we go to church?'"

Fifty years ago, this Trappist monk published the story of his conversion from being a young man with no religion to one who found Jesus and the Catholic Church. His autobiography, *The Seven Storey Mountain*, became a bestseller and has charmed and inspired thousands of people ever since. In examining the various ways in which God brought him to faith, Merton noted that the experience of beauty awakened his longing for God.

During a visit to Rome in the 1930s, the young seeker was surprised that he was much more inspired by the art and architecture of churches than by the temples and statues of imperial Rome.

"I found myself looking into churches rather than ruined temples. . . The effect of this discovery was tremendous. After all the vapid, boring semi-pornographic statuary of the empire, what a thing it was to come upon the genius of an art full of spiritual vitality . . . an art that was tremendously serious and alive and eloquent and urgent in all it had to say."

The ancient frescoes of saints moved him to a felt knowledge of the sacred. Divine beauty shone through the human art and sowed seeds of invitation to faith in the young seeker. "I was no longer visiting these churches merely for the art. There was something else that attracted me: a kind of interior peace. I loved to be in these holy places." This is how God our Father began to call Merton to a realization of his divine reality.[1]

Is it Possible for Us to Know Whether God Exists?

Some say... It is never possible to know God's existence. We cannot know something or someone that is beyond what we can see with our eyes or hear with our ears. Our mind is subject to the five senses and has been able to use this capacity to create the wonders of technology, but it cannot go further than that.

Karl Marx rightly taught that the notion of God, invented by religion, was used by the powerful to control the masses. The collusion of religion, politics, and economic interests enslaved the poor and used the idea of God and a so-called future life of happiness to distract them from dissatisfaction in this life. Religion was a drug, the opium of the people.

Sigmund Freud, in his examination of the subconscious, concluded that the idea of God was an illusion. God is a psychological projection, a creation of an inner need for a universal father figure. This illusion was an unhealthy way of avoiding personal responsibility and growing reflectively by facing one's unresolved conflicts. People needed a god, so they projected one.

Charles Darwin and his disciples argued that the idea of God belonged to a primitive phase of human evolution. It was an invention of people, in their early phase of evolving, designed to handle the cosmic threats of lightning, thunder, famine, storms at sea, the scorching sun, and the changing of the moon. Placating "God" helped them to deal with the mysteries of nature over which they seemed to have no control. Today, our advanced stage of evolution has swept away the need to have a god.

The thinkers of the Enlightenment in the eighteenth century prepared the way for this estrangement from God. They still retained the myth of God's existence, but claimed this God did little more than create the universe and leave the rest to us. God was a clockmaker who wound up the cosmic clock and then lost interest in us. Their belief system was called Deism. Logically, people concluded that if God ignored them, they would have no concern about him. Eventually, they concluded there was no God to be concerned about. Reason was all we needed to manage matters.

We cannot know God for there is no God to know.

The Catechism *teaches ...* "The desire for God is written in the human heart, because man is created by God and for God; and God never ceases to draw man to himself." (CCC 27)

People today are asking once again the deepest questions about the purpose of human life. What does it mean to be human? What is the meaning of sickness, evil, and death, which persist despite all the remarkable progress we have made? What are all these achievements worth? What can we do for the world and what can the world do for us? What will happen to us after death?

These questions about human existence are intimately related to the question about God's existence. The questions challenge the mind, one of our priceless human gifts. But the answers do not belong to the mind alone, essential though it be. We must also be aware of what the will demands of us, and above all, we must consult the mysterious drive of the human heart.

Blaise Pascal wrote that the heart has reasons of which the mind does not know. God has planted in our hearts the hunger and longing for the infinite, for nothing less than God. St. Augustine, the theologian of the heart, said it best: "Our hearts are restless until they rest in you." (CCC 30)

The *Catechism* presents two lines of argument that can guide us to know God. These approaches have been called "proofs" for the existence of God, not proofs in the sense that natural science uses the term, but "converging and convincing" (CCC 31)arguments that open us to the truth. These pathways to God are found in the physical world and in the experience of the human person.

(1) The World. St. Paul writes that the invisible things of God can be known from the visible results in creation. (Rom 1:19-20) St. Thomas Aquinas applied that scriptural principle in his analysis of five aspects of the world: motion, becoming, contingency, beauty, and order. He argued that these realities point back to a First Cause who is himself not caused. This cause we call God.

(2) The Human Person. When we examine our humanity we find five traits that ultimately involve God. They are signs of our inner spirituality. They are the seeds that lead us to know God and be open to faith.

a. We are basically open to truth and beauty.

b. We all sense the need to be morally good.

c. We treasure our freedom and are willing to defend it.

d. We experience the voice of our consciences.

e. We have longings that are limitless.

These messages from the world and the human person are voices that

open us to God. They represent the goodness within our nature that assures us our longing for God is a gift of love from God himself.

1. Have people always hungered for God?

"Throughout history down to the present day, men have given expression to their quest for God in their religious beliefs and behavior: in their
prayers, sacrifices, rituals, meditations, and so forth. These forms of religious expression, despite the ambiguities they often bring with them, are
so universal that one may well call man a *religious being*." (Cf. Acts 17:26-28)
(CCC 28)

2. Why do people reject God and religion?

"This 'intimate and vital bond of man to God' (GS 19,1) can be forgotten, overlooked, or even explicitly rejected by man.[GS 19,1] Such attitudes can have different causes: revolt against evil in the world; religious
ignorance or indifference; the cares and riches of the world; the scandal of
bad example on the part of believers; currents of thought hostile to religion; finally, the attitude of sinful man that makes him hide from God out
of fear and flee his call." (Cf. GS 19-21, Mt 13:22, Gen 3:8-10, Jon 1:3)
(CCC 29)

3. How do the world and the human person lead us to God?

"The world, and man, attest that they contain within themselves neither their first principle nor their final end, but rather that they participate in Being itself, which alone is without origin or end. Thus, in different ways, man can come to know there exists a reality which is the first
cause and final end of all things, a reality 'that everyone calls God.'" (St.
Thomas Aquinas, *Summa Theologica* 1,2,3) (CCC 34)

Response to objections

The rationalism that was held
by the Enlightenment thinkers
and carried to extremes by
Marx, Freud, Darwin, and others is gradually fading away. As this happens,
their militant atheism is also declining. If anything remains from that period, it is an agnosticism that is characterized by a seeking and searching
for spiritual realities. Rationalism had claimed that human knowledge is
primarily a sensory experience. Classical philosophy agreed about the role
of the senses in knowing. There is nothing in the mind that was not first in
the senses.

But that is not the end of the story. We know colors, melodies, shapes,
aromas, and sweet and salty foods. We also know extra-sensual and global
realities, something beyond the empirical. Newer scholars have opened
the way for us. Paul Ricoeur has probed the values and teachings of the
world of symbols. Mircea Eliade has given us a fresh slant on the philoso-

phy of religion from the aspect of anthropology. Martin Buber's analysis of dialogue, that our human existence is always a co-existing in relation to others, removes our attachment to a rationalistic view of human nature. We develop ourselves in I-Thou relationships, and above all, as scripture teaches, in an I-THOU relationship with God.

These post-Enlightenment developments that explore the human dimension in depth are welcome initiatives that should both encourage those who search for God and lay the groundwork for rediscovering God's presence in creation and the human person. They are the pre-dispositions for coming to a personal relationship with God that is made possible by revelation.

For dialog

1. If you wanted to persuade an unbeliever — but one who was also a searcher for truth — to come to a knowledge of God's existence, how would you go about it? Which five paths to God's existence have the greater appeal for you: St. Thomas Aquinas' analysis of the world or the *Catechism's* traits of the human person? Explain the reasons for your choice. Or, are they equally attractive?

2. Read again paragraph 29 of the *Catechism* which lists six reasons why people either forget their religious nature or never became aware of it in the first place. From your experience, how are people you know affected by one or other of these attitudes? What might you do to help them back to God?

3. What signs do you see in today's culture of a return to God? Why is this happening?

Prayer

O God, you are my God, for you I long;
for you my soul is thirsting.
My body pines for you
like a dry weary land without water.
So I gaze on you in the sanctuary
to see your strength and your glory.

Psalm 63: 2-3

Glossary

Proofs for God's Existence — "Proofs" drawn from the world and the human person, not in the sense of proofs from natural science, but "converging and convincing" paths that draw people to the truth.

Religious Nature — The *Catechism* teaches that every man and woman is born with a religious impulse and drive toward God.

Summa Theologica — St. Thomas Aquinas (1225-1274), Dominican teacher and writer, authored this explanation of Catholic theology in 1323. It still stands as a primary doctrinal defense for Catholic belief and teaching.

"The world is charged with the grandeur of God."
Gerard Manley Hopkins

Endnote
1. Thomas Merton, *The Seven Storey Mountain* (Harvest, 1999).

Chapter 2

GOD REVEALS HIS LOVING PLAN
CCC 36-143

"O Wisdom, O holy Word of God, you govern all creation with your strong yet tender care. Come and show your people the way to salvation."
Canticle of Mary Antiphon for December 17

Look for the Son — That's the Plan

A man who lived in New York was rich in almost every way. His estate was worth millions. He owned houses, land, antiques, and cattle. Although on the outside he had it all, he was very unhappy on the inside. His wife was growing old, and the couple was childless. He had always wanted a little boy to carry on the family legacy.

Miraculously, his wife became pregnant in her later years and she gave birth to a little boy. The boy was severely handicapped, but the father loved him with his whole heart. When the boy was five, his mom died. The dad drew closer to his special son. At age thirteen, the boy's birth defects cost him his life and the father died soon after from a broken heart.

The estate was auctioned before hundreds of bidders. The first item offered was a painting of the boy. No one bid. They waited like vultures for the riches.

Finally, the poor housemaid, who had helped raise the boy offered $5 for the picture and easily took the bid. To everyone's shock, the auctioneer ripped open a handwritten note from the back of the picture. This is what it said — "To the person who thinks enough of my son to buy this painting, to this person I give my entire estate."

The auction was over. The greedy crowd walked away in shock and dismay.

In God's loving plan for us, we will discover that God is personal, a Father who is prepared to give us his entire estate if we believe in and accept his only Son. God loves us so much he knew he would have to reveal this secret to us.

Is Divine Revelation Necessary?

Some say... Divine revelation is not needed. If we want to find God we have all the human resources to make this possible. Even the Catholic Church claims that we can discover God on our own through observing the world and the dynamics of the human person. These are "converging and convincing" (CCC 31) arguments that are fully sufficient to produce all we need to know about God. St. Thomas Aquinas himself wrote that beings should not be multiplied without necessity. So, why have a special revelation when we already possess the skills to come to God?

Moreover, what people say is revelation in the Bible introduces more problems than it appears to solve. The texts are often repetitive, contradictory, and contrary to what we know from science and history. Because of this there are a large number of competing interpretations of God, producing rival religions, which are mutually exclusive. Would it not be better to stay with reason, which would offer people an orderly understanding of God?

Finally, revelation has complicated what ought to be simple. Reason can demonstrate the utter simplicity of God. Revelation asks us to accept views of God that are obscure and unnecessarily resistant to plausible explanations. How is the modern mind going to cope with imponderable revelations about a holy Trinity, an Incarnation, a virgin birth? Reason can deal with God in a pure and simple manner.

Revelation is not needed.

The Catechism teaches ... "It pleased God in his goodness and wisdom, to reveal himself and make known the mystery of his will. His will was that men should have access to the Father, through Christ the Word made flesh, in the Holy Spirit, and thus become sharers in the divine nature." (*Dei Verbum* 2; cf. Eph 1:9, 2:18; 2Pt 1:4) (CCC 51)

Reason can know a good deal *about* God, but revelation makes it possible to know and love God himself. Revelation unfolds God's loving plan to save us from our sins and to invite us to share in divine life itself. No amount of unaided thinking could arrive at such a truth. God freely chose to share these wondrous secrets with us; otherwise, we could not know them. Love does such things.

Over many centuries, through words and deeds, God gradually revealed his inner life and his concern for our salvation. In this history of salvation, God formed covenants with Noah, Abraham, Isaac, Jacob, and Joseph. After the patriarchs, God selected the people of Israel as his living witness to the world. Through Moses he established a covenant with them at Sinai and gave them the commandments by which they would understand how to live the covenant.

When they fell away from covenant living, God raised up the prophets — Elijah, Isaiah, Jeremiah, Ezekiel, Daniel, and others — to call them back to the paths of virtue and maintain their faith that a Messiah would come one day to save them. When they needed insight into the puzzles and mysteries of suffering, exile, death, and evil, God brought them the wisdom of Job and Sirach and the wise witness of holy women such as Sarah, Rebecca, Miriam, Rachel, Ruth, Deborah, Hannah, Judith, and Esther. The greatest woman among them is Mary. All these holy people sustained the hope for a Messiah.

Finally, in the fullness of time, God sent Jesus Christ, the Son of God made man to be the savior of the world and the complete revelation of God. St. John of the Cross described this truth in the following words:

"In giving us his Son, his only Word (for he possesses no other) he spoke everything to us at once in his sole Word — and he had no more to say. . . because what he spoke before to the prophets in parts, he has now spoken all at once by giving us the All Who is His Son."[1]

Handing on the Faith — How Revelation Was Transmitted

Revelation comes to us through *Apostolic Tradition*. What does this mean? Jesus Christ was the fullness of revelation by his words and deeds. He trained and commissioned his apostles to preach and witness this revelation: his gospel of salvation from sin and the gift of divine life.

He showed them how to proclaim and witness the kingdom of love, justice, and mercy, promised by the prophets and fulfilled in the paschal mystery. He sent them the Holy Spirit to remind them of this Great Commission, to give them the spiritual boldness they would need, and to teach them how to apply it in their evangelizing.

Filled with the graces of Christ and the Spirit, the apostles heard and obeyed the commands of Christ to communicate and witness the revelation they received. They did this in four ways: orally, in writing, by the heroic sanctity of their lives, and by apostolic succession.

(1) Orally: They began their mission by preaching revelation in terms of the arrival of the kingdom of love, justice, and mercy and a gospel of salvation from sin and participation in God's own life. They called for the obedience of faith in this message and reception of baptism, the formation of a community of believers, the breaking of the Bread, and generosity to the

poor. They preached what Jesus taught them and what the Holy Spirit prompted them.

(2) In Writing: This message of salvation was written down by the apostles and other men associated with them, under the guidance of the Holy Spirit. The message was written in the four gospels, the Acts of the Apostles, the various epistles, and the book of Revelation.

(3) By Witnessing: The apostles practiced what they preached and lived the message of salvation and the kingdom. All of them, except St. John, suffered blood martyrdom. And St. John's mystical-like writings disclose a man magnificently united to the love of God.

(4) By Apostolic Succession: To assure the continued transmission of revelation, the apostles ordained bishops as their successors and gave them their own teaching authority as well as the power to ordain their successors.

Jesus had promised he would be with the Church until the end of time. He sent the Holy Spirit to make that possible. The visible evidence of this promise is seen in the Apostolic Tradition, characterized in the four steps outlined above.

The Way Tradition and Scripture Are Related

A. Sacred Tradition and Sacred Scripture are essentially connected. They both flow from the same wellspring — divine revelation.

B. Sacred Scripture is God's Word put down in writing by the inspiration of the Holy Spirit. At first there was no written New Testament. It took a number of years before the New Testament was completed.

C. Sacred Tradition passes on the Word of God that was entrusted to the apostles by Jesus and the Spirit. The New Testament vividly demonstrates the process of a living Tradition.

D. How is revelation to be interpreted, whether in Tradition or Scripture? The responsibility has been given to the bishops, the successors of the apostles, in communion with the pope, the successor of St. Peter, chief of the apostles. We call this teaching office the *Magisterium*.

1. What is the Apostolic Tradition?

"Christ the Lord, in whom the entire Revelation of the most high God is summed up, commanded the apostles to preach the Gospel, which had been promised beforehand by the prophets, and which he fulfilled in his own person and promulgated with his own lips. In preaching the Gospel, they were to communicate the gifts of God to all men. This Gospel was to be the source of all saving truth and moral discipline." (*Dei Verbum*, [Divine Revelation] 7; cf. Mt 28:19-20; Mk 16:15) (CCC 75)

2. How are Sacred Tradition and Sacred Scripture related?

"Sacred Tradition and Sacred Scripture, then, are bound closely together and communicate one with the other. For both of them, flowing out from the same divine well-spring, come together in some fashion to form one thing and move towards the same goal. Each of them makes present and fruitful in the Church the mystery of Christ, who promised to remain with his own "always, to the close of the age." (*Dei Verbum*, 9; Mt 28:20) (CCC 80)

3. What is the meaning of the Magisterium of the Church?

"'The task of giving an authentic interpretation of the Word of God, whether in its written form or in the form of Tradition, has been entrusted to the living, teaching office of the Church alone. Its authority in this matter has been exercised in the name of Jesus Christ.'[2] This means that the task of interpretation has been entrusted to the bishops in communion with the successor of Peter, the Bishop of Rome." (*Dei Verbum*, 10,2) (CCC 85)

Response to objections

At the first Vatican Council the bishops declared that God can be known with certainty by the exercise of human reason.[3] It is a truth of faith that we can know God — his providence and the natural law — from reason. But this is not as easy as it sounds. The effects of original sin darken the mind, weaken the will, and produce disorder in the passions. The gift of revelation offers us truths that are beyond our understanding, but also strengthens our reason to know religious and moral truths that are within its scope. Revelation helps reason to do its job such as speaking of God to all peoples, including philosophers, scientists, unbelievers, and those of other religions.

Revelation is necessary because God wants to have a loving union with us. God wants intimacy. To know about God is not the same as being in love with God. Divine Love wants to share secrets not available to reason alone. The intellect can know that God exists and that there are moral laws that bring peace, order, and happiness. But the mind alone cannot know the inner life of God and the loving plan that would save us from sin and bring us divine life.

God is indeed simplicity itself, but our path to simplicity is through complexity, as any mature person can testify. The record of revelation in the Bible is admittedly filled with many challenges regarding interpretation. That is why Christ gave the Church a Spirit-guided authority to determine true meanings. This goal is augmented by the results of the contemplation of the saints, the abiding faith of all God's people, and the rigorous work of authentic scholarship and theological research.

For dialog

1. While you know that God's existence can be known from reason reflecting on the world and human nature, you also know that revelation is a path to knowing and loving God. How would you express the need for revelation? How might revelation aid reason's own search for God? How does revelation surpass reason's quest for God?

2. Revelation comes to us in Apostolic Tradition and Scripture. Why can we say that Christianity is more than a "religion of the book"? In your own words describe how Tradition is a source of God's Word in today's Catholic Church? Why does the Church insist that Jesus and the Spirit have been with her from the start?

3. How do you see God's revelation gradually unfolding? In what ways has Scripture been a guiding force in your life? Why is the Church's teaching office (Magisterium) a true spiritual gift for us?

Prayer

We praise you, Lord, for the gift of revelation. We thank you for sharing with us the mystery of your inner life and for telling us about your loving plan to save us from our sins and invite us to share in your divine love and life. We are grateful for the revelation found in Jesus Christ and its transmission in Apostolic Tradition and Sacred Scripture. We are made confident by the grace of the Church's teaching office — the Magisterium — that enables us to have an authentic interpretation of our faith. Thank you for the love that made all of this possible.

Glossary

Revelation — The name given to the various ways that God has made known the mystery of his inner life, his loving plan to save us from our sins and give us divine life as gradually disclosed to the patriarchs, prophets, and men and women of wisdom — and above all, perfectly in Jesus Christ, Son of God made man.

Apostolic Tradition — Christ entrusted his revelation to the apostles. They communicated this in their preaching and witness. Guided by the Spirit, they passed this on to their successors, the bishops, in communion with the popes, the successors of St. Peter.

Sacred Deposit of God's Revelation — Revelation is expressed in Sacred Tradition and Sacred Scripture, which make up a single sacred deposit of God's revelation.

Magisterium — The Magisterium is the name given to the teaching office of the pope and bishops. This teaching office has been entrusted to them by Christ for the purpose of giving an authentic interpretation of God's revelation in Tradition and Scripture.

"But above all it's the Gospels that occupy my mind when I'm at prayer; my poor soul has so many needs, and yet this is the one thing needful. I'm always finding fresh lights there, hidden and enthralling meanings."

St. Thérèse of Lisieux[4]

Endnotes

1. St. John of the Cross, *The Ascent of Mount Carmel*, 2, 22, 3-5, in *The Collected Works*, tr. K. Kavanaugh, OCD, and O. Rodriguez, OCD (Washington, DC: Institute of Carmelite Studies, 1979), 179-180: LH, OR Advent, wk 2, Mon. Cf. CCC 65.
2. *Dei Verbum* 10,1; cf. Acts 2:42 (Greek); Pius XII apostolic constitution, *Munifentissimus Deus*, Nov.1, 1950, 756, taken along with the words of St. Cyprian, Letter 66,8:CSEL 3,2, 733: "The Church is the people united to its priests, the flock adhering to its Shepherd." Cf. CCC 85.
3. *Dei Filius*, 2, DS 3015.
4. St. Thérèse of Lisieux, *Story of a Soul* (Tan Books).

JOAN OF ARC

Chapter 3

FAITH IS A "YES" TO GOD AND HIS MESSAGE

CCC 144-184

"Help then, O Lord, my unbelief
And make my faith abound
To come to you when you are near
And seek where you are found."[1]

Joan of Arc Lived by Faith

The following dialogue occurred at the trial of Joan of Arc.

Bishop: Joan, are you in the state of grace?

Joan: If I am, may God keep me there. If I am not, may God put me there.[2]

These are words of a woman of faith.

When we first meet Joan of Arc, it is the early 1400s. France and England are locked into the Hundred Years War. Life in rural France is as bleak as the landscape. Joan is a determined young woman, profoundly religious. After the English burn her village, she receives a divine vision calling her to help break the siege of Orléans and see that King Charles is formally crowned and the invading army expelled from France.

How did this sixteen-year-old, uneducated peasant girl muster the maturity to save her country? Religious faith gave her both the imagination and the courage to accomplish so great a feat.

She had trouble convincing the king and the soldiers of her godly mission. But they were political pragmatists and they believed she could be useful to them. The common people rallied around her, impressed by her spirituality as well as her bravery and blunt speech.

Joan's miraculous successes on the battlefield won no great gratitude from the French King or the jealous military. No less resentful were the English who hunted her down and eventually captured her. But Joan never wavered from her commitment to God's plan.

She is captured by the English, tried by a Church court, found guilty of heresy, and burned at the stake — abandoned by the French. But God never left her side, nor did she compromise her faith. The pope revoked this sentence twenty-five years after her death. In 1920 she was canonized a saint and declared patroness of France.

God revealed a plan to her.

She responded in faith both to God and his message.

Can We Get Along Without Faith?

Some say... We do not need faith. It is better for us to live by common sense and a practical outlook on life. Faith tends to make people impractical and out of touch with the real world. Often they pay so much attention to the so-called next world, they miss what should be done in this world. It is not uncommon for them to be seen as dreamers who are out of touch. Dreamers usually waste their lives, fail to support their families properly, and cause discontent.

On the other hand there are people who claim to have faith, but in fact live a pragmatic lifestyle, compartmentalizing faith to an hour of worship a week. They are living proof that faith is useless for getting on in the world. What has faith to do with building a strong economy, discovering new ways to feed the world, and finding a cure for cancer? No, it is better to have a lively imagination, a creative impulse, and a bundle of energy to make these achievements possible.

Lastly, a positive mindset will do more good for others than faith can accomplish. Positive thinking produces healthy results. People with this attitude are always unearthing the possibilities of life. Those who start with faith seem to be occupied with the negative side of life, lamenting sin and placing burdens of guilt on those around them. They would be better off walking tall, whistling a happy tune, and putting a smile on their faces.

We can get along quite well without faith.

The Catechism teaches ... "Though faith is above reason, there can never be any real discrepancy between faith and reason. Since the same God who reveals mysteries and infuses faith has bestowed the light of reason on the human mind, God cannot deny himself, nor can truth ever contradict truth."(*Dei Filius* 4: DS 3017) (CCC 159)

Everyone agrees that reason is a way of knowing facts, truth, and reality. Not everyone realizes that faith is also a way of knowing. The difference is that faith is a way to know truths that are beyond the natural realm. Faith is the knowing process we use to apprehend the God of revelation and his revealed truths. Put more simply, faith is our capacity to respond to revelation.

If all goes as hoped for in our lives, we will receive three lights from God:

— the light of reason to know natural truths.

— the light of faith to know revealed truths.

— the light of glory to know God face to face in heaven.

The light of faith makes it possible to give our minds and hearts to God. St. Paul calls this the "obedience of faith." (Rom 1:5; 16:26) Scripture identifies Abraham as our father in faith because he obeyed God's call to leave his homeland and become the founder of a new people. (Gen 12:1-4) Read the eleventh chapter of Hebrews where the writer celebrates a number of Old Testament people who were models of the obedience of faith.

The Virgin Mary perfectly embodies this life of faith. Elizabeth said to her, "Blessed are you for having believed that what was spoken to you by the Lord would be fulfilled." (Lk 1:45) From her yes to God at the Annunciation to her silent assent at the Cross, Mary's faith never wavered. This is why the Church venerates Mary as the purest example of faith.

Faith is a Multi-Splendored Act

In paragraphs 150-175, the *Catechism* explores ten aspects of Christian faith:

(1) *Faith is personal.* The first words of the Apostles' Creed are "I believe." The "I" indicates that faith is a relationship between a human being and God. The believer effectively says, "Father, Son, and Holy Spirit, you have invited me by your act of self revelation to intimacy with you. In faith I believe you and give you my mind, heart, soul, and body. I love you."

(2) *Faith is communal.* The first words of the Nicene Creed, which we recite on Sundays are "We believe." Faith is not just an isolated act between an individual and God; it is also communal. The *Catechism* uses the expression "ecclesial," to show that faith takes place in the context of the Church. Why? Because Christ established the Church to be a community of believers and each of us needs the moral and spiritual support for our faith from others in the Church.

(3) *Faith is a human act.* Faith is a form of knowing and loving God. The Holy Spirit enlarges our minds and our hearts so that these human faculties have the ability to respond to revelation. Thus grace builds on our human nature and expands its capacities.

(4) *Faith seeks understanding.* The mysteries of faith — Trinity, Incarnation, Salvation, Church, Sacraments — are so full of meaning and depth that they invite a continuous, life-long prayerful effort to understand them and see how they apply to our lives. I may believe that Jesus is my savior, but I need years of mature reflection to appreciate what this means and how I should live because of this great gift. Theology and catechesis are two methods to help our faith seek an understanding of the richness of revelation.

(5) *Faith is certain.* Real faith fills us with conviction because God is the guarantee of the truthfulness of revelation. The truths of faith may puzzle us at times, but God's grace moves our hearts to help our minds accept their truthfulness. Cardinal Newman says that ten thousand difficulties do not make one doubt.

(6) *Faith is a friend of reason.* Faith and reason both deal with truth. God's truth does not contradict human truth since God is the author of truth wherever it appears. Research in all branches of knowledge, so long as it does not break moral laws, is not in conflict with faith.

(7) *Faith is free.* By its nature faith is a free act, hence it may never be forced on anyone. We propose faith to others. We should not try to impose on them. We offer people the option for Christ's love. We do our best to make the case for Jesus Christ by our personal witness and the energetic arts of persuasion, but we should not try compel others to believe.

(8) *Faith is belief in a message.* We have seen that faith should be personal, communal, trusting, and free. These qualities deal with faith as a relationship with God. Faith also encompasses belief in the message of revelation. Jesus said, "I am the truth." Jesus also taught, "I have the truth." Where do we find the messages of faith?

• In the Bible.
• In the Apostles' Creed, which dates from the second century and was used at baptisms.
• In the Nicene Creed, which dates from the fourth-century ecumenical councils (Nicaea and Constantinople) and clarified the doctrines of Christ's humanity and divinity and the divinity of the Holy Spirit.
• In the works of great theologians such as St. Augustine and St. Thomas Aquinas.
• In the various teachings of ecumenical councils and the Magisterium.
• In the *Catechism of the Catholic Church*.

(9) *Faith is a gift.* When St. Peter confessed that Jesus is the Messiah and

Son of God, Christ praised God for giving Peter the grace to see this. It was a gift. Peter did not know this from reason alone, from "flesh and blood," but by a gift of grace from God. Our own faith is just such a gift and grace.

(10) *Faith tastes eternal life.* Faith makes us taste in advance the light of glory by which we will see God in heaven. We are already participants in the divine life because of grace and faith. Still, this is only a hint. We walk by faith and not by sight and perceive God as in a mirror, dimly. Our experiences of injustice, evil, and death can shake our faith in the gospel. This is why we need the heroes and heroines of faith such as Mother Teresa and Maximilian Kolbe and hundreds of others. Their example bolsters our faith.

1. What is Christian faith?

"Faith is a personal adherence of the whole man to God who reveals himself. It involves an assent of the intellect and will to the self-revelation God has made through his deeds and words." (CCC 176) "[This] faith is a supernatural gift from God. In order to believe, man needs the interior helps of the Holy Spirit." (CCC 179)

2. Why is faith necessary?

"Faith is necessary for salvation. The Lord himself affirms, 'He who believes and is baptized will be saved; but he who does not believe will be condemned.'" (Mk 16:16) (CCC 183)

3. How can we persevere in faith?

"To live, grow, and persevere in the faith until the end we must nourish it with the word of God; we must beg the Lord to increase our faith. [Cf. Mk 9:24; Lk 17:5; 22:32]; it must be 'working through charity,' abounding in hope, and rooted in the faith of the Church." (Gal 5:6; Rom 15:13; cf. Jas 2:14-26) (CCC 162)

Response to objections

It is a recurrent temptation to think we can save ourselves by our own efforts. There is something appealing in the thought that common sense is the best and only guide for developing ourselves and overcoming the perplexities of life. Without a doubt common sense is a treasure and the world would be a better place if all people had more of it. Unfortunately, common sense is often in short supply and it is insufficient for achieving our salvation from sin and participating in divine life. For that we need faith.

Self-salvation is an idea that has attracted people since the fourth century when it was first promoted by Pelagius. Independence of mind and self-reliance, valuable in many ways, frequently become substitutes for grace and faith. Successful self-starters attribute their prosperity to their own energies and perseverance and they are probably right in many cases.

But everyone eventually comes up against the problems of evil, injustice, death, and sin.

To face these intractable and ever present difficulties, we need a savior, a higher power to liberate us from profound spiritual problems. God loved us enough to reveal a plan to save us in Jesus Christ. He provided us with grace and faith through his paschal mystery to overcome the evil of the world. These beautiful gifts make our common sense more sensible and our attitudes more positive. Eventually we learn that to God alone belongs the glory.

For dialog

1. How would you compare your faith as a child with the kind of faith you have today? Read again the ten characteristics of faith in this chapter. Why is it important to view faith from so many aspects? Which of these elements of faith need to develop in your own life?

2. Why do you think many people settle for self-salvation through common sense, personal effort, and a positive mental attitude? Share some stories of people you know who fit this profile. What approach would open them up to see the essential role of grace and faith in the process of salvation?

3. In your own experience what are areas where your faith needs a deeper understanding of a given teaching of revelation? How would you go about a faith search for deeper understanding in these cases? What do you think is the difference between a childlike faith and a childish one?

Prayer

Jesus, the centurion once said to you, "I believe, Lord, help my unbelief." Today I wish to echo his humble prayer and trust you will show me where my faith needs to be deepened. Give me the graces that would make this possible. Show me how faith is the right response to your gift of revelation. I repeat the words of St. Thomas the Apostle who praised you in great faith, "My Lord and my God."[3]

Glossary

Faith — Faith is the surrender of our whole human person to God. This happens individually and communally, in a free, trusting and certain manner. This gift of faith seeks understanding, works with reason, and gives us a taste of eternal life.

Apostles' Creed — This creed was developed in the second century for the Church of Rome to be used in the sacrament of baptism and it accurately reflects the faith of the apostles.

Nicene Creed — This creed resulted from the outcomes of the Councils of Nicaea (325) and First Constantinople (381) that clarified Church teachings about the humanity and divinity of Christ and the divinity of the Holy Spirit.

"Ten thousand difficulties do not make one doubt."

John Cardinal Newman

Endnotes

1. "I Walk by Faith and Not By Sight," author unknown.
2. See *Butler's Lives of the Saints*, Michael Walsh, ed. (Harper, 1991).

Chapter 4

GLORY TO THE FATHER, SON, AND SPIRIT

CCC 198-267

"Holy, Holy, Holy, Though the darkness hide thee,
Though the eye made blind by sin thy glory may not see,
Only thou art holy, there is none beside thee,
God in three Persons, blessed Trinity."

Richard Herber[1]

"Yes, I believe in God"

Cassie Bernall walked into Columbine High School on a Tuesday morning, a spring day, in 1999. She was carried out more than twenty-four hours later, a Christian witness to her faith in God.

"Do you believe in God?" a heavily armed gunman asked of the shy blond girl reading her Bible.

"Yes, I believe in God," she replied in a voice strong enough to be heard by classmates cowering under nearby tables and chairs.

"Why?" laughed the gunman wearing a long, black trenchcoat. He raised his gun and shot and killed the seventeen-year-old girl.

Her favorite movie was "Braveheart," the story of a man willing to die for what he believed.

Cassie had long blond hair and she planned to have it cut off to make wigs for cancer patients who had lost their hair through chemotherapy.

She was active in her parish youth group and was known for carrying her Bible to school. She was in the school library, reading her Bible when the two killers burst in.

A few years before, Cassie had dabbled in the occult and witchcraft. But then she gave that up, dedicated her life to Christ, and turned her life around. Upon hearing of her death, her pastor said, "Cassie has graduated, but we have assignments to complete."

Who is this God in whom she believed?

Who is the God for whom she gave her life?

Our fundamental response is in the meditation that follows.

Is God One Person or Three Persons?

Some say... God is one person. To say otherwise is to retreat to the polytheism that preceded the rise to monotheism. As Scripture itself testifies, the ancient world was filled with many gods. The journey to the purest and highest religion meant discarding the simplistic gods that were identified with the sun and moon, stars, skies, rain, trees, rocks, lightning, and mythical dragons.

God revealed himself to Abraham and Moses as a divinity who was personal and one. God is an "I" a personal divinity. God has a name. He is not an anonymous force. In disclosing his name, God became accessible, capable of being known and addressed personally.

The most powerful act of faith among the people of Israel professes the oneness of God. "Hear, O Israel, the Lord our God is one Lord."[2] The expression "one" refers both to the uniqueness of God — meaning there is no other god — and to the truth that God is one person.

The biblical history of God's people is filled with stories of their going after other gods. They were tempted time and again to worship idols made of gold and silver. Through the prophets God taught the people to return to him who is the one and only God — and the one divine person in whom they could rely.

"Turn to me and be safe,

all you ends of the earth,

for I am God: there is no other!

To me every knee shall bend;

by me every tongue shall swear." (Is 45:22, 23b)

Judaism has preserved this teaching about God's oneness. Hundreds of millions of Moslems profess that God is one, the only God. The Unitarian religion likewise insists on the oneness of God. Therefore, it is clear that Jesus is not God and the Holy Spirit is not God. Jesus is a prophet, indeed the greatest of the prophets, but he is not divine. The Holy Spirit is not a separate divine person, but rather a symbol of God's creativity. We experience the one God as creator, savior, and sanctifier. We should not turn these acts of God into persons. The result would be three gods. That obscures the unity of God who is one and unique.

The Catechism *teaches* ...

God is One. Scripture is clear about the oneness of God. "I am God, there is no other!" (Is 45:22)

The creed always begins our with faith in the oneness of God. "I believe in one God." This means there are no competing gods. They do not exist. Gods made of wood and stone, silver and gold are illusions. Gods identified with trees, mountains, caves, or cosmic realities are purely imaginary. Contemporary gods of sex, money and power are fools' gold. There is only one God. All others are false.

What shall we say of this one and only God?

(1) God is MYSTERY. At the burning bush God revealed his name. "I AM." This mysterious name tells us several truths about God.

(a) God is living and personal.

(b) God is closer to us than we are to ourselves. No one could be more intimate with us than God who creates, sustains, and loves us. At the same time, God is "totally other," divine, grand, magnificent, mysterious, and infinite in all directions. We cannot domesticate God.

(c) God communicates himself to us through our experience of created things or particular persons. "The heavens declare the glory of God." (Ps 19:2) God also lets us know about himself through revelations to prophets, saints, and other outstanding people of faith.

(d) Finally, God speaks to our hearts. Scripture mentions the heart over a thousand times. It is in our hearts, the source of loving and being loved, that we encounter God most warmly and personally. We are driven to love and be loved. In that sacred act we have an opportunity to be touched by God.

(2) God is TRUTH. This means God tells us the absolute truth and never lies to us. Such truth is more than abstract ideas. God's truth also implies utter fidelity to us. So God will never betray us or let us down. God is loyal and acts out the truth he speaks. No one else is more trustworthy than God. Because God is truthful and faithful, we can be that way too. God is the origin and source of truth and fidelity

(3) God is LOVE. As we experience the unfolding of the biblical story of God's saving acts, it becomes clear that love is his motive for saving us from our sins and giving us divine life. Scripture compares God's love to a father's affection for his daughter, a mother's love of her son, a bridegroom's passionate commitment to his beloved. God's love is stronger than any of our infidelities. St. John summarizes all this with his eloquent statement, "God is love." (1 Jn 4:8) As we now turn to God as Trinity, we may note that God is an eternal exchange of love among Father, Son, and Holy Spirit. God has destined us to participate in that exchange.

God is Trinity. All Christians are baptized in the name of the Father, and of the Son, and of the Holy Spirit.

The faith of all Christians rests on the Trinity. This is the most ancient and deepest of all the mysteries of faith. How was the mystery of the Trinity revealed?

The Old Testament called God father inasmuch as he is the creator of the world. "Is he not your father who created you?" (Dt 32:6)

God is also father due to making a covenant with his people. "Israel is my son, my first-born." (Ex 4:22)

Lastly, God is father of the poor, the orphan, and the widow. "The Father of orphans and the defender of widows is God." (Ps 68:6)

Jesus revealed God as father in a new sense. God is father in relation to his only Son, Jesus. In the Last Supper discourse (Jn 13-17) Jesus calls God "Father" forty-five times. The Son is as divine as the Father. "No one knows the Son except the Father, and no one knows the Father except the Son and anyone to whom the Son wishes to reveal him." (Mt 11:27) The Father testified to the divinity of his Son at the Baptism and Transfiguration. "This is my beloved Son." (Mt 3:17; 17:5) In the creed we state that we believe in Jesus Christ as God's only Son and Lord.

Before his passion, Jesus promised that he would send the Holy Spirit to the apostles and disciples. The Spirit would abide with them, teaching, guiding, and consoling them and giving them the courage to be witnesses to the Gospel and the Kingdom. The revelation of the Spirit at Pentecost and in the young Church in action throughout the remaining pages of the New Testament gives ample evidence of his distinct personal and divine nature. The Spirit's appearance and acts reveal the reality and work of the Father and the Son. In the creed we affirm, "We believe in the Holy Spirit, the Lord and giver of life."

How did the Church proceed to articulate the doctrine? Baptismal faith from apostolic times drew attention to the mystery of the Trinity. As time passed the Church needed to clarify her understanding of the mystery especially when faced with those who denied or deformed it.

Theologians borrowed three terms from philosophy to help her with this task. They used substance or nature to speak of the unity of God. They applied the terms person or hypostasis to Father, Son, and Spirit to illustrate the real distinctions among them. They chose the concept of relation to illustrate the truth that their distinctiveness lies in their relationship to one another.

Thus the doctrine of the Trinity includes three truths of faith:

(1) The Trinity is One. We do not speak of three gods, but one God. Each person is fully God. All three share the same divine nature or substance.

(2) The divine persons are truly distinct from one another. Father, Son, and Spirit are not just three shapes or modes of God, but three real identifiable persons. The Father is not the Son. The Son is not the Father. The Holy Spirit is neither Father nor Son.

(3) The divine persons relate to one another. Because of the manner in which they relate, we can identify each person by that relationship.

What are the missions of the persons of the Trinity? God's loving plan to save us is the common work of the three divine persons. Each divine person performs this common mission in a unique manner. We speak of the Father as Creator, the Son as Redeemer, and the Spirit as Sanctifier, even though all three work together in these missions. When we glorify and praise one person, we praise all three.

1. What are some implications of faith in the one God?
- "*It means living in thanksgiving*: if God is the only One, everything we are and have comes from him: "What have you that you did not receive?" [1 Cor 4:7] "What shall I render to the LORD for all his bounty to me?" [Ps 116:12]
- "*It means knowing the unity and true dignity of all men*: everyone is made in the image and likeness of God. [Gen 1:26]
- "*It means making good use of created things*: faith in God, the only One, leads us to use everything that is not God only insofar as it brings us closer to him, and to detach ourselves from it insofar as it turns us away from him" (CCC 224-226)

2. How may we speak of the Trinity?
"The mystery of the Most Holy Trinity is the central mystery of the Christian faith and of Christian life. God alone can make it known to us by revealing himself as Father, Son, and Holy Spirit." (CCC 261)

3. What is the relationship of baptism and faith in the Trinity?
"By the grace of Baptism 'in the name of the Father and of the Son and of the Holy Spirit,' we are called to share in the life of the Blessed Trinity, here on earth in the obscurity of faith, and after death in eternal light (cf. Paul VI, CPG # 9). (CCC 265)

Response to objections

One of the peculiarities of popular religion is attention to one person of the Trinity to the exclusion of the other. Some are Jesus-centered. Others are Spirit-followers. A smaller number are Father-oriented. While all the persons of the Trinity are implicitly honored in these cases, it is better for our spiritual development to become more aware of all three persons and their dynamic influence upon our lives.

Follow the example of the liturgy, which places our attention on the Trinity in all the prayers. In worship we address the Father through the Son in the Spirit. The flow of the liturgy is toward the Father. Our lives, too, should be oriented to the Father. Liturgical prayer draws us to be identified with Jesus Christ who acts upon us and applies to us the saving effects of his redemption. In the liturgy we are transformed by the power of the Spirit into holy people and prepared to witness this by acts of love, justice, and mercy.

A spirituality based upon the Trinity with ever deeper acts of faith begins to reveal to us the immense majesty of God as a divine family of Love. This Love arises out of the intimacy of the Trinity and results in creation, redemption, and providence. These three acts of the Trinity oversee and underpin the whole cosmos and each one of us.

We are always the focus of a continuing creation.
• The graces of salvation ever surround us.
• The joyful providence of God consistently nourishes us.

While we honor those whose faith is on the oneness of God alone, we respectfully invite them to open their hearts to the further revelation of God as Trinity. It is a grace we have received and a faith for which we thank Father, Son, and Spirit.

For dialog

1. What examples of fatherhood could you cite which will help you and others to appreciate the fatherhood of God? In those unfortunate cases where there is an absent father, what could be done to provide father figures for children and why is this needed? In even more severe instances of an unloving human father, what would you suggest be done? Since human fatherhood derives from divine fatherhood, what steps would you take to enhance the role of fathers in today's family based on our faith?

2. Since Jesus taught that no one knows the Father but the Son and no one knows the Son but the Father, what are some ways or prayers that would help you sense the love that exists between them? To see Jesus is to see the Father. What do we learn about God in this saying of Christ? God revealed his Name to Moses. Jesus adds more when he reveals God's name. What is new about Christ's revelation? Why is it important for our faith?

3. How much does the Holy Spirit mean to you? How attentive are you to the presence of the Spirit in your life? Whom do you know who clearly shows the influence of the Spirit in their behavior? Why do enthusiastic Christians trace their energy to the Spirit?

Prayer

Loving God, you are one in nature and substance. You are the only true God. At the same time, I praise you for revealing that you are also three persons involved in a relationship of infinite love. I thank you for the revelation and for the graces of faith that enable me to acknowledge such richness and depth in your inner life. I give you glory for the outpouring of your love as Father, Son, and Spirit, creating, redeeming, and sanctifying me and the world. Holy, Holy, Holy are you, Lord God almighty!

Glossary

Person in the Trinity — The church uses the term person to designate Father, Son, and Spirit as well as the true and real distinction among them. The Church has taken philosophical terms and given them an unprecedented meaning to signify an ineffable mystery.

Substance or Nature in the Trinity — The Church again borrows a philosophical term to describe the divine "being" in its unity. This is why we may speak of three divine persons in one divine nature or substance.

Relation in Trinity — The Church uses this term to say that the persons of the Trinity are distinct and identifiable by reason of their relationships to one another.

Cassie Bernall, the Christian witness at Columbine High School, wrote the following testimony faith, the Sunday before she was killed:

"Now I have given up on everything else — I have found it to be the only way to really know Christ and to experience the mighty power that brought him back to life again, and to find out what it means to suffer and to die with him. So, whatever it takes I will be the one who lives in the fresh nearness of life of those who are alive from the dead."[3]

Endnotes

1. Richard Herber, "Holy, Holy, Holy."
2. Deuteronomy 6:4 (RSV).
3. Cassie Bernall, in *She Said Yes : The Unlikely Martyrdom of Cassie Bernall,* by Misty Bernall and Madeleine L' Engle, Plough Publishing House, 1999.

Chapter 5

IN THE BEGINNING GOD CREATED THE WORLD

CCC 279-354

*"Let your every creature serve you;
for you spoke and they were made,
You sent forth your spirit and they were created;
no one can resist your word."*

Judith 16:14

Float Like a Butterfly

"My youngest daughter came back from a music camp in Massachusetts carrying some monarch caterpillars in a jar. She found them feeding on milkweed near the camp. We also have milkweed growing in Princeton and so she was able to keep the caterpillars alive. After a few days they stopped feeding, hung themselves up by their tails and began to pupate.

"The process of pupation is delightful to watch. They squeeze themselves up into the skin of the pupa, like a fat boy wriggling into a sleeping bag that is three sizes too small for him. At the beginning you cannot believe that the caterpillar will ever fit inside, and at the end it turns out that the sleeping bag was exactly the right size.

"Two or three weeks later the butterflies emerge. The emergence is even more spectacular than the pupation. Out of the sleeping bag crawls the bedraggled remnant of the caterpillar, much reduced in size and with wet black stubs for wings. Then, in a few minutes, the body dries, the legs and antennae stiffen and the wings unfurl. The bedraggled little creature springs to life as a shimmering beauty of orange, white, and black.

"We set her free in a nearby field and she flies high over the trees, disappearing into the sky. We hope that the move from Massachusetts to Princeton will not have disrupted the pattern of her autumn migration. With luck she will find companions to share with her the long journey to the southwest. She has a long way to go, most of it against the prevailing winds.

"The world of biology is full of miracles, but nothing I have seen is as miraculous as this metamorphosis of the Monarch caterpillar. Her brain is a speck of neural tissue a few millimeters long, about a million times smaller than the human brain. With this almost microscopic clump of nerve cells she knows how to manage her new legs and wings, to walk and to fly, to find her way by some unknown means of navigation over thousands of miles from Massachusetts to Mexico."[1]

Freeman Dyson's poetic story about the butterfly awakens in us the wonder evoked by the mysteries of the universe. We are prompted to ask a host of questions. Where have we come from? Where are we going? What is the purpose of it all? What does it mean? Questions about the origin and end of the world and life are inseparable. These are the interesting and provocative thoughts that we encounter in the story of creation.

Where Did We Come From?

Some say... New Age disciples seem to believe that we do not come from anywhere. We are part of God who is in the process of "becoming." There is no beginning so much as a flow of divine energy that always is. Trees, clouds, lakes, lions, deer, fish, bluebirds, boys, girls, men and women are all "emanations" of God. Everyone and everything is a part of God. The old term for this perspective is pantheism, based on the Greek words "pan" (all) and "theos" (god). In some mysterious way "we" are the origin of the universe and all it contains.

Modern materialists argue that the world did not begin; it always was. What we call creation is actually the slow interplay of visible and invisible material forces whose interaction resulted in the separation of land and water, the emergence of hills and valleys, the slow evolving of life forms from fish to land animals to birds and eventually the appearance of prehumans, followed by humans themselves.

No divine being had anything to do with this. The earth and the cosmos have always been here in some kind of "steady state" that was affected by a "big bang" at some point, resulting in the universe as we know it. There was no eternal, spiritual God to create this. There has only been an eternal material cosmos that evolved on its own to the present state of reality.

Another group is the creationists. They espouse an explanation called "creationism." They believe God created the world and all creatures and human beings without any intervening process of evolution to make it happen. Hence they do not accept the belief that God placed within creation the sources of development and oversees its unfolding with love and providential care. The creationists seek to have their teachings introduced into public schools' science classes either to supplant or to be taught alongside of theories of evolution, which exclude any role of God in the process of creation.

The Catechism *teaches* ...

We start with the first line of the Bible. "In the beginning God created the heavens and the earth." (Gn 1:1 RSV) This was the first step in God's loving plan to save us. The key to understanding the Genesis creation story must be found in the "new creation" story caused by the life, ministry, and saving acts of Jesus Christ. This is why John begins his Gospel with the words, "In the beginning. . . ." (Jn 1:1) Creation only makes sense against the background of redemption. In divine revelation the beginning is defined by the end. Purpose gives ultimate meaning.

The first ecstasy of God pouring out his love through the creative act of producing the universe and all it contains is an unfinished story. It needs to be matched by the narrative of the goal. This is the ecstasy of the Son of God, incarnate in Jesus Christ, whose outpouring of love for the Father and for us resulted in the salvation of the human race. We are pressed to ask not just who created the world, but why?

"Creation is the foundation of all 'God's saving plans' (GCD 51), the 'beginning of the history of salvation' (Gen 1:1; Rom 8:18-23), that culminates in Christ. Conversely, the mystery of Christ casts conclusive light on the mystery of creation. . . ." (CCC 280)

At the same time we correctly want to know how the world happened. What processes did God use to unfold his creative act? Natural sciences have extensively investigated human origins, the development of the earth, and the cosmos itself. Pope John Paul II has stated that the Church acknowledges the value of some theories of evolution. He also insists on our faith that God is the Creator of the world and presides over its developmental processes — and God is the Creator of the human soul.

Read and study paragraphs 283-286 of the *Catechism* for its analysis of the differences between the ways natural science, philosophy, and religion treat the topic of creation and the processes of its development.

Take time to meditate with faith on Genesis 1-3, the biblical account of creation. These chapters contain all the grand themes that command our attention about creation: "its origin and its end in God, its order and goodness, the vocation of man, and finally, the drama of sin and the hope of salvation." (CCC 289) Read these passages in the light of what Jesus has done and the living Tradition of the Church.

In our next chapter will look at the creation of man and woman in the image of God and the story of the Fall. Here we continue with five teachings from the *Catechism* about God's creation.

What is the relationship of God to his creation?

1. Love motivates God's creativity. To those who claim the world is the result of chance or blind fate, we reply that our faith tells us God created the world out of love. While we attribute creation to the Father, we affirm that the whole Trinity is the one principle of creation. Creation is more than a mechanical event; it is the outcome of God's wisdom. Who can observe the soaring beauty of the mountains or the awesome depth of the oceans or the poetry of nature's complexity and not break out into song?

"How manifold are your works, O Lord,

In wisdom you made them all." (Ps 104:24)

2. God created the world out of nothing. If you want to build a house you must use existing materials: wood, wire, bricks, glass, plaster, steel, iron, plastics, ceramics, and tiles. God had no preexisting materials. God created from nothing — from "no thing." God has given us the gift of imagination, art, and craft to imitate his creativity and participate in the ongoing process of creation. At the same time the Holy Spirit continues creation in the gifts of faith and many other divine blessings that cause us to grow in holiness and enable us to build up the Body of Christ. When God created the world, he rejoiced and said, "That's good!" Any time we participate in his authentic creativity we extend the goodness of God in the world.

3. God's plan includes providence. Creation has not occurred in its perfection. It is in process towards its divinely destined fulfillment. God remains present to creation to care for it and oversee its destiny. God is present to the process. Divine providence is the name we give to the dispositions by which God guides creation towards what it is meant to be. Jesus taught that the beauty of the lilies of the field comes from God's attention to them. If God takes care of the flowers, will he not take care of humans who are more important than all else in creation? We share in God's providential care of creation when we respect the environment and make a garden of the universe, not a wasteland.

4. God's providence prevails despite the problem of evil. Why is there evil if God has created a good and ordered world and cares for it and us? There is no quick or easy answer. Faith gives us a partial answer. People use their freedom to sin and cause evil towards others. God never causes evil, but does permit it in the sense that he does not take away human freedom. God can and often does bring good out of evil. Such is the case in the story of Joseph of Egypt. (Gen 45:8; 50:20) Paragraph 309 of the *Catechism* lists the following elements of faith life that provide us with the context for dealing with evil:

a. Goodness of creation
b. Drama of sin
c. Patient love of God
d. Gift of the Spirit
e. Redemptive Incarnation of the Son
f. Gathering of the Church
g. Power of the Sacraments
h. Call to eternal life

The above eight truths form a pattern that sheds light on ways we can respond to the existence and impact of evil. On earth our insight is always partial. In heaven we will gain the full understanding we seek.

5. God created angels. Angels are spiritual beings who serve as messengers of God. From Genesis to Apocalypse, Scripture contains numerous accounts about angels. An angel announced the Incarnation to Mary. Angels sang at Christ's birth and proclaimed his resurrection. Angels comforted Jesus after the temptations in the desert and during his agony in the garden. At every Eucharist angels join us in praising the thrice-holy God. The liturgical feast of the Guardian Angels reminds us that each of us has a special angel to look after us. The last book of the Bible tells us that angels will announce Christ's return and serve him during the last judgment.

1. What does God witness in his creation?

"In the creation of the world and of man, God gave the first and universal witness to his almighty love and wisdom, the first proclamation of the 'plan of his loving goodness,' which finds its goal in the new creation in Christ." (CCC 315)

2. How does the whole Trinity participate in creation?

"God created the universe and keeps it in existence by his Word, the Son 'upholding the universe by his word of power' (Heb 1:3) and by his creator Spirit, the giver of life." (CCC 320)

3. What is divine providence?

"Divine providence consists of the dispositions by which God guides all his creatures with wisdom and love to their ultimate end.... Divine providence works also through the actions of creatures. To human beings God grants the ability to cooperate freely with his plans." (CCC 321, 323)

Response to objections

The New Age view of creation that asserts all beings are emanations of the divine fails to distinguish between creatures and the creator. In effect this belief eliminates both the inherent majesty and utter freedom of God, as well as the authentic dignity of being human. It is not helpful to dissolve all creation into a vague identification with God. Proper distinctions are lost and the order of the universe basically becomes meaningless.

The materialistic solution to the mystery of creation excludes God and the spiritual dimension of humans. This is an unsatisfying mechanical understanding of creation that has no legitimate answers to the perennial questions about morality, spiritual yearning, the basis for human dignity, or the questions about the purpose and meaning of life. Blind chance, governed by an anonymous force, is just that — blind. But the history of humanity is a search for light.

Creationists are right to affirm that God created the world. They are also correct in rejecting theories of evolution that explicitly deny any role for God in the development of the universe or the creation of the human soul. But they seem to have an underdeveloped sense of divine providence that created and presides over the evolving processes whereby the world attains its fulfillment. In so doing they fail to see the rightful autonomy of natural sciences which have contributed greatly to our understanding of human and cosmic origins.

For dialog

1. Share some examples from your life where goals influenced projects you started or jobs you began. Explain how beginnings and ends have been connected in your life. In your own words describe how the work of Jesus Christ gives meaning to the beginning of the world. When you think of the term "create" what comes to your mind? What is the difference between the way God creates and the way humans create?

2. Deists claim that God created the world and gave people all they needed to take care of everything after that. We believe that God continued to have an interest in the world through his providential acts. Why is our position more consistent with our faith in God? Why is a providential God more truly caring than a "clockwork" God, that is, one who winds up the universe and then leaves it to itself?

3. Above we gave five points about God's relationship to the world and humans. Discuss how each truth could be applied in everyday life. How can we participate in God's own ongoing involvement in creation?

Prayer Creator Father, you made the world out of love for us. Your wisdom designed the world and arranged that all creation be part of your loving plan to save us. With the Son and the Holy Spirit you have providentially been with us ever since time began. You have planted within the universe the seeds of development which through the centuries have unfolded according to your wise and loving will. We praise and glorify you for your creation through which we perceive your loving presence. Grant us the graces we need to participate in the ongoing processes of creation for your greater honor and glory and the good of all people.

Glossary **Creation** — God — Father, Son, and Holy Spirit — created the world out of nothing. Motivated by love, the original creation became a "new creation" in Jesus Christ and his work of salvation.

Providence — God did not abandon the world after creation, but remains present to it and guides all creatures, including humans, with his wisdom and love to their ultimate destiny.

"The world will never starve for wonders — only for want of wonder."

G. K. Chesterton

Endnote

1. Freeman Dyson, *Infinite in all Directions* (New York: Harper & Row, 1988), p. 33.

Chapter 6

MAN AND WOMAN — IMAGES OF GOD
CCC 279-354

"What a piece of work is man!
How noble in reason! how infinite in faculty!
In action how like an angel!
In apprehension how like a god!"

William Shakespeare, *Hamlet*

"You are lovely. Give me your hand"

This story is from *Tuesdays with Morrie* by Mitch Albom.[1] Mitch has brought his wife Janine to visit his dying professor. . . .

"So, Janine," Morrie said.

She smiled.

"You are lovely. Give me your hand."

She did.

"Mitch says that you're a professional singer."

"Yes," Janine said.

"He says you're great."

"Oh," she laughed. "No. He just says that."

"Will you sing something for me?"

Now I have heard people ask this of Janine for almost as long as I have known her. When people find out you sing for a living, they always say, "Sing something for us." Shy about her talent and a perfectionist about conditions, Janine never did. She would politely decline. Which is what I expected now.

Which is when she began to sing.

"The very thought of you

and I forget to do
the little ordinary things that everyone ought to do."

It was a 1930's standard written by Ray Noble, and Janine sang it sweetly, looking straight at Morrie. I was amazed once again at his ability to draw emotion from people who otherwise kept it locked away. . .

"I see your face in every flower,
your eyes in the stars above,
it's just the thought of you,
the very thought of you,
my love. . ."

When she finished, Morrie opened his eyes and tears rolled down his cheeks. In all the years I have listened to my wife sing, I never heard her the way he did at that moment.

The simplicity of this scene, with the modesty of the singer, the direct sentiment of a love song and the appreciative pull of a dying man illumines a moment of humanity. It is one of life's little surprises that permission to be human can also reveal God's image shining through our humanity.

What Does it Mean to Be God's Image?

Some say... We are not images of God. It is quite enough to be human. We have all the faculties and physical abilities we need to get along in this world. To speak of us as images of God muddies the picture and diminishes the grandeur of being human. Science has helped us to understand that we have evolved into being human from pre-human forms. There is no need for us to claim an origin from God. The origin of the species is a wondrous process of natural selection. Our roots are in the earth, air, fire, and water that released energies and combinations through eons of time that eventually yielded man and woman. We are born good. Education and culture remove the obstacles to discovering this truth about ourselves and foster our personal development.

Others say that not only are we not images of God, we are little more than superior animals. Control of the world belongs to the strongest and most attractive of human-like animals. In this century such a view allows us to experiment on weaker people such as the mentally impaired, to dehumanize babies in the womb and so dispose of unwanted "fetuses," and to justify genocide. In this view the world is a jungle and its law should prevail. Rawanda and Kosovo come to mind.

Another group of people ignore the idea of being an image of God. Their interest is in what they call the image of self. In many cases they seem to ignore God and animal alike in the quest for finding a proper self image. The only reference is self — no one or nothing else. Bookstores are filled with self-help texts. The cultivation of a positive and fulfilling self-image is a major human goal. There is no need to be bothered with being an image of God — or even to explore one's kinship with animals.

The Catechism *teaches ...*

"God created man in his image...male and female he created them." (Gen 1:27)

Every human being is an image of God. Within all humans are surges, drives, energies that propel them to hungers and thirsts that are ultimately satisfied with nothing less than God.

The source of this interior energy is God's image planted in the soul at its creation.

The attraction to truth, the longing for beauty, the enchantment with goodness, found in every human being, expressed in a greater or lesser degree, may be traced to this marvelous gift in the shrine of every soul — God's image.

We should not imagine God's image as a static picture stamped on our souls. This is the biggest mistake made by most people about God's image. It is better to think of it as a field of energy, swarming with potential, moving, driving, pulsing, striving for a fulfillment that can ultimately be sated by God.

The image of God is a power surge, pushing us toward the light, the love, the poetry created by God and satisfying us even as we rush onward for more.

The process is liberating, not enslaving. Addictions are similar to the powers generated by God's image. But addictions close us in, deprive us of freedom, and disappoint us to the edge of despair. The drives that arise from God's image open us to fields of freedom and horizons that are at first unimaginable.

Perhaps the picture of an archer, a bow, and an arrow may help. The archer is God who holds the bow. This is God within each of us as *Imago Dei*. We are the arrows. The goal is the bulls-eye who happens to be God. Hence God is both behind us thrusting us forth and in front of us luring us onward. We are not inanimate arrows, but rather free human beings invited into the greatest of all adventures.

It is essential that you hold onto this energizing vision of being the *Imago Dei*, Image of God, when reading the following characteristics of this gift described in the *Catechism*.

(*Note: This chapter should be understood in the light of the Fall and Original Sin, which will be treated in the next chapter. Both themes then need to be seen in the light of Christ's redemption.*)

The *Catechism* tells us that we image God in five ways:

1. We can know truth and know God. We all experience the process of knowing and gathering knowledge in a classroom. Beyond this we need to notice that within us is a limitless drive to know and be known. We should become aware of the inner push to know, a dynamic outreach not just for book knowledge, self-knowledge or truths about God. As an image of God we are drawn to know God himself.

2. We can love people, ourselves, and God. The most powerful movement in any human being is the longing to love and be loved. Acceptance and rejection face us from infancy to old age. We want to be loved. We want to love. No one can escape this hunger. We are unrestricted drives to love and be loved. Where does this come from? Its source is the Image of God as the radiant warmth of love reaching out for others and eventually for God. The divine archer wants to send us on a journey of a love that never ends.

3. We understand ourselves as persons, not things. When Adam was by himself in the garden of paradise, he had the animals for company. But they were not enough. Adam realized he was not an animal. They seemed content with their own kind. He felt alone and lonely. God said that it is not good for a man to be alone. He needs human company. So God created Eve and presented her to Adam much to his great joy. "This one at last is bone of my bones and flesh of my flesh." (Gen 2:23) In other words she is a human person just as Adam is. They discover their common humanity. Being God's image confirms our human dignity. We are not animals nor things.

4. We are called to form community with each other. God is a community of love in which Father, Son, and Spirit relate to each other in infinite love. Hence the image of God within us awakens our need to imitate the divine community by living in solidarity with our family, friends, strangers and the whole of humanity. We are not meant to be lone rangers, indifferent to the needs of others and refusing the gifts of others' humanity in shaping our own growth.

5. We are called by grace to communion with God. The final outcome of the multiple energies that surge from our being images of God is a faith union with God on earth and a permanent love union with God in heaven. The divine archer is also the goal of the affections that he plants within us. As the Irish prayer puts it, "Christ behind us . . . Christ in front of us." We are enfolded with the beauty of God who loves us and never forces us. This whole process takes place in respect for our freedom. We learn from experience that the more we give ourselves to this process the more free we are.

1. What did God intend for man and woman in creation ?

"[God] destined all material creatures for the good of the human race. Man, and through him all creation, is destined for the glory of God" (CCC 353).

"Man is predestined to reproduce the image of God's Son made man, the 'image of the invisible God.' " (Col 1:15) (CCC 381)

2. Did God make man and women equal to each other?

"Man and woman have been *created*, which is to say, *willed* by God . . . in perfect equality as human persons . . . man and woman possess an inalienable dignity which comes to them immediately from God their Creator. (Cf. Gen 2: 7, 22)

"In marriage God unites them in such a way that, by forming 'one flesh' (Gen 2:24), they can transmit human life. . . By transmitting human life to their descendants, man and woman as spouses and parents cooperate in a unique way in the Creator's work (Cf. GS 50,1)." (CCC 369, 372)

3. How should we see the relationship of our souls and bodies?

" 'Man, though made of body and soul is a unity' (GS 14, 1). The doctrine of faith affirms that the spiritual and immortal soul is created immediately by God: 'God did not create man a solitary being. From the beginning, 'male and female he created them' (Gen 1:27). This partnership of man and woman constitutes the first form of communion between persons' (GS 12, 4)." (CCC 382-383)

Response to objections

It is a comforting illusion to believe that we are not images of God. Those who claim it is enough to be human close out a number of questions and possibilities that have engaged philosophers and saints throughout all of history. The mysteries of death, suffering, loss of health and loved ones are not easily coped with in a world that shuts God out of the picture. So long as we are healthy, strong, and prosperous, we believe we can delay any serious dialogue about ultimate questions. Eventually, the great issues of life and death, origin and destiny come to each person's consciousness. Denial only works for a while. The pity of it all is that the life-giving energies of being images of God have been squandered. Too much was lost.

Tragically, a certain number of people believe the best way to be human is to identify with the animal world. Expectation determines destiny. If I look upward to the angels, I can be more than I am. If I look downward to the animals, I shall become less than I am. The brutish behavior of tyrants, abusers, beaters, liars, swindlers, betrayers, killers, thieves, torturers is the bitter fruit of lives based on immoral and amoral self-concepts. When we reject the pure stream of life that comes from being God's image, we live by the darkness of our chaotic evil impulses.

Those who stare for years at the image of self while ignoring their potential for greatness as images of God — and, more dangerously, their leanings to evil — are stalled. They never really grow. Their relationships are shallow. Their commitments are soft. They consume personality junk food. In terms of maturity they are eternal children, but without the charm and buoyancy of youth. Their god is Narcissus. Its sweet flower is decadent. Missing is the sturdy life of conflict that leads to growth.

For dialog

1. What is your learning style? Is it fueled by curiosity or wonder? Do you sense an eagerness to know? Or have you lost interest in life? God's image within you urges you to the adventure of knowing and learning. How could you image God more effectively by a pursuit of truth?

2. If someone asked you to name five qualities of love what would you say? How did you learn to love? Which are you better at: loving others or seeking to be loved? What needs improvement? How will you do it? When faced with rejection, how do you react? As God's image, you have an unrestricted capacity to love and be loved. What plans could you make to live this truth more effectively?

3. If you know some people who are loners what do you think about them? Why is involvement in community more life-enriching than individualism? What would you say to someone who objects that he or she fears to be "lost in a crowd"? Why do we point to the Trinity as a model for community? How can you image God by becoming more communal?

Prayer

We praise you, O God, for creating us in your image. By your grace we have been given sources of energy that move us to know truth, love you and others, be involved in community, sense our solidarity with all peoples, and appreciate our human dignity. Ultimately, we experience a loving attraction to you who alone can give us permanent joy. Teach us how to image you. Strengthen us in the quest to make you, dear Lord, our goal and purpose in life.

Glossary

Image of God — When God creates our souls, he plants within them capacities to know truth, love others and God and self, be committed to community, be aware of solidarity with all people, and seek final union with God. These drives are divinely given energies that push us toward the light, the truth, the love, the community and eternal life that makes life worth living and purposeful.

Self-Realization — Contemporary culture is filled with the call to fulfill ourselves, to have true self-worth. While there are many positive and useful suggestions about how to do this, they will fall short if they are not rooted in acting as images of God with the help of the Holy Spirit.

" The heart benevolent and kind
The most resembles God."

Robert Burns

Endnote

1. Adapted from *Tuesdays with Morrie*, Mitch Albom (New York: Doubleday, 1997).

Chapter 7

ADAM, EVE, AND THE SERPENT
CCC 396-421

"Sin is not simply a weakness we can overcome, but rather a condition from which we have to be saved."

Robert Barron[1]

Enjoy the Whole Garden, Except. . .

God created Adam and Eve and placed them in the garden of Eden. God told them to enjoy the goods of creation, including the beauty and company of each other. They were to cultivate the garden and use their gifts of mind, will, and imagination to make the world flourish around them.

They could eat the fruit of all the trees, including presumably the Tree of Life. But they should not eat of the Tree of the Knowledge of Good and Evil. God set a limit to their earthly achievements. God gave them a drive to a goal that surpassed their natural powers to see and understand. To reach that end they would need revelation.

They could grasp a lot. But they needed obedience and prayerful submission so they could be led forward by God and given the gift of a vision they could not attain on their own.

The forbidden Tree was a symbol of human limits and mastery. We have an infinite hunger that cannot be satisfied by finite means. Trust alone in the Mystery of God makes possible the next step.

The serpent persuaded Eve that human aggressiveness can acquire whatever it wants by its own power. He painted God as a jealous rival. He introduced fear into paradise. She should fear that God will crush us with laws. The serpent intimated to her that God is afraid that we would threaten him and his control of us.

Eve surrendered to the serpent's temptation. Fear replaced the innocence that was based on love of and trust in God. She convinced Adam to do the same.

The man and woman immediately hid their genitals, sign of what was most personal and intimate between them. For the first time they wore the armor of defensiveness.

Next, they heard God's voice seeking them out, and they hid in the bushes. They had declared independence from God. They wanted to live where God could not find them and interfere with them.

Of course, God easily found them.

"Where are you?"

"I was afraid, because I was naked, so I hid," says Adam.

There we have the story of Original Sin. Afraid. Naked. Hidden. Fear has replaced trust. A cover-up of the self is needed to defend the ego from God. Hiding is running from God so we can be independent of him.

The blame game began. The serpent blamed God. Eve blamed the serpent. Adam blamed Eve. Personal responsibility was abdicated.

Adam and Eve lost the garden. Childbirth would be painful. Farming the garden of a fallen world would be difficult. Suffering and death would be part of life.

In this dark moment God promised a new creation, a redemption that would be greater than the first creation. To the serpent God says, "I will put enmity between you and the woman, and between your offspring and hers. He will strike at your head while you strike at his heel." (Gen 3:15)

In our previous chapter we looked at man and woman as images of God. The story of Adam, Eve, and the serpent explains how the originating evil came about and affects us to this day. This is the topic that now lies before us.

What Are We to Think About Original Sin?

Some say... We should forget about original sin. When God made us he said, "That's good!" We are born good. Anyone who looks at the fresh innocence of a baby can tell that. We are not conceived or born in sin. We are original blessings, not shadowed by sin. Baptism is not needed to take away any sin for our birth is an event of goodness. We are intrinsically good. Of course we are not perfect, but that is due to a psychological weakness that can be corrected by therapy. Or it could be traced to a flaw in our development that can be healed by patient education and recourse to positive thinking.

Others conclude that if one is pressed to describe original sin, it should be attributed to a sinful situation. Inadequate social structures, violent homes and neighborhoods, ignorance of leaders, and similar social problems are the real original sin. It is a social problem, not a personal moral flaw. It is the bad vibrations of a society gone awry rather than any assumed internal moral weakness due to inherited original sin. We arrive good. We learn how to be bad from the sinful environment around us.

The Catechism *teaches* ...

"By one man's disobedience many (that is all) were made sinners. . . Then as one man's trespass led to condemnation for all men, so one man's (Christ's) act of righteousness leads to acquittal and life for all men." (Rom 5:12;19)

What was the original state of Adam and Eve?

They lived in a state of original holiness and justice. Their spiritual powers controlled their bodies and passions. The union of man and woman was marked by harmony and love. They related to creation peacefully and fruitfully. They related to God with love, trust, and obedience.

What was lost through their disobedience?

They were deprived of original holiness and justice. The flesh now warred against the spirit. Husband and wife began to experience tensions, lust, and the quest for domination. Nature became a hostile environment that needed to be tamed. Their attitudes to God were colored by fear, the cover-up of self, and a "hiding" from God to gain independence from the Lord. Suffering and death entered history.

How did Adam's sin become the sin of his descendants?

All humanity is contained in Adam as one man. Because of the unity of the human race everyone is touched by Adam's sin, just as each person is affected by Christ's justice. The Council of Trent teaches that original sin is transmitted by propagation, not by imitation. *But the transmission of original sin is a mystery we cannot fully understand.* Following St. Paul, the Church's faith has always believed that Adam's sin is transmitted to us when we are conceived.

Do we commit original sin? No. We inherit it. It is a deprivation of original holiness and justice.

Is our human nature totally corrupted or just wounded? Our human nature is wounded, not fully corrupted. St. Thomas Aquinas speaks of five wounds of original sin:

(1) Ignorance. We have difficulty in knowing the truth.

(2) Malice. We are inclined to act from uncharitable motives.

(3) Weakness in Will. We find it hard to choose the good.

(4) Disorder in Passions. We let emotions control behavior.

(5) Suffering and Death. We face pain and the finality of death.

Is original sin a stain on our souls?

The image of stain has a long history in religious language. Since the soul is spiritual it cannot have a physical mark. The use of the term "stain" was meant as an image of the deprivation of original holiness and justice due to the disobedience of Adam and Eve.

What is another way to imagine original sin's impact on us?

Another possibility is to envision the effect of original sin as a source of evil energy within us. We endure an originating evil that pulls us away from God. Baptism takes away original sin, but not the damage. The wounds mentioned above remain as powers, movements, surges that incline us to evil thoughts words and deeds.

Why did not God prevent Adam and Eve from sinning?

God would not take away the freedom that assures our humanity. Thomas Aquinas wrote, "There is nothing to prevent human nature's being raised up to something greater even after sin. . . Thus St. Paul says, 'Where sin increased, grace abounded all the more (Rom 5:20).' And the Exultet sings, 'O happy fault, . . . which gained for us so great a Redeemer!'"

1. What was the substance of the first sin?

"Man, tempted by the devil, let his trust in his Creator die in his heart and, abusing his freedom, disobeyed God's command. This is what man's first sin consisted of. (Cf. Gen 3:1-11; Rom 5:19) All subsequent sin would be disobedience toward God and lack of trust in his goodness." (CCC 397)

2. What did the Church adopt from Augustine on original sin?

"The Church's teaching on the transmission of original sin was articulated more precisely in the fifth century, especially under the impulse of Augustine's reflections against Pelagianism . . . Pelagius held that man could, by the natural power of free will and without the necessary help of God's grace, lead a morally good life; he thus reduced the influence of Adam's fault to bad example. . .We therefore hold with the Council of Trent that original sin is transmitted with human nature 'by propagation, not by imitation...' (Paul VI CPG,16)." (CCC 406, 419)

3. What are we to say about Mary and original sin?

"Many Fathers and Doctors of the Church have seen the woman announced in the *Protoevangelium* as Mary, the mother of Christ, the 'new Eve.' Mary benefited first of all and uniquely from Christ's victory over sin: she was preserved from all stain of original sin and by a special grace of God committed no sin of any kind during her whole earthly life (Cf. Pius IX, *Ineffabilis Deus*: DS 2803; Council of Trent: DS 1573)." (CCC 411)

Response to objections

One assumption behind the rejection of the doctrine of original sin is that we are born totally and intrinsically good. This was one of the principles of Enlightenment thinking. Even if one was born rough hewn — a noble savage — the person was fundamentally good, with no sin or moral flaw. This view puts great stock in the role of education and culture, which is intended to smooth out the rough edges of the "savage" by evoking the inherent goodness already there.

The Church, following the development of St. Augustine on this matter, teaches that we are born good, but flawed, because we are deprived of the gifts of original holiness and justice. Hence there is need to be born again of water and the Holy Spirit in Baptism. The sacrament removes the deprivation caused by original sin and introduces us to the life of God in grace. But Baptism does not erase the damage due to original sin. That is why we speak of the traces or wounds of the primal sin that remain. We require growth in spirituality and moral virtues to be liberated from the damage.

A second proposal claims that original sin is the environment of sin into which all people are born. Society's evils and the bad example of others are the real meaning of original sin. This makes the sin a social problem rather than a personal inheritance from which we need salvation by the work of Christ and the sacrament of Baptism. There is no doubt that a sinful milieu is a great moral challenge for people. But this does not account for the depth of evil to which a person may be prone even in homes and neighborhoods where the best example is given. In the final analysis our acceptance of the teaching on inherited sin as found in St. Paul and St. Augustine and articulated at length in the Council of Trent is based on our religious faith and understood in the light of Christ's redeeming acts in the paschal mystery.

For dialog

1. Share some stories from your experience that detail what you might call impenetrable and unaccountable evil. What are you to make of it? The poet T. S. Eliot coined the phrase "motiveless malignity" to describe unspeakable evil. What do you think of his expression? How would the Nazi holocaust, the Rwanda genocide, the Serbian ethnic cleansing and the Cambodian killing fields fit in a discussion on original sin?

2. What is there about the story of Adam and Eve and the serpent that rings as true today as when it was written centuries ago? What thoughts occur to you as you think about the Tree of the knowledge of good and evil, the words of the serpent that Adam and Eve would be as gods, the wearing of a loincloth to cover the genitals, the hiding in the bushes?

3. St. Paul wrote of inner conflicts he experienced, doing what he should not do, not doing what he should. How would you relate our chapters on Image of God and Original Sin to Paul's inner warfare? What is the value of seeing Image of God and Original Sin as sources of good and bad energy fields driving your inner life and seeking domination of your inner self? What would you do to overcome the effects of the wounds of original sin on your life?

Prayer

Lord Jesus, my Redeemer, thank you for your incarnation, life, teachings, passion, death, and resurrection. By your paschal mystery, you have made possible our liberation from original and actual sin. We thus can know from our experience that where sin abounds, grace does more abound. Your love is stronger than any sin or evil, whether inherited or actual. We therefore realize that reflection on original sin must include your saving work for you are the center and Lord of history. Through you must be seen the whole picture of the drama of salvation. Praise be to you, Lord Jesus Christ now and forever Amen!

Glossary

Original Holiness and Justice — Revelation teaches us that before sin occurred, man and woman lived in a state of original holiness and justice. There was no suffering or death and they lived in harmony with themselves, creation, and God.

Original Sin — By their disobedience, Adam and Eve were deprived of original holiness and justice. We inherit from them this deprivation, which is called original sin.

Effects of Original Sin — Because of original sin, human nature is weakened. We are affected by ignorance, suffering, and death and the inclination to sin which is called concupiscence.

Devils — Satan (the devil) and other demons are fallen angels who defied God. They tempt us to revolt against God.

Protoevangelium, "First Gospel" — God did not abandon us after the Fall, but announced that a Messiah would come, that there would be a battle between the serpent and the woman's descendant who would achieve the final victory over evil. (Cf Gen 3:9,15) (CCC 410)

"Adam was but human — this explains it all. He did not want the apple for the apple's sake, he wanted it only because it was forbidden."
Mark Twain

Endnote

1. Robert Barron, *And Now I See: A Theology of Tranformation* (New York: Crossroads, 1998), p. 50.

Chapter 8

JESUS COMES TO LOVE AND SAVE US
CCC 442-570

"Shepherd of souls, in love come feed us,
Life-giving Bread for hungry hearts!
To those refreshing waters lead us
Where dwells that peace your love imparts."

Omer Westendorf[1]

Brother Bill Stands in the Line of Fire

There is a sixty-something Catholic layman in Chicago who has an un-usual mission: to stop gang warfare between the Gansta Disciples and the Vice Lords.

Chicago has one hundred twenty-five gangs with seventy thousand members.

How does Bill do it?

He will get a call from a gang member ordered to kill someone.

"Bill, I don't want to kill nobody. I don't want to die. Nothin's gonna happen if you come. Help me, man."

Bill pulls on a blue robe made up of cut-up pieces of old blue jeans. He begins to pray.

The shooting has started by the time he arrives. Bill walks into the cen-ter of the street — right into the line of fire.

He hears the crack of the bullets.

He knows he could be killed.

He feels absolute peace.

He's been doing this for over fifteen years.

"Get out of the way, Brother Bill."

"No I won't . . . Because I love you."

Gradually the gunfire stops. A gang member says, "If Bill is willing to take a bullet because he loves you that much, it makes it harder for you to hate the other side."

Who is Bill? William Wylie Tomes.

How did he get his mission?

He is a middle class Catholic raised in Evanston, Illinois. He attended Jesuit Loyola Prep and Notre Dame University. He worked fifteen years with Catholic Charities when he decided to get a doctorate in psychology. When he obtained his degree, he was offered jobs as chief therapist for a hospital and executive trainer for an airline.

He visited St. Joseph's Ukrainian Church and knelt before an icon of Jesus and prayed for guidance. A voice came from the image:

"Bill, love! Do nothing but love. I'll lead. You follow. Don't be afraid. Give me your trust. Forgive everyone. Take nothing for the journey."

Amazed, Bill returned to that image many times for the next three months and heard the same message. His spiritual director concluded, "Jesus wants you to give away all you own."

Bill eventually surrendered. He gave away his art collection, media center, expensive clothes, all he owned. He went to work as a youth minister in an inner city parish working with the gangs. It was there he discovered his call to stand in the line of fire for the sake of peace.

Recently he found a twenty-one-year-old gang member dying in a stairwell, with four bullets in his chest. The paramedics would be too late. Bill whispered in the young man's ears the last word he would hear.

"God made you. God loves you. God wants you to be with him forever."

Jesus came to save us from our evil. His graces are a thousand points of light in a dark world, one that Brother Bill knows all too well. He has been called to be Christ's peace in a world of violence and poverty and despair.

Do We Need a Savior?

Some say... We do not need a savior. When God created us he gave us all the resources we need to live a good, productive, and moral life. What people call sin is a weakness that can be overcome by determination, discipline, and proper motivation. What some people call grace is the good example of outstanding men and women. Their heroic life stories assure us that we have inside us all we need to triumph over adversity and evil.

Jesus himself taught that the kingdom of God is within us. He meant by this the talents, energies, and drive that come with being human. Above all, this describes the gifts of intelligence and imagination that help us figure out how to master ourselves. When these gifts are wedded to our will power we possess the secret of saving ourselves from the forces that would enslave us.

God honored us by giving us freedom. With this exquisite gift we have the capacity to choose good over evil. When we have the will to believe in our own creativity, there is nothing that can stop us from ultimately making our light shine in the darkness. God never wanted us to be so dependent on him that he would have to send a savior to rescue us. At our birth we received all we need to save ourselves. Our freedom is the keystone of our liberation. To say otherwise is to foster a self-defeating attitude. If we begin our lives imagining we can't, then we will approach moral challenges helplessly. We will depend on a messiah to take over our lives and substitute his strength for our weakness. The result is dehumanizing. We become less human. In reality we become more human the more we exercise our ability to liberate ourselves.

Everyone is an image of God. Does this not affirm that we own the mind, heart, will and imagination to achieve the goal to which God has destined us? Why then would we need a savior?

The truth of the matter is — we don't.

The Catechism *teaches* ...

"God so loved the world that he gave his only Son, that whosoever believes in him should not perish but have eternal life" (Jn 3:16).

We needed a savior for the following four reasons.

(1) *The Son of God became flesh for us to save us from sin and reconcile us to God.* Sin is more than a human failing that can be overcome by effort, imagination, and will power. Sin is a condition from which we need to be saved. Sin alienates us from God as well as from one another. Sin is an evil so profound that it ruptured our relationship with God. Only God can restore this relationship.

(2) *By the power of the Holy Spirit the Son of God became incarnate and was born of the Virgin Mary. Why? That we may know that God is love and that he loves us.* Scripture gradually reveals to us the inner life of God. From the promise of a savior to Adam and Eve, to the covenants with Noah, Abraham, Moses, and the people of Israel, we experience God's loving care for people. But the greatest manifestation of divine love for us was the humble generosity of the Son of God to become a man like us in all things except sin.

(3) *The Word became flesh to show us how to be holy. Every act of Jesus taught us the way to holiness.* "The whole of Christ's life was a continual teaching: his silences, his miracles, his gestures, his prayer, his love for people, his special affection for the little and the poor, his acceptance of the total sacrifice on the Cross for the redemption of the world, and his

resurrection are the actualization of his word and the fulfillment of Revelation."[2]

(4) *The Son of God became man to make it possible for us to share his divine life.* Love transforms the beloved so long as the one loved is receptive. When the lover happens to be God, the transformation brings to the beloved the gift of divine life. Hence Jesus Christ not only empties us of sin but fills us with grace, that is, divine life. The marvel is that Jesus does more than heal a relationship. Jesus elevates us to a participation in God's own life if we are willing and open to be saved through the graces of faith, sacraments, and initiation into the Church.

Who is Jesus Christ? He is the Son of God and the son of Mary — true God and true man. The term *incarnation* means that the Son of God assumed a full human nature, like us in all things except sin. (Cf. Jn 1:14; Phil 2:5-6; Heb 10:5-7; I Tim 3:16)

Jesus Christ is not part man and part God, nor a confused mixture of humanity and divinity. He is fully human and fully divine. While this was the faith of the New Testament believers, it was clarified through responses to various heresies.

The first heresies (Gnosticism, Docetism) denied his humanity. Christian faith asserted Christ's true coming in the flesh, being really born of the Virgin Mary and truly dying on the Cross.

The next major heresy, Arianism, claimed that Jesus was not truly divine. Arius argued that the "Word," which was incarnated in Jesus, was a created being — noble indeed, but not divine.

The Council of Nicaea (325) reaffirmed that Jesus was really God, "begotten, not made, of the same substance as the Father."

A third heresy, Nestorianism, said that Jesus had a human person that was joined to his divine person. The Council of Ephesus (431) proclaimed that the faith of the Church holds that Christ's humanity — body and soul — has no other subject than the divine person of the Son of God from the moment of his conception by Mary. She is therefore truly the mother of God.

A fourth heresy, Monophysitism, argued that Christ's human nature disappeared when the divine person assumed it. The Council of Chalcedon (451) declared that Christ's human nature remained intact at the Incarnation. Christ's divine and human natures remained together without change, confusion, or division — united by the divine person of the Son of God.

How may we speak of Christ's humanity? Vatican II states, "The Son of God . . . worked with human hands, he thought with a human mind, acted by human choice, and loved with a human heart. Born of the Virgin Mary, he has truly been made one of us, like us in all things except sin."[3]

Jesus learned and grew humanly. He "increased in wisdom and in stature, and favor with God and man." (Lk 2:52) At the same time, the Son of God in his human knowledge displayed the divine penetration he had into the secrets of the human heart.

"By its union to the divine wisdom in the person of the Word incarnate, Christ enjoyed in his human knowledge the fullness of understanding of the eternal plans he had come to reveal. [Cf. Mk 8:31; 9:31; 10:33-34; 14:18-20, 26-30]. What he admitted to not knowing in this area, he elsewhere declared himself not sent to reveal [Mk 13:32; Acts 1:7]." (CCC 474)

Jesus possessed a human will as well as a divine one. Jesus willed humanly in obedience to the Father what he had decided divinely with the Father and the Spirit for our salvation.

Jesus had a real human body. In Christ's body we see our God made visible to help us love the God we cannot see.

1. What does the name Jesus mean?

"The Name Jesus means 'God saves.' The child born of the Virgin Mary is called Jesus, 'for he will save his people from their sins' (Mt 1:21): 'there is no other name under heaven given among men by which we must be saved' (Acts 4:12)." (CCC 452)

2. Why is Jesus called Christ?

"The title 'Christ' means 'Anointed One' (Messiah). Jesus is the Christ, for 'God anointed Jesus of Nazareth with the Holy Spirit and with power' (Acts 10:38). He was the one 'who is to come' (Lk 7:19), the object of 'the hope of Israel' (Acts 28:20)." (CCC 453)

3. What do we mean when we call Jesus Son of God?

"The title 'Son of God' signifies the unique and eternal relationship of Jesus Christ to God his Father: he is the only Son of the Father (cf. Jn 1:14, 18; 3:16, 18); he is God himself (cf. Jn 1:1). To be a Christian, one must believe that Jesus Christ is the Son of God (cf. Acts 8:37; I Jn 2:23)." (CCC 454)

Response to objections

By creating us in his image, God has given every person the potential for doing good and avoiding evil. We all have intelligence, imagination, creativity, and will power — talents meant to recognize and enhance our human dignity. The energies that flow within us from being God's image are considerable and filled with promise. And often they do produce the desired results.

But history and everyday experience have demonstrated that logic and human striving alone seem insufficient for dealing with a number of life's weaknesses and mysteries. Death, suffering, wars, holocausts, the vagaries of love, betrayal, cycles of disappointment, failures, rejections, pain, fears, nameless dread, addictions to alcohol and drugs, ethnic cleansing, and a host of similar evils are commonplace.

We have developed prisons, punishments, laws, education, art, culture, sanitariums, therapies, pills, rational inspiration, self-help nostrums, bombs, defense budgets, police forces, customs and social standards to contain and protect ourselves from the evil that lies just below the apparent, controlled, calm surface of life. Yet every day the news programs report murders, rapes, lies, thefts, marital disasters, natural catastrophes, suicides, and other woes that constitute the dark side of human behavior.

We do what we can to save ourselves. Yet it is clear we need something more. Recovery programs remind us that there are hundreds of thousands of cases that rely on a "higher power" for healing. Rich people have created "gated communities," contemporary gardens of paradise, but guards and trained dogs and coded keypads cannot eliminate the virus of evil that roams freely in the prettiest of places.

Eventually, we must come to grips with the mysteries of sin and death. These are not temporary afflictions that will be overcome by human ingenuity. The twentieth century was the cleverest era of history. Never was intelligence triumphant more evident. Never has history seen more horror and suffering. Evil is not a momentary setback that can be overcome by human effort. Evil and sin are a condition from which we need to be saved.

That is why a loving God sent his Son, Jesus Christ, to save us from our sin and to overcome death. Jesus offers us reconciliation with God, deliverance from sin, a revelation of God's undying love, the way to be holy, and a share in divine life. To receive these gifts we need the graces of faith, sacraments, Church, and the abiding presence of the Holy Spirit.

For dialog 1. Share some stories of cases where evil seems to have an intransigent control of a given person's life. In telling such tales, protect — if needed — the privacy of these people. The purpose is not to feel superior or judgmental, but to reflect on "close to home" examples of evil. Balance this with inspiring anecdotes such as those narrated in *Chicken Soup for the Soul*.

2. Discuss the teaching that sin is more than a weakness that can be overcome by human effort, but rather a condition from which we need to be saved. Give testimony about how Jesus Christ has reconciled you to God, shown you the love of God, opened to you the way to holiness and

shared divine life with you. If you are unable to do this, what do you see as the road toward such a possibility?

3. Popular entertainment is filled with stories of violence, lust, betrayal, murder, greed, lies, depression, arrogance, and other human frailties and works of evil. Why do millions want to watch these portrayals of the dark side of humanity, the underworld of human consciousness? Paradoxically, there is also a widespread denial of sin and personal responsibility for evil. Why is this so? Why does the doctrine of Jesus the Savior begin to look better and better in this odd situation?

(The doctrines concerning the Blessed Virgin Mary, Mother of God — and her relationship to Christ and the Church — will be discussed in a separate chapter.)

Prayer

Glory be to you, Lord Jesus Christ, Son of the living God. We thank you for the graces of your incarnation in the womb of Mary, the saving mysteries of your life on earth, and the salvation from sin gained by your death and resurrection. We are grateful for the gift of divine life won by your paschal mystery and the sending of the Holy Spirit. Enable us to confront our sinfulness honestly with all its destructive power. Awaken in us the desire for the salvation that you so graciously offer to us. Wean us away from our resistance to grace. Fill us with faith, hope, and love.

Glossary

Jesus — The name *Jesus* means, "God saves." There is no other name by which we can be saved.

Christ — The word *Christ* means "Messiah" or "Anointed One."

Son of God — In Scripture, the term "Son of God" may refer to angels, the chosen people, and their kings. It implied intimacy between God and his creatures. But when Peter and Paul call Jesus the *Son of God*, they attribute to him actual divine sonship. The same truth is taught at the Baptism and Transfiguration of Jesus when the Father speaks of Jesus as his *Beloved Son*.

Lord — At Sinai. Moses heard God's name as *YHWH* (Yahweh). This name is *Kyrios* in Greek and *Lord* in English. The New Testament calls both the Father and Jesus *Lord*. "To confess or invoke Jesus as Lord is to believe in his divinity." (CCC 455)

"Love the sinner, but hate the sin."

St. Augustine

Endnotes

1. Omer Westendorf, "Shepherd of Souls."

2. John Paul II, *On Catechism*, 9.

3. *Gaudium et Spes* (GS) ("The Church in the Modern World"), 22. Flannery, O.P., General Editor, *Vatican II: The Conciliar and Post Conciliar Documents* (Northport, NY: Costello Publishing, 1975).

Chapter 9

BEHOLD THE WONDROUS CROSS!
CCC 571-637

"Cross of Jesus, cross of sorrow,
Where the blood of Christ was shed.
Perfect man on thee did suffer,
Perfect God on thee hast bled."

William J. Sparrow-Simpson[1]

The Parable of the Three Trees

Three young trees stood on a mountain and dreamed of their future.

Pondering the sparkling stars, the first said, "I want to be a treasure chest, covered with gold and filled with jewels."

Looking at the ocean, the second tree mused, "I want to be a ship and travel mighty waters and carry powerful kings."

Surveying the valley below, the third tree reflected, "I never want to leave this mountaintop. I want to become the world's tallest tree and make people think of God."

Years passed and the three trees reached their maturity.

Then the woodcutters came.

One cut down the first tree who dreamed of being a treasure chest. He brought it to a carpenter's shop. The carpenter fashioned it into a feed box for animals. The once lovely tree was not covered with gold, but coated with sawdust and filled with hay as for hungry farm animals.

Another lumberjack cut down the second tree who dreamed of being an ocean-going ship for kings. Instead the once strong tree was hammered and sawed into a simple fishing boat. Too weak for the ocean, the boat was taken to a small lake.

The third tree that dreamed of soaring on the mountaintop was cut down and divided into beams and left in the lumberyard.

Years passed.

One night a star poured light over the first tree as a young mother put her newborn baby into the feedbox. "I wish I could make a cradle," said the father. The mother smiled and touched the smooth and sturdy wood. "The manger is beautiful." The first tree realized it was carrying the world's greatest treasure.

One evening a tired traveler and his friends crowded into an old fishing boat. The traveler fell asleep. A thrashing storm arose. The little boat shuddered. The tired man awoke. He stood up and said, "Peace." The storm stopped as suddenly as it started. The second tree realized it was carrying the king of heaven and earth.

On Friday morning the beams of the third tree were yanked from the forgotten woodpile. The third tree flinched as she was carried through a jeering crowd. She shuddered when soldiers nailed a man's hands to her. She felt ugly, harsh, and cruel.

But on Sunday morning when the sun rose and the earth trembled with joy beneath her, she knew God's love had changed everything. From now on when people thought of the third tree, they would think of God. This was better than being the world's tallest tree.

The next time you feel down because you did not get what you want, sit tight and be content because God is thinking of something better to give you.

Did Jesus Need to Die to Save Us?

Some say... Jesus did not need to suffer and die to redeem us. Because he was Son of God he could choose a number of less devastating ways to reconcile us to God and demonstrate his love. There was some wisdom spoken by those at the foot of the cross who said to him, "Then save yourself if you are God's son and come down from the cross!" (Mt 27:40) Their tone was mocking but the truth of what they said remains. God's Son did not need to die to save us.

There is something repellent in selecting suffering as a means of salvation. Such purposeful pain would appear to many as psychologically unhealthy. After all, suffering is an evil. Why would an all-good God submit to an evil in order to overcome evil? It doesn't make sense.

It seems even worse to claim that the Father willed such agony for his Son. Is this good modeling for human fathers? Could we admire fathers inflicting pain on their children? The introduction of excruciating pain and humiliating death into the plan of salvation seems like a shortsighted and ill-advised solution.

There is a genuine charm in having the Son of God become a man and share our lives on earth. He was able to show us the ideal path to happiness and teach us the wisdom that could make it happen. In his story we could see exactly what we should do to overcome sin and find inner peace and joy.

He trained leaders to witness his life and teachings and form a community to sustain the dream. He created sacraments to give us saving graces. All he needed to do after that was to say farewell and return to heaven, much as he finally did in his Ascension. Angels sang his glory when he was born. Angels escorted him back to heaven at the conclusion of his earthly ministry.

The interlude of the passion and death does not seem to add much and in fact becomes distracting and puzzling. What point was there in his deciding to submit to suffering and death? Do we not have a right not to suffer? Could he not have supported this human right and given us an example of a pain-free life?

No, Jesus did not need to die to save us. He could have chosen a more creative and positive path.

The Catechism teaches …

"Christ died for our sins in accordance with the scriptures." (1 Cor 15:3) The Apostles and the Church which follows them have made the paschal mystery of the death and resurrection of Jesus the center of the Good News of salvation proclaimed to the world. We will consider first the passion and death of Jesus and then his resurrection from the dead. Though considered separately, they form one redeeming act.

It is a consoling illusion for some to think that Jesus could have passed through this life without facing lethal opposition. Jesus was pure goodness. He was the only person on earth who was both really human and yet with no sin. We need to appreciate that sinfulness cannot be indifferent to goodness. Nor can goodness ignore evil. Good and evil can never be "strange bedfellows" practicing an easy truce of "live and let live."

Once Jesus began to preach and witness the kingdom of salvation, he encountered opposition from the religious leaders of his time. They misunderstood his teaching on the Law of Moses and the temple. They were scandalized by his claim to forgive sins, to be indeed a savior God.

In reality Jesus upheld the Mosaic Law, arguing that he came to fulfill its true meaning. Second, Jesus honored the temple, made pilgrimages to it, prayed there and protected it as God's house. His prophecy of its destruction symbolized his own death and the arrival of a new age in which his Body would be the definitive temple.

When Jesus forgave sins he disclosed himself as the savior God. He socialized with sinners, not because he approved of their sinfulness, but because he wanted to save them from sin. He invited the religious authorities to believe in him. But they were too scandalized. They needed an act of faith in Jesus that required a death to self and a rebirth influenced by grace. Tragically, they misunderstood him, saw him as a threat, and accused him of blasphemy. They acted partly out of ignorance but also from the hardness of unbelief.

Some leaders privately supported him, namely, Nicodemus and Joseph of Arimathea, who were secret disciples. Still, Caiphas and the Sanhedrin declared Jesus a blasphemer and handed him over to the Romans, accusing him of political revolt.

However, the Jewish people should not be held collectively responsible for the death of Jesus. ". . . what happened in his passion cannot be blamed upon all Jews then living, without distinction, nor upon Jews today . . . the Jews should not be presented as repudiated or cursed by God, as if such views followed from holy Scripture."[2] The truth is that ". . . *sinners were the authors and ministers the divine Redeemer endured*" [emphasis added].[3]

Love made Him do it. What did we need to be saved from?

We needed to be saved from sin and its effects, especially alienation from God, suffering, and death.

The Father's loving plan to save us included the Son's entering into our state in every way except sinning. Jesus Christ would redeem everything about us. Why? Because he loves us. How? Because he had a divine person — incarnate in a human nature — he could take our universal humanity and start it over.

He taught this truth. Jesus said the greatest form of love is to die for the beloved. He held up the example of the Good Shepherd who goes after the lost sheep and risks his life to save it.

Can there be value in suffering? Jesus embraced sacrificial love to rescue us. Like the Suffering Servant in Isaiah 53, Jesus silently allowed himself to be led to the slaughter as the real Paschal Lamb. He showed us how to use pain for healing. He did this for every one of us.

"There is not, never has been, and never will be a single human being for whom Christ did not suffer." (Council of Quiercy, A.D. 853) (CCC 605)

Is there an amazing grace in dying for one you love? Certainly there was in the redemptive death of Jesus. This did not make it easy for him. At

Gethsemane he expressed the repulsiveness that death meant for his human nature when he asked the Father to remove this "cup." But freely and lovingly he accepted the Father's will. "He himself bore our sins in his body on the tree." (1 Pt 2:24)

Jesus did not exempt himself from the pain and death all humans know. But he transformed suffering and dying into a redemptive act by his love, freedom, and obedience. He substituted his obedience for our disobedience. No corner or shadow of the human heart was left untouched by Christ's willing presence.

The unassumed would be unhealed.

Jesus assumed effects of our sinfulness, and so healed us.

1. Was the crucifixion of Jesus an unintended accident?

"Jesus' violent death was not the result of chance in an unfortunate coincidence of circumstances, but is part of the mystery of God's plan, as St. Peter explains to the Jews of Jerusalem in his first sermon on Pentecost: 'This Jesus [was] delivered up according to the definite plan and foreknowledge of God.' " (Acts 2:23) (CCC 599)

2. Did Jesus freely embrace the Father's redeeming love for us?

"By embracing in his human heart the Father's love for men, Jesus 'loved them to the end,' for 'greater love has no man than this, that a man lay down his life for his friends.' [Jn 13:1; 15:13] In suffering and death his humanity became the free and perfect instrument of his divine love which desires the salvation of men . . . 'No one takes [my life] from me, but I lay it down of my own accord.'" (Jn 10:18) (CCC 609)

3. Was Christ's death a sacrificial event?

"Christ's death is both the *Paschal sacrifice* that accomplishes the definitive redemption of men, through 'the Lamb of God who takes away the sin of the world' [Jn 1:29; cf. 8:34-36; 1Cor 5:7; 1Pet 1:19] and the *sacrifice of the New Covenant*, which restores man to communion with God by reconciling him to God through the 'blood of the covenant, which was poured out for many for the forgiveness of sins.' (Mt 26:28; cf. Ex 24:8; Lev 16:15-16; 1Cor 11:25)" (CCC 613)

Response to objections

At the heart of Christ's redeeming act is his forgiving love. There is no love without sacrifice in this world. The divine plan of salvation was born of the Father's love for us. Once love entered the picture there was no way of avoiding the sacrifice it would require.

No one has ever loved in this world without the pain that inevitably accompanies it. Loving parents sacrifice for their children. Loving spouses freely and willingly embrace the daunting challenges, the sickness and health, the good times and bad, that belong to the growth of any love. True friends will bicker and make up, but one thing is certain — the path of real affection never runs smooth.

Once it is accepted that love is the key to God's plan of salvation then the role of betrayal, reconciliation, suffering, and death and the dream of immortality — elements present in every love story — is bound to be found in Christ's redeeming work. As soon as the Son of God entered our world, the days of our lives, he would experience all the follies, beauties, craziness, sanity, cravenness, nobility, sins, and graciousness that is our human lot — though without sin himself.

To imagine Jesus breezing through our lives unaffected by the impact of evil, pain, and ultimately death is to construe a spiritual fantasy that would appeal to no one. It is precisely because he saved us in and through all the galvanic forces that human nature — both admirable and detestable — could throw at him, that millions of men and women for two thousand years have thrilled to his story and trooped to his colors, and even died for love of him.

In most of history the heroic has stirred and inspired people's hearts. What is there about the present age that would even remotely approve a standard of unheroic behavior? Heroes and heroines love boldly, suffer grandly, and march larger than life on the world's stage. Why would anyone advocate a bland, sweet, painless life squeezed free of the juices of daring, passion, scaling dizzying heights? Who knows?

One thing is sure, theirs is not a story that has much of a shelf life. The canvases in cathedrals, palaces, and museums surge with the rising aspirations of the human spirit, the hunger for spirituality and redemption. All of those journeys include a Way of the Cross before the resurrection.

It was always so. It always will be until the end of time.

For dialog   1. Share examples of sacrificial love and the impact they have had on your life. What is there about love that demands sacrifice? Why would someone propose a Christ who would save us without suffering on our behalf? Who are your heroes? Your heroines? What do they do for you? What would life be like without them?

2. Read again one of the accounts of the passion and death of Christ from the gospels. What incidents tend to touch you the most? Why are these accounts so durable and influential after two thousand years? What is the secret of their impact on people? We know that Jesus was willing to die for our salvation. Why have Christian martyrs been willing to die for Christ? Why do we say that the "blood of the martyrs is the seed of the Church?"

3. Do you think you could overcome sin by your own efforts and energies? Has this actually happened in your life? How do people discover that in reality they need to be saved from their sinfulness? Is salvation from sin a humbling or exhilirating experience? What would we say to people who deny they have ever sinned?

Prayer

Lord Jesus, my Savior, I honor the holy Cross on which you were impaled to save me from my sins and obtain for me the gift of divine life. I revere the mystery of your passion and death by which you liberated me and every man and woman from the slavery of sin. I stand in awe before your crucified presence and welcome the graces of glory that flow from your wounds. With St. Thomas the Apostle I touch your scars and pray, "My Lord and my God." Give me the graces to participate in your paschal mystery. Help me to take up my cross and follow you.

Glossary

Paschal Mystery — The paschal mystery refers to the saving death and resurrection of Jesus Christ. We experience this mystery and its effects especially in the celebration of the sacraments.

Redemption — The act by which Jesus Christ liberated us from original and actual sin and death and brought us the gift of divine life. This was accomplished above all by his death and resurrection.

"Apart from the cross there is no other ladder
by which we may get to heaven."

St. Rose of Lima

Endnotes

1. William J. Sparrow-Simpson, "Cross of Jesus."
2. *Nostra Aetate* (Declaration on the Relation of the Church to Non-Christian Religions), 4, in Austin Flannery, O.P., ed., *Vatican Council II* (Northport, NY: Costello Publishing Co.: 1975).
3. *Roman Catechism*, I.11.

Chapter 10

JESUS CHRIST IS RISEN TODAY!
ALLELUIA!

CCC 638-658

*"Forth he came at Easter like the risen grain,
He that for three days in the grave had lain.
Raised from the dead my living Lord is seen;
Love is come again like wheat arising green."*

John M. Crum[1]

The Resurrection of Faith in Eastern Europe

In 1988 the churches of Eastern Europe celebrated the thousandth anniversary of the bringing of Christianity to their territories by Saints Cyril and Methodius. The shadow of Communist persecution and opposition to Christianity hung over the commemoration.

In no place was this more evident than in Czechoslovakia.

The secular minister of culture controlled every aspect of Church life. Religious orders were suppressed and went underground for survival. Parish priests could not wear the collar or any visible sign of their calling. Nor could they engage in acts of charity and mercy outside the confines of their churches. For example, they were forbidden to visit the nursing homes or bring Communion to the sick.

Local superintendents of religion monitored priests' sermons to make sure no criticisms of the government occurred. These bosses also kept an account of who went to Church regularly. High school-age youth who were observant Catholics were denied a college education and doomed to low paying jobs.

When the thousandth anniversary of Saints Cyril and Methodius arrived, the minister of culture went to the revered religious shrine of Vellehrad to give a speech marking the occasion. To everyone's surprise, one hundred thousand Catholics showed up, the majority of them college-age students.

The minister droned on talking about "Mr." Cyril and "Mr." Methodius, ignoring any contributions that were made to religion and faith; instead he connected them only to the cultural roots of the nation. The students grew impatient and angry. The started shouting, "Saint" Cyril! and "Saint" Methodius!

Finally, the flustered minister, shocked by this ourburst, gathered up his papers and left the podium. The students cheered and yelled, "Bring us the pope!" Four years later Communism collapsed and the Berlin Wall came tumbling down. And Pope John Paul II went to St. Vitus Cathedral in Prague to celebrate the resurrection of faith and freedom in that nation.

The faithful people arose from the death of persecution to the life of freedom. In a very real way they had lived through the death and resurrection of Jesus in their own history.

What Really Happened On the First Easter Sunday?

Some say... Something happened to the apostles and disciples. They overcame their fear. They spoke of Jesus as being "risen." What did they mean? Several plausible explanations seem acceptable.

First, they had a religious experience of Christ's presence. They did not see him but they felt him as a spiritual presence. They sensed he was alive. He had promised he would return to them and he did so by touching their souls with his love. His resurrection was a felt-spiritual experience.

Second, they meant that Jesus survived in their memories. The impact of his life was so great that they could never forget him. Their temporary sorrow during the passion and crucifixion faded away as the warm glow of his life and teachings flooded into their memories. He would always live there and they would pass this memory onto others. His resurrection was a memory.

Third, those who "saw" Jesus risen were having either a vision or a hallucination. In either case the visual event was purely subjective, meaning that they did not actually encounter a physical body of Christ that could be touched.

Various psychological pressures were probably at work. Peter's vision could be attributed to his guilt about the denial. This drove him to imagine he saw Jesus. Similarly, Paul's vision was most likely the outcome of an obsession with Christ. The story of the five hundred who claimed they saw a risen body of Christ could plausibly be explained as a classic case of mass hysteria.

The resurrection was a subjective event. Something happened to the apostles and disciples. Nothing happened to Christ's body.

How then shall we read the resurrection narratives of the gospels?

The gospel stories of the empty tomb and the resurrection appearances are fictional accounts, composed long after Christ's death to justify his claims to divinity. They embarrass the modern mind and are a disservice to Jesus.

The Catechism *teaches* ...

"If Christ has not been raised, then empty [too] is our preaching; empty, too, your faith." (1Cor 15:14) At dawn on the Sunday morning after his death, Jesus Christ rose from the dead in his glorified body. The resurrection of Jesus is the central truth of our faith. It was believed and lived by the first Christian community, passed on by Apostolic Tradition, confirmed in the New Testament, and preached as an essential part of the paschal mystery along with the Cross.

Christ's resurrection really happened historically as evidenced by his appearances and the testimony of numerous witnesses. (1Cor 15:3-4) The empty tomb prepared the holy women and the apostles to encounter the risen Lord. When St. John looked at the empty grave and linen cloth, "... he saw and believed." (Jn 20:8)

Mary Magdalene and the holy women came at dawn to complete the anointing of Jesus' body. The original anointing had been interrupted by the arrival of Passover. Mary Magdalene met the risen Jesus in the garden by the tomb. She brought this great news of the resurrection to the apostles. Hence she is called the *Apostola Apostolorum*, the Apostle to the Apostles. Next, Peter and the apostles saw the crucified and risen Jesus and became witnesses. Lastly, St. Paul, St. James, and five hundred others testified they met the crucified and risen Lord.

What was Christ's body like? He could be touched, seen and be able to eat a meal. He was not a ghost. The risen Christ said to the apostles, "Why do questions arise in your hearts? Look at my hands and my feet, that it is I myself. Touch me and see, because a ghost does not have flesh and bones as you see I have. . . Have you anything to eat?" (*Lk* 24:38-9; 41) They gave him a piece of baked fish and he ate it in front of them. He even bore the scars of the nail marks from the crucifixion.

But he also carried the qualities of a **glorified body**.

He was not limited by space or time, but able to be present how and where he willed. He was different from Lazarus and the daughter of Jairus whose bodies were resuscitated. They came back from the dead to ordinary life and would die again. Jesus rose from death to another life beyond space and time. The Holy Spirit permeated his body. Jesus is now a man of heaven.

While the resurrection of Christ is an event of history, it is also a transcendent event beyond the realm of history. No one saw the resurrection event itself. No evangelist describes it. No one can tell us how it happened physically. Nor can hand or eye or ear perceive how the essence of Christ's life passed over into another form. Though he could be seen, heard and touched, his Resurrection is essentially a religious mystery which requires our faith to accept. The New Testament always speaks of having faith in the Resurrection even by those who saw, touched and ate with Jesus.

Easter was a work of the Holy Trinity.

The Father's power raised Jesus.

The Son used his divine power to rise from the dead.

The Holy Spirit gave life to Christ's dead humanity.

What is the meaning of Christ's Resurrection for us?
1. Our faith would be senseless if Jesus had not risen.
2. It fulfilled the promises of the Old Testament and of Jesus.
3. The Resurrection demonstrates the divinity of Jesus. "When you lift up the Son of Man then you will realize that I AM." (Jn 8:28)
4. Easter completes the paschal mystery. At Calvary Jesus freed us from sin. At Easter he offers us divine life.
5. The Resurrection is the principle and source of our own bodily resurrection, first by the justification of our souls, then by new life for our bodies at the general resurrection of the dead.

1. How is the Resurrection historical and transcendent?
"Faith in the Resurrection has as its object an event which is historically attested to by the disciples, who really encountered the Risen One. At the same time, this event is mysteriously transcendent insofar as it is the entry of Christ's humanity into the glory of God." (CCC 656)

2. What is the lesson of the empty tomb?
"The empty tomb and the linen cloths lying there signify in themselves that by God's power Christ's body had escaped the bonds of death and corruption. They prepared the disciples to encounter the Risen Lord." (CCC 657)

3. How is Christ's Resurrection the principle of our resurrection?
"Christ, 'the first born from the dead' (Col 1:18), is the principle of our own resurrection, even now by the justification of our souls (cf. Rom 6:4), and one day by the new life he will impart to our bodies (cf. Rom 8:11)." (CCC 658)

Response to objections

People from the beginning have doubted the truth of the bodily Resurrection of Christ from the dead. Jewish leaders considered he was already guilty of blasphemy and cursed for having been crucified. Greeks only believed in the immortality of the soul. It was repugnant to them that the body should rise again. The first heretics (Gnostics and Docetists) denied that Jesus had a real body, for God would never literally take on a body. Hence no resurrection was possible.

But the Crucified and Risen Christ is the center of the Christian faith. Without this mystery there would be no Church, no hope of eternal life, no living Christ to encounter in his Eucharistic body and blood. It is very unlikely that people would have died as Christian martyrs who believed in the bodily Resurrection of Jesus if all it meant was a subjective experience with no objective foundation.

The contemporary deniers of the Resurrection twist the language of the New Testament to suit their own biases. They look at the gospel stories of the Resurrection and reject what the authors said and meant.

Instead they claim, "This is what the Resurrection narratives mean, regardless of what the New Testament said or meant." If we were to apply this principle to modern law, psychology, or philosophy we would not be surprised that lawyers, psychologists, and philosophers would be angry and outraged.

When some people say the Resurrection was just a memory, a totally inward spiritual experience, or a fiction to defend Christ's divinity, they are denying the evidence of the text that obviously says otherwise. Basically, they are saying, "It could not have happened, therefore it did not happen."

Old time skeptics, like Celsus or David Hume, recognized what the New Testament writers said and meant. On grounds of common sense or rational judgment, they found the teaching unacceptable, but they never denied that is what the scriptural texts said.

As Rabbi Jacob Neusner has asked, if we dismiss most of the gospels as unhistorical, how will we save Moses? Religion does more than state secular facts. Faith speaks of God's action in the world. That cannot come under the court of secular history that claims such action is "unhistorical."

Christ's Resurrection is both historical, as witnesses testify, and transcendent — beyond history — as a mystery of faith.

For dialog

1. What are your childhood memories of Easter? What were you taught about Christ's Resurrection? As you have grown older in your faith journey, how has your faith in the Res-

urrection matured? What does St. Paul's statement, without the Resurrection our faith is in vain, mean to you today?

2. Have you read or heard about "near death" experiences, stories of people who apparently died and then returned to tell the tale of seeing light and vague visions of relatives and friends? What do you think of this? What impact might this have on your faith in the immortality of your soul and the eventual resurrection of your body? Are such experiences "proofs" of resurrection or interesting indicators of a hunger for life after life?

3. What do the pyramids of Egypt, vast tombs, monuments to kings, queens, and generals and other similar ways of remembering the dead indicate to you? What other ways do we express our yearning for immortality, for life after death? Why is the resurrection of our bodies important? What is the connection between Christ's Resurrection and ours?

Prayer Crucified and Risen Jesus, we join the angels, saints, and the Church in singing alleluias to celebrate this historic and transcendent event. We rejoice in your glory and thank you for this gift that enables us to die to our sins and be filled with the Holy Spirit. We are filled with confidence in the face of the Good News that is greater than all other news. Because of Easter, our faith is justified and filled with assurance. May we now walk in your peace, safe from all that could harm us.

Glossary **Resuscitation** — The body is temporarily restored to life after death, as in the case of Lazarus and the daughter of Jairus. They lived for a while and died again.

Reincarnation — This is a belief that we emerge after our death and live again in some other body. Hence our existence is a journey in which we live, die, and live once more in another "incarnation."

Resurrection — Our Christian faith tells us that because of Christ's bodily Resurrection we are already justified in our souls if we have come to Jesus in faith, and that our bodies will rise again on the last day in a permanent glorified form and be united with our souls.

"To behold the risen Christ was an experience that burst the bounds of the ordinary."

Romano Guardin[2]

Endnotes

1. John M. Crum, "Now the Green Blade Rises."
2. Romano Guardin, *The Lord* (Washington, D.C.: Regnery Gateway, 1982), p. 409.

Chapter 11

COME, HOLY SPIRIT
CCC 683-747

"On Pentecost they gathered quite early in the day.
A band of Christ's disciples to worship, sing, and pray.
A mighty wind came blowing, filled all the swirling air.
And tongues of fire a-glowing inspired each person there."

Jane Parker Huber[1]

The Third Age — That of the Spirit

Around the year 1190, a fervent young man went to the Holy Land on a pilgrimage. While there, he had several mystical experiences that influenced him profoundly some years later. Upon his return, he trained as a canon lawyer and worked in a chancery in Italy. Eventually he became a Cistercian monk and acquired some modest fame for his spirituality. Several popes and cardinals became his friends.

When he was fifty, he left the Cistercians and founded his own monastery at Fiore. He became known as Joachim of Fiore. Soon thereafter he wrote a prophecy whose content was based on his visions in the Holy Land.

His prophecy included an interpretation of history. He claimed that all history is divided into three ages. The first was the Age of the Father, which occurred in the Old Testament. The second was the Age of the Son, which began with the New Testament and would continue until 1260.

In 1260 the third period would start — the Age of the Spirit. He predicted that in this era the visible Church would become invisible, for all Christians would become a community in the Spirit. Popes, bishops, and priests would acquire new roles since no visible organization or administration would be needed for an invisible Church. Finally, this would be a period in which love would prevail and war would disappear.

At first his work caused little excitement or opposition. He was never censured or called to correct his prophecy. After his death, however, and as the year 1260 approached there was more controversy about it. A branch of Franciscans went off by themselves and awaited the Age of the Spirit, believing their way of life perfectly fit the prediction of Joachim.

Thomas Aquinas rejected the whole idea. For him, yes, the Old Testament was the Age of the Father. But the second Age was that of the Son who sent the Spirit to inaugurate the Church. The third age would be heaven.

Well, 1260 came and nothing radical happened. No millennium occurred. But the dream of Joachim lived on. Many of the Protestant reformers in the sixteenth century believed their new faith was the Age of the Spirit. They stressed the invisible and spiritual side of the Church over against visible popes, bishops, priests, and other vast Catholic structures. They played down sacraments other than Baptism and Communion, and added that the real priesthood was that of the faithful.

Fascination with Joachim's scenario continued so that even secular paradise models developed such as Communism's "workers' paradise" and Nazism's thousand years of Aryan supremacy. There is always a hunger to have a perfect society on earth, an era of the Spirit. It certainly is an admirable ideal to make life on earth as close to heaven as we can in a sinful world. But we should never expect a utopia in the present scheme of things.

Still, in quite another sense, we are already in the Age of the Spirit and the catechesis of the Spirit shows us what that means.

Is the Holy Spirit God?

Some say... There is only one God. We should do all we can to support the monotheism so clearly upheld by the Jewish and Moslem religions. To claim the Holy Spirit is God in the sense of being a separate person contradicts monotheistic belief. Scripture itself describes the Holy Spirit always in terms of how the One God affects the world.

The Spirit is God "breathing." This breath of God hovers over the dark abyss in the first chapter of Genesis and blows into it the life forms that eventually emerge. In one scene God takes a lump of clay and breathes life into it after which Adam appears. This breathing of God makes creation possible. The Spirit is a way of illustrating the creativity of the One God.

This breath of God swept into the souls of the prophets inflaming them with a social conscience and penetrating their spirits with the courage to confront kings and shape a nation's moral fiber. The Spirit was a scriptural device to help readers understand God's action in history. When God breathed on the prophets he shaped their ability to bring the People of God back to a sound covenant relationship.

In the life of Jesus, God's influence continued much as it had with the prophets. As always the image that describes this action best was the Spirit. This Spirit led Jesus into the desert to be tempted. Christ's teachings, ministry, miracles, and witness all reflected God's Spirit action in his life. The Spirit was not a separate divine person, so much as a method by which God exercised divine power in the world.

Pentecost is another excellent example of this truth about the One God. Fire and wind are images drawn from nature, pictures that show how God's remarkable power flooded the Upper Room and changed a scared group of apostles and disciples into fiery and courageous evangelizers of the world. The remaining pages of the New Testament testify to the force by which God shaped the destiny of the Church. God's spiritual force, symbolized by the Spirit, prompted, prodded, inspired, and encouraged the boldness of the apostles and disciples as they went forth to convert the known world to Christ.

The image of the Spirit was an excellent tool for showing how the One God behaved in the world and also preserved the truth about the spiritual nature of God. The true God is not some kind of natural, physical force, rather this God is pure spirit, yes, a Holy Spirit.

This is the real meaning of Holy Spirit.

The Catechism teaches ...

The Holy Spirit is God, one of the three persons of the Holy Trinity. In the Nicene Creed, we profess our belief that the Holy Spirit is the Lord (that is, God) and giver of life.

In the fourth century, some had denied that the Spirit was divine. The Church convened the First Council of Constantinople (381 AD) at the church of Holy Peace (Hagia Irena) where the bishops reaffirmed the New Testament faith that the Spirit was as divine as the Father and the Son.

The Holy Spirit is the last of the persons of the Trinity to be revealed. St. Gregory of Nazianzus outlines the divine teaching method by which the Trinity was slowly revealed:

"The Old Testament revealed the Father clearly, but the Son more obscurely. The New Testament revealed the Son and gave us a glimpse of the divinity of the Spirit. Now the Spirit dwells among us [in the Church] and grants us a clearer vision of himself."

St. Gregory taught that we needed first to grasp God as Father; then, we could proceed in faith to accept the revelation of the divinity of the Son. Finally, we would be ready to receive the disclosure of the divinity of the

Spirit. In this way we advanced slowly in appreciating the mystery of the Trinity.

The Spirit is always involved in the plan of salvation. The Holy Spirit is involved in the plan of salvation from the beginning just as much as the Father and the Son. The Spirit is really God. The Spirit is "consubstantial with the Father and the Son" and is inseparable from them. (cf. CCC 689) The Spirit has the same "substance" or divine nature as they do. The Spirit has the same mission as the Son in the cause of salvation. When the Father sends the Son he also sends the Spirit to save us from sin and give us divine life.

The word Spirit comes from the Hebrew *ruah* which means "breath, air, wind." The Spirit is God's breath, filling us with divine life, purifying our souls, sustaining our immortality until we love what God loves, do what God wants of us until this earthly part of us glows with divine fire.

Scripture calls the Spirit the *paraclete*, meaning our advocate and consoler. Jesus asked the Father to send us the Spirit to remind us of what Jesus taught and guide us into truth. On Easter night Jesus gave the Holy Spirit to the Apostles, breathing into them the third person of the Trinity. From that moment on the mission of Jesus and the Spirit becomes the mission of the Church.

Tradition uses many images to illustrate the Spirit's actions.

1. Water, signifying the Spirit's saving action at Baptism.

2. Oil and Seal, by which the Spirit anoints us at Confirmation.

3. Fire, by which the Spirit transforms us into Christ.

4. Cloud, the shining glory that led Israel in the desert, dwelt on the Ark of the Covenant, overshadowed Mary at the Annunciation, and was present at Christ's baptism and transfiguration. The cloud image emphasizes how the Spirit helps us experience the effective divine presence.

1. How close is the work of the Spirit to the Father and the Son?

"From the beginning to the end of time, whenever God sends his Son, he also sends his Spirit: their mission is conjoined and inseparable." (CCC 743)

The Holy Spirit, whom Christ the head pours out on his members, builds, animates, and sanctifies the Church." (CCC 747)

2. How do we experience the Spirit in our life in the Church?

"The Church, a communion living in the faith of the apostles which she transmits, is the place where we know the Holy Spirit:

• in the Scriptures he inspired;

• in the Tradition, to which the Church Fathers are always timely witnesses;

• in the Church's Magisterium, which he assists;

• in the sacramental liturgy, through its words and symbols, in which the Holy Spirit puts us into communion with Christ;

- in prayer, wherein he intercedes with us;
- in the charisms and ministries by which the Church is built up;
- in the signs of apostolic and missionary life;
- in the witness of the saints through whom he manifests his holiness and continues the work of salvation." (CCC 688)

3. *What did the Holy Spirit accomplish in Mary?*

"In the fullness of time the Holy Spirit completes in Mary all the preparations for the Christ's coming among the People of God. By the action of the Holy Spirit in her, the Father gives the world Emmanuel, 'God-with-us' (Mt 1:23)." (CCC 744)

Response to objections

The doctrine of the Trinity has always caused people to resist the tension between the unity of the Godhead and the trinity of persons. Monotheists such as Moslems and Jews emphasize the unity of God and the divine Oneness. They do not accept the divinity of Jesus Christ or the Holy Spirit.

Others want to preserve the unity of God by arguing that what we call a trinity of persons is actually a way of talking about the three major functions of God.

These divine behaviors are: creation, redemption, sanctification. God functions in our lives as a creator, savior, and sanctifier. It is intellectually convenient for us to symbolize these roles of God in terms of Father, Son, and Spirit. Catholic theology calls this approach "modalism." In other words there are three modes or methods by which the One God relates to us.

People who hold this view assume that God's inner life is totally unknowable. All we know is God's external behavior, functions by which he touches us as creator, redeemer, sanctifier. The One-personed God manifests himself in three ways for our benefit.

But this is a reading of Scripture that does not take seriously the words and meaning of revelation about God's inner life. We would not know this if God had not told us. Scripture plainly says that God is Father, that God is Son, and that God is Spirit, and that God is One. Scripture challenges us to have faith in God as one and three. This is an awesome mystery about which we can touch only the threshold.

We are not the first believers to find the mystery daunting. The first four councils of the Church were equally challenged by it. Read their history and conclusions. After several centuries of dialogue, debate, and prayerful outcomes the councils reaffirmed scriptural faith about three persons in one God.

Hence the argument that the Holy Spirit is only a function or role of one God is unacceptable to Catholic faith.

For dialog 1. If you have experienced Catholic charismatic renewal, share your experience with the group. If you were a member of a Pentecostal-style faith, tell the group what it was like. Of what value are such testimonies? If you have had a religious conversion in recent years, how has the experience of the Holy Spirit been part of that conversion? From your knowledge of Scripture, show how the Holy Spirit provided people with an experience of God.

2. Why might we be able to say that prayerful reading of Scripture and devout participation in Eucharist are fruitful sources for experiencing the impact of the Spirit? What are ways you have found which help you get in touch with the Holy Spirit? Shares stories about people you know or have read about who seem to be deeply influenced by the Spirit?

3. Read 1 Cor 12-14 which describes the gifts of the Spirit. Note that chapter thirteen teaches that love is the greatest Spirit gift. Note also in chapter fourteen that the ability to speak in tongues is a lesser gift and is only important if it strengthens Church community. Which gifts do you think you have received? What aspects of the gift of love have you experienced? As you review the gifts, which ones would you be motivated to pray for?

Prayer *. . . For the seven gifts of the Holy Spirit . . .*

Come, Holy Spirit, with the gift of Wisdom. Direct my every thought, word, and deed to your greater honor and glory.

Come, Holy Spirit, with the gift of Knowledge. I ask especially for a deeper knowledge of Jesus and Mary.

Come, Holy Spirit, with the gift of Understanding. Help me to know myself more deeply and You more profoundly.

Come, Holy Spirit, with the gift of Courage. May I serve you today with a cheerful heart.

Come, Holy Spirit, with the gift of Counsel. Shape my conscience according to your loving law.

Come, Holy Spirit, with the gift of Piety.
- By Christ's agony in the garden, help me to do God's will.
- By Christ's scourging at the pillar, make me pure.
- By Christ's crowning with thorns, make me love.
- By Christ's carrying of the cross, make me compassionate.
- By Christ's death and resurrection, redeem me from my sins and give me divine life.

Come, Holy Spirit, with the gift of Fear of the Lord.

- That I may fear to displease you, my God, and fear to be separated from the love of Christ.
- That I may be delivered from the false fears of failure, rejection, pain, and death.
- Give me the love that casts out fear.

Glossary

Charism — A scriptural term meaning gift, used to describe the Holy Spirit's gifts, especially those in 1 Cor 12-14.

Paraclete — In Jn 16:7, Jesus calls the Spirit the Advocate or Paraclete, referring to the Spirit's work of convincing us of our sinfulness, convicting us of it, and converting us from it.

"The Spirit comes gently and makes himself known by his fragrance. He is not a burden, for he is light."

St. Cyril of Jerusalem

Endnote

1. Jane Parker Huber, "Breaking Bread."

Chapter 12

THE CHURCH IS THE LIGHT
OF NATIONS

CCC 748-870

"About Jesus Christ and the Church, I simply know they're just one thing, and we shouldn't complicate the matter."

St. Joan of Arc

A Protestant Tribute to the Catholic Church

British Protestant and historian Thomas Macaulay wrote the following reflection on the durability of the Catholic Church.

"There is not and there never was on earth a work of human policy so well deserving of examination as the Roman Catholic Church. The history of that Church joins together two great ages of human civilization. No other institution is left standing, which carries the mind back to the times when the smoke of sacrifice rose from the Pantheon, and when cameleopards and tigers bounded in the Flavian Amphiteater.

"The proudest royal houses are but of yesterday, when compared to the line of Supreme Pontiffs. That line we trace back to an unbroken series from the Pope who crowned Napoleon in the nineteenth century to the Pope who crowned Pepin in the eighth; and far beyond the time of Pepin the august dynasty extended till it is lost in the twilight of fable. . .

The Church saw the commencement of all governments and of all the ecclesiastical establishments that now exist in the world; and we feel no assurance that she is not destined to see the end of them all. She was great and respected before the Saxon set foot on Britain, before the Frank had passed the Rhine, when Grecian eloquence still flourished at Antioch, when idols were still worshiped in the temple of Mecca.

"And she may still exist in undiminished vigor when some traveler from New Zealand shall, in the midst of a vast solitude, take his stand on a broken arch of London Bridge to sketch the ruins of St. Paul's." — Thomas B. Macaulay[1]

Should the Church Be an Institution?

Some say... The Church should stress its invisible, spiritual vocation. People are touched by a personal relationship with Jesus Christ and those who represent Jesus, particularly popes, bishops, priests, and religious. But the Church as an *institution* stands in the way. Too much money, energy, and effort are put into maintaining the organization of the Church from top to bottom.

To make sure the Church is an institution the Vatican has to support a vast bureaucracy. The same is true in every diocese, especially big ones in large metropolitan areas. Even local parishes, particularly large ones, require institutional trappings of committees, budgeting, planning, and other organizational traits.

All of this takes its toll on the personal and relational aspects of faith ministry. Maintaining the institution swallows up the time, money, and energy of the leadership. The hierarchical style of Church leadership distances the bishops and priests from the people. Ambition for titles and preferment dilutes the spiritual quality of the leaders.

Instead everyone should be insisting on the communal nature of the Church. At the base of the dome of St. Peter's Basilica in Rome are inscribed the words of Jesus to Peter, "Peter, do you love me?" "Yes, Lord." "Feed my sheep." (cf. Jn 21:15-17) This is the love model of Church leadership that should prevail. Love is what would give the Church the magnetism that would attract secular man and woman.

It is instructive to note that Vatican II spoke strongly about the Church being a People of God. The focus of the Church should be people, not buildings and committees and laws and rules. Love is what will make the Church an effective presence for all people. Jesus came to save people not organizational structures. The more the Church becomes a community of love, the closer it will fulfill what Jesus intended for her.

Whenever community is the priority there the Church grows. It has been claimed that eighty percent of parish effort is directed to maintaining the structure. Suppose this was reversed and eighty percent of parish energy was spent on fostering mutual love and the advancement of community and spiritual values of faith and hope?

The Church should be a community.

The Catechism *teaches* ... The Church is the People of God, the Body of Christ and the Temple of the Holy Spirit. The Church has a visible and invisible aspect. The visible Church is a public institution with a hierarchical government, laws, and customs. This is its earthly and human side. Its purpose is to serve the salvation needs of God's people. St. Robert Bellarmine said the Church is as visible as the kingdom of Naples.

The invisible Church is the Body of Christ, the Temple of the Holy Spirit — a divine reality maintained by the gifts and graces of God. It is present on earth and is seen in the holiness of its members but also transcends the earth. This visible and invisible truth about the Church is one complex reality ordered to the salvation and holiness of its members.

The Church is a mystery of faith. It is planned, founded, and sustained by God. It is the sacrament of salvation. A sacrament does three things by God's grace. (1) It points to a divine reality. (2) It contains this reality. (3) It produces this reality. When we speak of the Church as the sacrament of salvation we mean that it points to salvation and the kingdom of heaven, and it contains and produces these gifts by the power of the Holy Spirit. By the help of the Spirit we receive these gifts when our hearts are open to the Church and the sacraments.

How does this happen?

The Spirit communicates the graces of Jesus Christ to us through the Church and her seven sacraments. By the will of Christ the savior, the Church is the divinely appointed instrument of salvation in the world. "The Church, in Christ, is like a sacrament — a sign and instrument, that is, of communion with God and of unity among all men." (*Lumen Gentium*, 1) (CCC 775)

The Church as People of God contains seven traits:

1. God's people are called by God's Word not by self-choice.
2. They require a spiritual birth in faith, conversion, and Baptism.
3. They have for their head Jesus Christ and the pope as his vicar.
4. All members have dignity as sons and daughters of God in whom the Spirit dwells.
5. Their [the Church's] law: To love as Jesus did.
6. Their Mission: To be the salt and light of unity, hope, and salvation for everyone on earth.
7. Their Destiny: The kingdom of God begun on earth, perfected in heaven.

"The Church is the Body of Christ. Through the Spirit and his action in the sacraments, above all the Eucharist, Christ, who once was dead and is now risen, establishes the community of believers as his own Body. In the unity of this Body, there is a diversity of members and functions.

"All members are linked to one another, especially to those who are suffering, to the poor and persecuted."

"The Church is the Temple of the Holy Spirit. The Spirit is the soul, as it were, of the Mystical Body, the source of its life, of its unity in diversity, and of the riches of its gifts and charisms" (CCC 805, 806, 809).

The Church is one, holy, catholic, apostolic. The four marks of the Church — one, holy, catholic, apostolic — are inseparably linked to one another. They are always found in the Church and essential to her mission. Only faith can see this. The Church's history of saints, holiness, durability, stability, and charitable outreach testify to her credibility and divine mission.

But because of the sinfulness of the membership, these marks are not always wholly realized. The marks are both a reality and a challenge.

The Church is one. She reflects the unity of the Trinity. The Spirit works to unify the Church and reconcile its members. This unity includes a diversity of gifts, talents, cultures, and rites. The bonds of unity contain the one faith received from the apostles, the sacraments, and the Christian community as well as the apostolic succession with the bishops as signs of unity and the pope as vicar of Christ. This unity has been injured by heresy, apostasy, and schism. The ecumenical movement is designed to restore the unity of the Church (cf. CCC 818-819 for principles of ecumenism).

The Church is holy. Christ the founder is holy. Jesus makes holiness, which is freedom from sin and participation in divine life, available to us by his paschal mystery. The Holy Spirit imparts this holiness to us. But though the Church is holy, there is sinfulness in its members, sins that can be forgiven in the sacrament of Reconciliation. The Church confirms its holiness when it canonizes saints.

The Church is catholic. Catholic means universal. All the means of salvation are found in the Church. We have the fullness of the faith, the sacraments, and apostolic succession. We have a universal mission to all countries. Christ commissions us to speak to the consciences of all people. The Church strives to relate to every nation, culture, and religion. The challenge is to make this a reality to the several billion people for whom the case for Christ has not yet been made.

The Church is apostolic. This means the Church is founded by and built upon the twelve apostles who were called and trained by Christ and established by him as a the foundation of the Church. We have received the teaching of the apostles. The Church continues to be taught by the successors of the apostles: the college of bishops, assisted by the priests and united to the pope, the successor of Peter. The Church is also apostolic in the missionary meaning of the word.

Study the *Catechism's* treatment of the Church's Magisterium, CCC 888-892.

1. How is the Church of Christ in the Catholic Church?
"'The sole Church of Christ which in the Creed we profess to be one, holy, catholic, and apostolic, . . . subsists in the Catholic Church, which is governed by the successor of Peter and by the bishops in communion with him. Nevertheless, many elements of sanctification and of truth are found outside its visible confines' (LG 8)." (CCC 870)

2. What is the relation of pope, bishops, priests, and deacons?
"The Bishops, established by the Holy Spirit, succeed the apostles. They are 'the visible source and foundation of unity in their own particular Churches' (LG 23).

"Helped by the priests, their co-workers, and by the deacons, the bishops have the duty of authentically teaching the faith, celebrating divine worship, above all the Eucharist, and guiding their Churches as true pastors. Their responsibility also includes concern for all the Churches, with and under the Pope." (CCC 938-939)

3. What is the role of the laity in the Church?
"Lay people share in Christ's priesthood: ever more united with him, they exhibit the grace of Baptism and Confirmation in all dimensions of their personal family, social, and ecclesial lives, and so fulfill the call to holiness addressed to all the baptized.

"By virtue of their prophetic mission, lay people 'are called . . . to be witnesses to Christ in all circumstances and at the very heart of the community of mankind' (GS 43, 4)." (CCC 941-942)

4. What is the Communion of Saints?
"The Church is a 'communion of saints': this expression refers first to the 'holy things' (*sancta*), above all the Eucharist, by which 'the unity of believers, who form one body in Christ, is both represented and brought about' (LG 3).

"The term 'communion of saints' refers also to the communion of 'holy persons' (*sancti*) in Christ who 'died for all,' so that what each one does or suffers in and for Christ bears fruit for all.

" 'We believe in the communion of all the faithful of Christ, those who are pilgrims on earth, the dead who are being purified, and the blessed in heaven, all together forming one Church; and we believe that in this communion, the merciful love of God and his saints is always [attentive] to our prayers' (Paul VI, CPG 30).' " (CCC 960-962)

Response to objections

There is no doubt that the Church ought to be a community of faith, hope, and love, called by the Father, centered in Jesus and held together by the Holy Spirit. We accept without reserve the love model of leadership determined by Jesus in his call to Peter in Jn 21:15-17.

However, we assert that the Church is both a community and an institution. Jesus called Peter to the institutional model of leadership at Caesarea Phillipi when he said, "You are Peter and upon this rock I will build my Church." (Mt 16:18) These words are also inscribed at the base of the dome of St. Peter's in Rome thus vividly dramatizing the balance of community and institution that gives us a comprehensive view of the Church.

It is common enough to argue that love is a charism of the Spirit and this is clearly taught in 1 Cor 1-13. But the institution is also a charism of the Spirit as exemplified by Christ's use of the "rock" image in Matthew 16 and also by St. Paul when he lists "administration" among the Spirit's gifts. (1 Cor 12:28)

The Church needs an institutional side to serve its stability, continuity, and order. So long as this is seen as a loving service to people, the institution will not be an obstacle to community nor a block to knowing and loving Jesus. Just as the soul needs a body, so the community needs an organization to serve it.

Abuse does not take away the use. Problems with the institution are not arguments for its removal, but rather for its renewal. We need the rock and we need the love. Together, working in harmony, they give us a holistic Church, much as Jesus intended.

The Church is both and community and an institution.

For dialog

1. If you are active in your campus parish, or also in your parish at home, what are you involved in? When you are participating in Church life, what are some values that proceed from that? What are the values and challenges you experience from your membership in the Church?

2. This lesson raises questions about whether the Church should be an institution or a community. How could the Church's communal life be enhanced? Why is it important that the Church always have an institutional aspect? If you were to explain the four marks of the Church, what stories or examples would you use to do so?

3. The Church should always be missionary in its outreach to others. In its basic form this would mean that the members are willing to share their faith in a friendly and invitational way. What opportunities to do this might

arise in your life? Why might we say that sharing faith is a sign of the vitality of the Church's members?

If you wanted to improve the Church what would you like to see?

How do you think that love for the Church can be fostered?

Prayer

Father, we praise you for calling the Church into existence. Jesus, we are grateful for your ministry in establishing the Church. Holy Spirit, we love you for manifesting and sustaining the Church from Pentecost to present day. We ask for the graces we need to be loving and active Catholics. May we contribute to the building of faith community and the strengthening of the Church's stability and continuity. Thank you, Lord, for this great gift.

Glossary

People of God — God calls the Church into existence thereby forming a community of faith, hope, and love centered in Christ and sustained by the Holy Spirit.

Body of Christ — Jesus Christ is head of the Church. We are the members of his Body. Each of us has been given particular gifts by the Holy Spirit to make the Body of Christ visible and accessible for all peoples.

Temple of the Holy Spirit — The Holy Spirit manifested the Church at Pentecost. The Spirit continues to be the cohesive force of the Church in favorable and unfavorable circumstances. Because of the Spirit the Church has stability and continuity and availability for the salvation of the world.

Sacrament of Salvation — The Church is the sacrament of salvation for through it Jesus Christ saves the world by the graces of the sacraments, the preaching of the Word of God, and the spiritual and moral witness of the members.

"Look for a moment at the whole panorama of twenty centuries of the Church. It begins in the wounded side of Christ, goes through the 'tempering' of Pentecostal fires, and comes onward like a burning flood to pass through each era."

Henri De Lubac, S.J.

Endnote

1. In *Faith of Millions*, Father John A. O'Brien (Huntington, IN: Our Sunday Visitor, 1993).

Chapter 13

MARY, OUR BELOVED

CCC 466; 484-511; 963-975; 2673-2679

"Who would know how to proclaim your grandeur?
You have embellished human nature,
You have surpassed angelic legions,
You have surpassed all creatures. . .
We acclaim you: Hail full of grace!"

Sophronius of Jerusalem

I Felt a Mother's Love Had Touched Me

A retreat master was giving a retreat. Toward the end of it a woman handed him a note. He put it in his pocket and forgot about it. After the retreat he found it, unfolded it, and read:

"For the past eight months I have been in psychotherapy.

"As a child I experienced overwhelming fear because of hatred and abuse. A major focus of my life right now is to overcome and transform that fear. The details are unnecessary, but much of my fear is centered on my mother. I had become so turned off to the concept of mothers that I consciously rejected the love of Mary, the mother of Jesus.

"After your talk I walked outside — feeling terribly alone. I prayed for the grace to break through the wall that was keeping me from trusting. I wanted to cry, but haven't in months.

"You may have noticed a small round building near the cemetery. Curiosity is one of my strongest traits. I walked to it and opened the door.

"When I looked inside, I was filled with fear. There stood a large statue of Mary. My first impulse was to run away in anger. But something drew me slowly to the kneeler at her feet. Then I fell to my knees, weeping into the folds of her robes.

"When it was over, I felt cleansed and new. I felt willing to be a trusting child. Even more important, I felt that a mother's love had touched me, leaving in me a true desire to forgive my natural mother."[1]

Unique in one way but universal in another, this young woman's story has been repeated thousands of times. The details of her journey are hers alone. The essence of it she shares with many others. Numberless lost souls have come to Mary and found the hope needed to start again. They found a spiritual mother in Mary.

Should We Practice Devotion to Mary?

Some say... We honor Mary much as we revere the mothers of other great figures of history. She solicits our reverence as the mother of Jesus who is so central to our lives. We all know that the greatness of sons reflects back upon their mothers, and this is true in the case of Mary. We cannot and should not forget Mary's maternal role toward her son Jesus.

However, when we face the issue of devotion to Mary, we believe this exceeds the regard we have for her as Christ's mother. As long as we linger on a filial relationship we are comfortable. But to ask us to pray to her and seek her mediation seems to cross a line clearly set out by the first letter to Timothy: "For there is one God. There is also one mediator between God and the human race. Christ Jesus, himself human who gave himself as ransom for all." (1 Tim 2:5)

Jesus Christ is the one and only mediator between God and ourselves. There is no other name under heaven by which we are to be saved. (Cf. Acts 4:12) The authority of Scripture, God's own word, makes it clear that we should never look elsewhere for salvation. Jesus alone is the savior. Because he is Son of God, the sacrificial act of his human nature obtained infinite value and was able to save us. The crucified and risen Christ now stands before God interceding for us and acting as our one mediator: "Therefore, he [Jesus] is always able to save those who approach God through him, since he lives forever to make intercession for them." (Heb 7:25)

It seems to us unfitting and even contrary to Scripture to ascribe any intercessory power to anyone but Jesus, even to one so venerable as Christ's mother. We disagree with prayers to Mary to gain her intercession. Moreover, we view devotion to Mary liable to excess and are uneasy about building shrines to her, enthroning her statue amid flowers and candles, or walking in processions to praise her.

No matter how well meaning this appears to those who practice such rituals and say such prayers, we can only speak with regret about it. These devotions distract people from Jesus and derail the true nature of mediating which belongs solely to Christ.

Devotion to Mary is inconsistent with biblical teaching.

The Catechism teaches ...

"What the Catholic faith believes about Mary is based on what it believes about Christ, and what it teaches about Mary illumines in turn its faith in Christ." CCC 487

The *Catechism* teaches about Mary principally in three places: the section dealing with Jesus Christ; the section about the Church; and in the fourth part dealing with prayer. We will touch here on five major teachings about Mary.

Conceived by the Spirit — Born of the Virgin Mary. When the angel Gabriel appeared to Mary at the Annunciation, the fullness of time had arrived. Scripture speaks of time in two ways: *chronos*, or clock time and kairos, or *fulfillment* time. The seconds and minutes of history flow inexorably, but there are moments full of grace when God accomplishes his will in history. This is *kairos*, the sacred moment. All the promises about a Messiah are now about to be accomplished in Mary of Nazareth. Gabriel tells the Virgin Mary she will conceive and bear a son.

"How can this be since I know not man?"

"The Holy Spirit will come upon you."

The moment is Trinitarian. The Father will send the Holy Spirit, Lord and giver of life, to sanctify the womb of Mary and cause her to conceive the Son of God in the flesh.

The Father willed that the incarnation be preceded by a "yes" from the predestined mother. From all eternity God had chosen Mary to be the mother of his Son. But he also willed that her cooperation be a free assent.

The mission of many holy women prepared for Mary. Despite her disobedience, Eve received the promise of a descendant who would conquer the evil one. Throughout the Old Testament God chose the powerless to give evidence of his promise: Sarah, Hannah, Deborah, Judith, and many other women. Mary, a daughter of Zion, stood out among all these poor and humble of the Lord who waited for the Messiah with confidence and hope (cf. CCC 490).

God enriched Mary with the graces she needed to be the mother of the Savior. Gabriel greets her as a woman, "full of grace." (Lk 1:28 RSV) Her "yes" to God, freely given was itself a testimony to grace.

Immaculate Conception. For centuries the Church meditated on this singular gift of Mary as the woman "full of grace." Under the guidance of the Spirit, the Church came to realize that Mary was immaculately conceived, meaning that she was conceived without inheriting original sin. Pope Pius IX proclaimed this teaching as a dogma of the Church in 1854. "The Blessed Virgin Mary was, from the first moment of her conception, by a singular grace and gift of almighty God and by virtue of the merits of Jesus Christ, savior of the human race, preserved immune from all stain of original sin."[2]

Mary needed to be redeemed by Jesus like everyone else. She was saved from original sin at her conception by the anticipated merits of Jesus Christ, which he achieved for everyone at the Cross and on Easter. Grace continued to work in Mary so that she remained sinless throughout her life. We should note here that the Immaculate Conception does not refer to the virginal birth of Christ, but rather to Mary's being conceived without inheriting original sin. The Fathers of the Eastern Church call her the "All Holy" (Panagia) and celebrate her as free from any sin.

Mary replied to Gabriel, "Be it done to me according to your word." Mary responded with the obedience of faith. Without a single sin to restrain her, she gave herself entirely to the work of her Son and served the mystery of salvation with him. Study and pray over the encyclical *The Mother of the Redeemer* by Pope John Paul II. He has given us an inspiring meditation on the faith of Mary first extolled and admired by Elizabeth when she said to Mary, "Blessed are you for having believed."

Mother of God — Theotokos. In the year 431, St. Cyril of Alexandria led a delegation of Egyptian bishops to the Council of Ephesus. The Bishop of Antioch led a contingent of bishops from Syria. Pope Celestine I sent three legates. St. Augustine was to chosen to attend but died before the Council opened. The best known decision of the Council was to declare that Mary was the *Mother of God (Theotokos, or God-Bearer)*.

Why were they moved to this development of the ancient faith of the Church about Mary? Because the Patriarch of Constantinople, Nestorius, was teaching that the child born of Mary was only human. Mary was simply the Christ-bearer, not the God-bearer. Nestorius could not accept the idea that Mary was God's mother. He explained his position by saying that there were two persons in Jesus, a human one and a divine one. After Jesus was born the divine person of the Word united himself to the human Jesus and so Jesus then became divine.

The Council Fathers rejected this teaching. They asserted that the Son of God was united to the humanity of Jesus at his conception. "He made the birth of his flesh into his own flesh. Thus we do not hesitate to call the Holy Virgin: Mother of God." Mary was the mother of the whole Jesus Christ, divine and human. The Fathers were making a statement primarily about Jesus. (Cf. CCC 466)

Mary Always a Virgin. The Church believes that the Holy Spirit's power made possible the conception of Jesus in Mary's womb. There was no human father. The gospels present the virginal conception of Jesus as a divine work that surpasses all human understanding. The meaning of this event is accessible only to faith.

As the Church's faith in this mystery deepened, it came to confess that Mary remained a virgin while giving birth to Jesus and also afterwards. The liturgy of the Church speaks of Mary as "ever virgin." Some have objected that this could not be true since the Scriptures speak of the "brothers and sisters" of Jesus. St. Jerome, in his book, "Against Helvidius," defended Mary's perpetual virginity, claiming that the word for siblings could also mean cousins. The Eastern Church had an alternate tradition that these brothers and sisters were the children of Joseph by a previous marriage.

At the Council of Capua in 392, St. Ambrose upheld the Church's position about Mary's perpetual virginity. This was reconfirmed by Pope Siricius. In 1992, Pope John Paul went to Capua to celebrate the sixteenth-hundredth anniversary of that Council. On that occasion he preached on the gift and mystery of Mary's total virginity. Jesus is Mary's only son, but her spiritual motherhood extends to all whom he came to save.

The *Catechism* gives five reasons for Mary's virginal motherhood:

1. It emphasizes God's absolute initiative in the Incarnation. Jesus has only God as Father.
2. It highlights that Jesus is the New Adam who begins the new creation. The Spirit dwells in him with divine fullness, from whom we receive a multitude of graces.
3. We are made participants in divine life, not from flesh or human intentions but by God alone. This life is virginal, for it comes only from God.
4. This is a sign of Mary's faith not diluted by any doubt. She gave God the undivided surrender of her whole self.
5. As both virgin and mother, Mary symbolizes the Church. In receiving God's Word, the Church preaches and baptizes and begets sons and daughters in Christ. The Church is virginal by her pure fidelity to Christ her spouse.

Mother of the Church. It was Vatican II which developed the title Mother of the Church for Mary. From Christ's conception until his death, Mary was united to her Son in his work of salvation. Her pilgrimage of faith brought her to the Cross, where she joined her son's sacrifice and lovingly consented to it. Jesus asked her to look at John, and by extension to all of us, and said, "Mother, behold, your son." (Jn 19:26-27)

Mary prayed with the apostles and disciples after the Ascension and begged for the Spirit who came at Pentecost. She was present at the Incarnation of the physical Christ — and at the manifestation of the Mystical Body at Pentecost.

In the mystery of her Assumption, Mary was granted a unique participation in her Son's Resurrection and a forecast of our resurrection. "The Immaculate Virgin . . . when the course of her earthly life was finished, was taken up body and soul into heavenly glory, and exalted by the Lord as Queen over all things, so that she might be more fully conformed to her Son, the Lord of lords and conqueror of death."[3]

Pope Paul VI has written a wonderful book — *Marialis Cultus* — on devotion to Mary, based on the Scriptures, councils, liturgy, and popular piety. His warm-hearted direction is inspiring and faith enriching and deserves our prayerful meditation.

Finally, in Mary we behold what the Church is already like during the pilgrimage of faith — and what the Church will become at the end of the journey. Mary is an icon of the Church as well as sign of hope and comfort for all of us.

1. What is the role of Mary's faith in the plan of salvation?

"The Virgin Mary 'cooperated through free faith and obedience in human salvation' (LG 56). She uttered her yes 'in the name of all human nature.' (St. Thomas Aquinas, *STh* III, 30, 1). By her obedience she became the new Eve, the mother of all the living." (CCC 511)

2. What is the Church's teaching about Mary's virginity?

"Mary 'remained a virgin in conceiving her Son, a virgin in giving birth to him, a virgin in carrying him, a virgin in nursing him at her breast, always a virgin.' (St. Augustine, *Sermon* 186, 1: *PL* 38, 999): with her whole being she is the 'handmaid of the Lord' (Lk 1:38)." (CCC 510)

3. What are ways to have devotion to Mary?

"The Church rightly honors 'the Blessed Virgin with special devotion. From the most ancient times the Blessed Virgin has been honored with the title 'Mother of God,' to whose protection the faithful fly in all their dangers and needs. . .This very special devotion . . . differs essentially from the adoration which is given to the incarnate Word and equally to the Father and the Holy Spirit, and greatly fosters this adoration." (LG, 66) The liturgical feasts dedicated to the Mother of God and Marian prayer, such as the rosary, an "epitome of the whole Gospel," express this devotion to the Virgin Mary." (cf. Paul VI, MC 42; SC 103) (CCC 971)

Response to objections

Jesus is indeed the one mediator between God and us, and Jesus is the only Savior. But this does not negate the possibility of subordinate mediation. Here on earth we routinely ask one another to pray for us. Carmelite convents receive a steady flow of petitions asking the contemplative sisters for their prayers. Instinctively we know that holy people who are near to God are likely to have their prayers answered.

Christ is not jealous of his position of mediator. It gives Jesus joy to see a host of prayers coming to him to present to the Father. Why is it that we have no trouble asking people to pray for us on earth, but once they go to heaven we stop doing it? Actually, it would be more logical to be even more willing to entreat them since they now actually behold God.

Acts of intercession in no way interfere with Christ's supreme mediation. In fact they enhance it in our eyes because each intercessory prayer is a blunt acknowledgement that Christ alone is the real mediator. We are reaching for the throne of the Father through Jesus by the power of the Spirit. That is the faith sequence spoken in every major prayer of the liturgy.

Now of all the humans outside of Christ, who is dearest to the heart of God? It is Mary the mother of Jesus, the mother of God. Catholic faith is so impatient to reach Christ that believers recite two billion Hail Marys everyday. The last words of Mary in the Bible are: "Do whatever he tells you." (Jn 2:5) Her final words on earth are a prayer of intercession. Mary's mediation refer directly and unambiguously to Christ. Mary does not draw attention to herself, but to her Son.

A popular story among Catholics is the case of the "strangers in heaven." Jesus is seen walking around the celestial city and noticing a number of people who do not seem to belong there. Jesus goes to Peter who guards the heavenly gates and handles admissions. He asks Peter, "Do you realize there are a number of people who have no business being here? Why did you let them in?"

"It's not my fault," replied Peter. "I didn't want to say anything because I thought it would upset you." Frustrated Jesus said, "I am the Lord. I have a right to know what's going on." Hesitant, Peter answered, "Well, I did tell them they couldn't get in. So they marched confidently around to the back door — and your mother let them in."

This lighthearted tale tells us how deeply Mary is embedded in the Catholic soul. The sons and daughters of Mary blithely go their way, knowing they have an affectionate mother who is interested in their salvation. They swell with conviction when they cry out, "Mary, pray for us!" They know she will never let them down. They also know that ultimately Jesus is the only Savior and that Mary invariably touches his heart.

Our present culture is booming with Hi-Tech — a world brooding over the monitor that yields virtual reality. It can be cold, impersonal, and even dehumanizing. To counter this we need Hi-Touch, a human world with real persons and feeling and warmth and the delight of relationship of love and affection.

Religion stands for all these values and reveals a God who has given us these opportunities. If at times God seems distant — like virtual reality — we have Mary to be our Hi-Touch, our personal, maternal friend who confides our deepest yearning to her Son on our behalf.

One last important distinction prompts us to note the difference between adoration and veneration. We adore God. We venerate Mary. Adoration belongs only to God. The honor we give to Mary is of a totally different order; it is a tribute given to a creature. We need to maintain the distinction to avoid confusion. Having said this, we are then liberated to pour out our love for Christ and Mary with a sense of abundance and the passion that accompanies true affection.

Holy Mary, mother of God, pray for us now, and at the hour of our death. Amen.

For dialog

1. Share with each other the stories of your relationship with Mary. How do you think this will affect your future devotion to Mary? Why can we say with confidence that the closer we get to Mary, the closer we will be to Christ and the Church? What is the reason for staying near Mary in order to approach God?

2. What Catholic teaching becomes more clear in the light of Mary's Immaculate Conception? When we meditate on Mary's glorious Assumption into heaven, what are we moved to consider about our own future after death? At the Cross Jesus asked Mary to be a mother to John. "Woman, behold, your son." Mary is also our spiritual mother. What impact could this have on your life?

3. Do you know how to say the rosary? How could you learn? What is the value of this prayer, especially with its repetition of Hail Marys and contemplation of Christ's mysteries? There is a feast of Mary almost every month of the year. See if you can name them and share a faith reflection about them. Why are the liturgies of Mary a sound foundation for devotion to Mary?

Prayer

Lord our God, through the Blessed Virgin Mary you have shown us an example of a disciple who is faithful to the words of life; open our hearts to receive your saving word, so that by the power of the Holy Spirit it may speak to us in our daily lives and bring forth a rich harvest of holiness. Amen.

— From the Mass of Mary, Disciple of the Lord

Glossary

Immaculate Conception — This is the Church's teaching that Mary was conceived without original sin. She was redeemed by the anticipated merits of Christ and lived her whole life without sin.

Ever Virgin — The Church's faith holds that Mary was a virgin in conceiving and bearing Jesus and remained a virgin for the rest of her life.

"If then we establish solid devotion to our Blessed Lady, it is only to establish more perfectly devotion to Jesus Christ, and to provide an easy and secure means for finding Jesus Christ."

St. Louis de Montfort

Endnotes

1. Quoted by Father Mark Link, S.J., in a homily for the feast of the Mother of God, Year C.
2. *Ineffabilis Deus*, 1854.
3. Pius XII, *Munificentissimus Deus*; DS 3903.

Chapter 14

THE FOUR LAST THINGS: DEATH, JUDGMENT, HEAVEN, AND HELL

CCC 988-1066

"I have come to consider death as a friend."

Joseph Cardinal Bernardin

Teaching Us How to Die

The late Cardinal Bernardin said he had three fears in life: the fear of being falsely accused, the fear of getting cancer like his father, the fear of dying. All that he feared happened to him. He was accused of sexual abuse by Stephen Cook, a young man dying of AIDS who subsequently retracted his accusation. The Cardinal met with Stephen, forgave him, and anointed him.

Bernardin then was afflicted with cancer and the prospect of a painful dying process. At one point his bones were so brittle due to stenosis that he snapped a rib when bending over. He noticed that illness tended to pull him inside himself focusing on his pain. He felt sorry for himself and depressed. He wanted to withdraw from people.

He learned to turn outward to Jesus and his message and open himself to God's grace. Christ helped him to begin thinking of other people and their needs. He decided to walk with them in their trials. When he arrived at the cancer clinic, he refused the offered private entrance and went into the waiting room with his fellow sufferers. He approached and comforted each one and followed this up with phone calls and notes. In the last three months of his life, he acquired a "special parish" of six hundred people like himself, giving them hope and love. He loved to go to parishes and conduct services for the anointing of the sick. For him death was not the end, but a transition to life eternal.

In his last week on earth he wrote three letters. The first he sent to the Supreme Court of the United States. He begged the justices not to approve of physician-assisted suicide. "As one who is dying, I have come to appreciate in a special way the gift of life." He added that to approve of a new right to assisted suicide would endanger America and send the false signal that a less than perfect life was not worth living.

His second letter was a handwritten one to the United States bishops assembled for their autumn meeting in Washington, D.C. He asked them for their prayers that God would give him the grace to make it through each day. Lastly, he sent out his Christmas cards early to his priests and many friends.

He taught us all that approaching death meant learning new lessons of faith and new lessons to share with others. He was well prepared. "I know that just as God called me to serve him to the best of my ability throughout my life on earth, he is now calling me home."[1]

Is There Life After Death?

Some say...
"In that sleep of death what dreams may come
When we have shuffled off this mortal coil. . .
The dread of something after death,
The undiscovered country, from whose bourn
No traveler returns, puzzles the will,
And makes us bear those ills we have,
Than fly to others that we know not of."

Hamlet, Act 3, Scene 1

Hamlet says it well. Who knows what dreams may come after death? We avoid death by bearing the ills we have in case there are worse things to come. He need not have worried. There is nothing after death. Our death will be our end. The dread of something after death may puzzle Hamlet. But he need not bother. This life is it. The answer to the old song, "Is that all there is?" is "Yes."

Hoping there is another life after death is a case of wish-fulfillment. We want it to be so, therefore it is so. Gravestones, be they as monumental as the pyramids of Egypt or as simple as a small marker in a Puritan cemetery, are respectful tributes to the dead, not assurances of a future life.

Is there any value in thinking of death? Yes. Death reminds us of the absolute limitation of our personal lives. We only have so much time. Instead of being distracted by some assumed reality after death, we should use the fact of our end as a motivation to live life to the fullest here. We ought to exercise our freedom to the maximum.

Death should motivate us to self-fulfillment, which is the best way to have happiness and peace here on earth. Knowing that our years will one day come to an end, we should turn every day into quality time. This means seeking reasonable prosperity for ourselves and our families. We should devote our energies to making the earth a better place for everyone.

Someone has suggested we write our obituary so we could begin to live now as we hope to be remembered. A variation of this exercise is to imagine what people will say of us as they pause by our coffins just before our burial. "He was a good, husband, father, and neighbor." "She was a loving mother, wife, and volunteer to the community." Visualizing how we want to be remembered urges us to be that way now.

The best we can hope for is a little bit of heaven on earth right now, not in the so-called next world. We also reject what has been called pie-in-the-sky theology which uses the myth of a future life to make the poor accept their lot with the promise of a better life elsewhere. We should help them now, for this is all we have.

There is no life after death.

The Catechism teaches ...

"[At death] life is changed not taken away" (Preface for the Mass for the Dead).

Death intrigues the believer and unbeliever alike.

Two of the best-known philosophers of the twentieth century, Sartre and Heidegger, claimed that meditation on death inspired their lifelong quest to find meaning in life. Sartre said, "I am free to make meaning out of my life despite my mortality." His mental brush with death awoke in him the passion to make sense out of life.

Heidegger, too, contemplated the role of death in his life. He saw his life inevitably moving toward death. He noted that death would cancel out all the things he would still like to do. Instead of being depressed by this, he resolved to look at all of life's possibilities, thus to fulfill himself as much as he could.

What these men discovered at the human level about death's effect on life is even more true for the believer in Jesus. Christ resolutely looked at death and did not deny it. He taught us that this brings a divine meaning to our lives and that it called us to see the possibilities which life on earth holds for us. But far more, Jesus instructed us to see that death is not the cancellation of possibilities, but the prelude to an even greater life beyond the grave. The soul is immortal. And one day, in Jesus, our bodies will rise again.

Death is a result of sin. The Church's Magisterium interprets Scripture and Tradition to mean that sin caused death to enter the world. Had we not sinned, we would not die.

Death is transformed by Jesus. Accepting death by a free submission to the Father's will, Jesus transformed death into an act that both conquered sin and overcame death for us. Jesus took the experience of death, which frightens so many people and removed its finality. It is not the end. It is the beginning of a new life. In death we are not obliterated. We pass into a new world where we can live with God in eternal rest and joy.

Listen to the saints:

"My earthly desire has been crucified . . . there is living water in me, water that murmurs and says within me: come to the Father." (St. Ignatius of Antioch)

"I want to see God. In order to see him, I must die." (St. Teresa of Avila)

"I am not dying. I am entering into eternal life." (St. Thérèse of Lisieux)

We should prepare for death by avoiding sin and living a life of virtue. Since we will die as we have lived, it makes sense to spend each day full of love for others and always deepening our friendship with God. So when death comes we will not have to rage against the dying of the light, for death shall have no dominion over us. We can go gently into that good night. As a ripe fruit falls quietly from the tree, so we will fall peacefully into the heart of God. Cardinal Bernardin said it best, "I learned to treat death as a friend."

I believe in the resurrection of the body. "On no point does the Christian faith encounter more opposition than the resurrection of the body." God revealed the resurrection of the body gradually. Faith in God as creator of body as well as soul led the believing community to confess the resurrection of the dead. The Maccabean martyrs were clear, "The King of the universe will raise us up to an everlasting renewal of life, because we have died for his laws." (2 Mac 7:9)

The Pharisees looked for resurrection, but the Sadducees did not.

Jesus raised the dead to life in his own ministry as a symbol of future resurrection. Strictly speaking the raising of Lazarus and the daughter of Jairus were resuscitations, not resurrections, for they died again. Jesus associated resurrection of the body with himself. "I am the resurrection and the life." (Jn 11:25)

What is resurrection? At death the soul leaves the body to meet God. The soul waits for reunion with the body.

Who will rise? All dead people will rise. The good will rise to life with God. The evil will rise to the eternal death of hell.

How will this happen? Jesus received his own body back, even with the scars of the crucifixion. But his body was a glorified one with new supernatural qualities. The same will be true of us. One of the best scriptural passages for this teaching is First Corinthians, chapter fifteen.

Though we attempt many ways to explain resurrection, the "how it happens" exceeds our imagination and understanding. The seed-flower image can be useful because it establishes identity between the old and new body. It shows the glorious difference. It describes the change in dynamic terms.

When will the resurrection happen? At the last day at the end of the world, a date unknown to us.

Through our baptism we know by faith that we have already begun the process of resurrection because we have been united to the risen Jesus. Therefore our bodies deserve reverence as well as other peoples' bodies, especially the suffering in hospitals, nursing homes, and hospices.

Judgment: Purgatory, Heaven, Hell. The Church stands with the dying to absolve them from their sins, to anoint them with spiritual strength, and to give them Jesus in the Eucharist (Viaticum) as food for the final journey. At the funeral liturgy, the Church commends the person to God in these beautiful words: "May holy Mary, the angels, and all the saints come to meet you as you go forth from this life. . . May you see your Redeemer face to face."

Immediately after death we face the *particular judgment*. Depending on the state of our souls, we enter heaven, purgatory, or hell. St. John of the Cross sums up the judgment in this touching sentence, "At the evening of life, we shall be judged by our love." (cf. CCC 1022)

Purgatory. Those who die in the state of grace and friendship with God, but who are not fully purified from their sinfulness, are assured of their eternal salvation. They must undergo a purification to obtain the holiness needed to enter heaven. This is purgatory. In the liturgy of All Souls, the Church remembers this teaching and recommends Eucharist, prayer, charitable giving, and works of penance on behalf of the departed.

Heaven. If we die in the grace of God and have no need of further purification we will go straight to heaven. In heaven we will find perfect and unending happiness at last. This will be caused by a perfect communion with the Holy Trinity, the Blessed Mother, the angels and saints. Jesus Christ opened heaven to us by his death and resurrection. We will enjoy the results of what Jesus accomplished for us.

What is heaven like in concrete terms? Scripture uses a variety of pictures to help us understand heaven, such as: wedding party, wine, life, light, peace, paradise, the Father's house. But the real heaven is beyond any picture we can paint of it. "No eye has seen, nor ear heard, nor the heart of man conceived, what God has prepared for those who love him." (1 Cor 2:9)

Seeing God face to face in all his glory is an essential aspect of heaven.

This is called the "beatific vision." To make this possible God must reveal himself and give us the capacity to behold him.

Hell. Hell is eternal separation from God. It is impossible to be united with God if we refuse to love him. When we sin seriously against God, neighbor, or self, we have failed to love God. The great Last Judgment scene in Matthew 25:31-46 reminds us that we will go to hell if we fail to meet the serious needs of the poor and helpless. Freely chosen self-exclusion from communion with God is called hell.

Immediately after death, the souls of those who die in a state of mortal sin go to hell. The principal suffering of hell is absolute and eternal separation from God. While images of fire are used to picture hell, the reality exceeds our ability to describe the pain that truly comes from rejecting God's love.

Scripture and the teaching of the Church regarding heaven and hell emphasize a call to personal responsibility by which we use our freedom, aided by divine grace, to affect our eternal destiny. There is always an urgent call to conversion and repentance. "God predestines no one to go to hell." (CCC 1037) Only a free turning away from God in mortal sin and persistence in this attitude leads to hell. The Church prays everyday in her liturgy for the conversion of her members. "The Lord . . . is patient with you, not wishing that any should perish but that all should come to repentance." (2 Pt 3:9)

The Last Judgment. "The Last Judgment will come when Christ returns in glory. Only the Father knows the day and the hour; only he determines the moment of his coming. Then through his Son Jesus Christ he will pronounce the final word on all history. We shall know the ultimate meaning of the whole work of creation and of the entire economy of salvation and understand the marvelous ways by which his Providence led everything to its final end. The Last Judgment will reveal that God's justice triumphs over all the injustices committed by his creatures and that God's love is stronger than death." (CCC 1040)

New Heaven and New Earth. Once the kingdom of God arrives in its completion at the end of time there will be a renewal of the universe itself in Christ. Scripture uses many images to describe this mysterious reality. There will be a new heavens and a new earth. "Creation itself will be set free from its bondage to decay." (Cf. Rom 8:19-23) The holy city will descend from heaven to earth. We do not know when or how this will happen. But we do believe that God will make this happen. At the end of time, "The universe itself, which is so closely related to man and which attains its destiny through him, will be perfectly re-established in Christ." (LG, 48; 2 Pt 3:10-13)

1. How are the souls in purgatory helped by us?

"By virtue of the 'communion of saints,' the Church commends the dead to God's mercy and offers her prayers, especially the holy sacrifice of the Eucharist, on their behalf." (CCC 1055)

2. What happens at the Last Judgment?

"'The Holy Roman Church firmly believes and confesses that on the Day of Judgment all men will appear in their own bodies before Christ's tribunal to render an account of their own deeds' (Council of Lyons II [1274]: DS 859; cf. DS 1549)." (CCC 1059).

3. What will the full Kingdom of God be like?

"At the end of time, the Kingdom of God will come in its fullness. Then the just will reign with Christ forever, glorified in body and soul, and the material universe itself will be transformed. God will then be 'all in all' (1 Cor 15:28) in eternal life. (CCC 1060)

Response to objections

Many people find it hard to believe there is life after death. That is the crux of the matter. Death raises all the ultimate questions about our existence. We hate the thought of disappearing altogether. We rebel against death because there is something in us that we intuitively know cannot be reduced to mere matter. The Bishops at Vatican II expressed the universal unease with death. But only faith can help us see beyond the barrier of death to the life that lies ahead:

"It is in the face of death that the riddle of human existence grows most acute. Not only is man tormented by pain and by the advancing deterioration of his body, but even more so by a dread of perpetual extinction. He rightly follows the intuition of his heart when he abhors and repudiates the utter ruin and total disappearance of his own person. He rebels against death because he bears in himself an eternal seed which cannot be reduced to sheer matter. All the endeavors of technology, though useful in the extreme, cannot calm his anxiety; for prolongation of biological life is unable to satisfy that desire for higher life which is inescapably lodged in his breast."[2]

"Although the mystery of death utterly beggars the imagination, the Church has been taught by divine revelation and firmly teaches that man has been created by God for a blissful purpose beyond the reach of earthly misery."[3]

We note that some claim that death can be a motivation for enhancing human dignity and proper self-realization, without believing in an afterlife. And a certain number of people of good will have committed themselves to this goal. But the long history of how humans cope with death demonstrates that they either share Hamlet's tortured ambiguity about death's aftermath or more explicitly affirm faith in an afterlife.

For most thoughtful people, a solid faith provides the answer to their anxiety about what the future after death holds for them. This same faith enables them to be in touch through Christ with loved ones who have died. Faith arouses the hope they have found in true life with God.

In his very public death, Cardinal Bernardin showed how a person of faith can make friends with death, and he helped millions who walked with him on his last journey to believe this is but one step into a future life.

For dialog 1. It has been said that the younger we are the more "immortal" we think we are. Youthful energy and strength tend to make the young less aware of death and functionally deny it. How true is this? Why is it so? If true, what can be done to incorporate the role of death in life with faith? Often there are tragic deaths among the young. Does this make a difference in youthful attitudes to death?

2. Violence as entertainment in movies, TV, video games, novels, and grisly reports about murders and wars in the media regularly inoculate us, distance us from real death. This is not only death without faith, but death de-sensitized. What are we to think of this? What happens when death is trivialized?

3. Pope John Paul II has written that we live in a "culture of death" that legalizes abortion and capital punishment — and cheapens life in general. He urges us to create a "culture of life." How can we do that? How can we accomplish this personally, in our families and neighborhoods and in the laws and customs of our nation?

Prayer Father . . . in Christ who rose from the dead, our hope of resurrection dawned. The sadness of death gives way to the bright promise of immortality. Lord, for yourfaithful people life is changed not ended. When the body of our earthly dwelling lies in death we gain an everlasting dwelling place in heaven. And so, with all the choirs of angels in heaven we proclaim your glory and join in their unending hymn of praise.

"In addition, that bodily death from which man would have been immune had he not sinned[14] will be vanquished, according to the Christian faith, when man who was ruined by his own doing is restored to wholeness by an almighty and merciful Saviour. For God has called man and still calls him so that with his entire being he might be joined to Him

in an endless sharing of a divine life beyond all corruption. Christ won this victory when He rose to life, for by His death He freed man from death.[15] Hence to every thoughtful man a solidly established faith provides the answer to his anxiety about what the future holds for him. At the same time faith gives him the power to be united in Christ with his loved ones who have already been snatched away by death; faith arouses the hope that they have found true life with God."[4]

Endnotes

1. Joseph Cardinal Bernardin, *The Gift of Peace* (Bantam Doubleday Dell, 1998).
2. GS, 18, *Vatican II* (Northport, NY: 1975).
3. Ibid., 19.
4. Ibid., 18.

Chapter 15

COME, LET US WORSHIP THE LORD
CCC 1066-1209

"Sing to the Lord a new song
of praise in the assembly of the faithful."

Ps 149:1

A Liturgy of Angels — A People's Worship

Washington, D.C.'s Library of Congress celebrated the restoration of its grand reading room with a display of ancient manuscripts on loan from the Vatican Library. An additional feature of the celebration was a series of special lectures. One of these was titled "The Theology of the Renaissance Popes," delivered by Jesuit historian Father O'Malley.

He said that a clue to the religious vision of these popes could be obtained from nineteenth century English novels in which the second son of an upper class family was often destined for the ministry. This pastor was expected to do three things. First, he should have financial competence so he could protect the inheritance of the parish and assure its future stability. Second, he ought to be moderately pious, faithful to his prayers and have pastoral concern for his people. Third, he should supervise and celebrate the liturgy with great care and attention.

Father O'Malley applied these three expectations to the popes of the Renaissance. They were men who skillfully administered the finances of the Vatican and left behind the buildings and art works that attract millions of visitors every year. Generally, they were men of moderate piety who conserved the faith of the apostles. They paid attention to the liturgy and commissioned the building of the Sistine Chapel as well as a new St. Peter's Basilica. Their view of liturgy was its transcendent majesty. They looked at the heavenly aspect of worship, the presence of the invisible angels and saints at every Eucharist.

Because worship was the court of heaven present on earth, the popes wanted visible magnificence to symbolize the invisible holy assembly so that earthly participants could sense the divine presence. Fortunately, that period of history produced men of extraordinary artistic genius: architects like Bernini and Bramante, sculptors and fresco masters like Michelangelo and musicians such as Palestrina.

The popes recruited these artists to create settings and music for a liturgy of transcendence the like of which awes us to this present day. The spirit of today's Church tends more to prefer the human aspect of worship and the active role of the visible assembly. Both viewpoints are valid and together honor the full mystery of worship with its divine and human sides.

How Necessary Is Liturgy?

Some say... The greatest contribution religion can make to society is a moral code and good behavior. Decency, civility, and moral responsibility are virtues that assure strong families and healthy nations. Religion seems best suited to offering these qualities to individuals, families, local communities, and the country at large. This is the practical use of religion. When it functions best it shapes moral character.

Rituals and elaborate church buildings distract religion from its more promising contributions to society. Liturgies and large churches filled with art satisfy esthetic sensibilities. But our cities are filled with museums, concert halls, and theaters where the artistic hunger of people is already amply fed.

Drama more than adequately supplies the rituals some people need. Museums offer efficient collections of art works in climate-controlled, well-lighted settings for people who can appreciate these products of beauty. Concert halls have long produced the world's greatest music performed with professionalism and passion.

Religion does not have to use its energies for rituals and thousands of church buildings and solicit vast amounts of money required to build and maintain these structures. These projects divert clergy from what they have been called to do, namely, help the body politic with character education, inspiration for moral virtue, and civic responsibility.

If there must be church buildings let them be simple meeting halls where community formation is fostered, uplifting talks can be heard, and classes in moral fundamentals can be taught. Once a building is designed for ceremonies, vestments, altars, pulpits, baptismal fonts, confessional rooms, tabernacles, candles statuary, elaborate paintings and windows, choir stalls, robed choirs, gold vessels, a huge expense is incurred to create this and maintain it.

Yet all we need is a simple setting, a tasteful place to meet people, forge friendships, and hear reminders about how to do good and avoid evil. In our opinion liturgy is superfluous. It may have certain artistic benefits, but these can be better served in other locales that already exist.

For these reasons we do not see the need for liturgy.

The Catechism *teaches* ... For people of faith, liturgy is not an option. By the divine initiative, liturgy and worship are the true, God-chosen channels of salvation for our souls.

Book two, part one, of the *Catechism* lays out for us the basic teachings about liturgy. Part two will treat of the sacraments. In this chapter we will meditate on part one. In future chapters we will study the sacraments.

At Pentecost the Holy Spirit inaugurated the time of the Church. The Spirit made salvation present and communicated it through the liturgy which is ultimately the work of the Trinity:

- The Father, source and goal of liturgy, blesses us.
- The Son, at the heart of liturgy, redeems us.
- The Spirit, the soul of liturgy, sanctifies us.

The Father Blesses. In liturgy we associate the work of the Father with blessing. The Father blesses us from the liturgical hymn of creation in Genesis to the songs of the heavenly Jerusalem in the Apocalypse. The Father blessed Adam and Eve, Noah, Abraham, Moses and the holy people of Israel in the Exodus, Temple, Exile, and Return. Israel's liturgies used the Torah, the prophets, and the psalms to think of the Father's blessings and thank him.

All Christian liturgies are directed to the Father. United with Jesus and dependent on the Spirit, we assemble as the Church to praise God from whom all blessings flow.

The Son Redeems. At liturgy Jesus acts in the events of the sacraments to communicate the grace of divine life to us. Jesus enacts his paschal mystery, his dying and rising, so that we may share more deeply in salvation. Some people behave as though Jesus is an audience and the worshippers are the actors "doing something to Jesus." It is quite the opposite.

Jesus is the agent who acts on and in us. It is Jesus who baptizes, confirms, and offers the Eucharistic sacrifice through his visible ministers. At the Last Supper and on Easter night, Jesus gave to the apostles the power of sanctification and apostolic succession. All the worshippers are expected to participate actively in liturgy.

The Spirit Sanctifies. The Spirit teaches the faith to God's people and is the artist of God's masterpieces, the sacraments. The Spirit makes the mystery of Jesus present and real. The Spirit is the Church's living memory, reminding us of the teachings of Scripture and Tradition, which we tend to forget. The Spirit does more than put the teachings before us, but also gives life to the liturgical acts of proclamation, gestures, and symbols. At Eucharist the priest begs the Holy Spirit to come and change the bread and wine into the Body and Blood of Christ. A medieval poet said it this way:

"Come, Holy Spirit,
Bake this bread in your holy fire
Cook this wine in your holy flame."

Matthew of Riveaulx

The work of the Spirit at liturgy may be summarized this way:
- To prepare the assembly to encounter Christ.
- To manifest Jesus to the faith of the assembly.
- To make Christ's saving work present and active.
- To make the gift of Communion bear fruit in the Church.

The Sacraments of Salvation. The Church makes the sacraments. The sacraments make the Church. What are sacraments? They are:

(1) EFFICACIOUS SIGNS OF GRACE, which means they accomplish what they signify. Baptism washes away all our sins. Confirmation anoints us with the oil of the Spirit to strengthen us. Eucharist feeds us with the eternal life of Jesus.

(2) INSTITUTED BY CHRIST. It is Jesus who originates the sacraments and who acts in them today.

(3) ENTRUSTED TO THE CHURCH. We have seen already that the Church is the sacrament of salvation. By Christ's will, the Church oversees and celebrates the sacraments.

(4) SOURCES OF DIVINE LIFE. Sacraments are the divinely appointed events of salvation from sin and sources of divine life for us.

The sacraments of initiation are Baptism, Confirmation, and Eucharist. The sacraments of healing are Reconciliation and Anointing. The sacraments that build up the community of the Church are Matrimony and Holy Orders.

What is the purpose of the sacraments?

a. To call us to worship God
b. To make us holy
c. To build up the Church
d. To deepen our faith

e. To train us to pray

f. To incorporate us into the Church's Tradition

God works primarily through the sacraments, but God is not limited by the sacraments. (Cf. CCC, 1257) God also works through prayer, catechesis, evangelization, spirituality, good works, and social ministry. These activities orient us toward the Eucharist and help us to participate more vitally in that celebration. Liturgy is work, not entertainment. Liturgy is more like dieting, exercise, or the energies demanded by our professional lives. Liturgy is *work*!

Who Celebrates? The whole Body of Christ celebrates the liturgy. Jesus, our high priest, Mary, the angels, and the saints are present at our liturgy.

When we gather for liturgy we are an ordered and structured community. The *Catechism* gives us this powerful passage on the dignity of the liturgical assembly:

"Forming 'as it were one mystical person' with Christ the head, the Church acts in the sacraments 'as an organically structured priestly community. [*LG* 11; cf. Pius XII, *Mystici Corporis* (1943)]. Through Baptism and Confirmation the priestly people is enabled to celebrate the liturgy, while those of the faithful 'who have received Holy Orders, are appointed to nourish the Church with the word and grace of God in the name of Christ. [LG 11, 2]' " (CCC 1119)

Hence we have a hierarchical model of liturgy that respects the varying roles and responsibilities of those at liturgy.

There are "diverse liturgical traditions or rites, legitimately recognized, [which] manifest the catholicity of the Church, because they signify and communicate the same mystery of Christ. (Cf. CCC 1208)

How do we celebrate? We use signs and symbols, such as candles, water, and fire in our celebration. We take these symbols from creation, which reflects the Creator. We relate them to our human life, so at liturgy we wash sins away, eat and drink the Body and Blood of Christ. We relate these symbols to the history of salvation. Hence at Baptism we recall God's liberation of the Israelites from political slavery at the crossing of the Red Sea and see ourselves liberated from spiritual slavery by the power of Christ as we cross over the waters of redemption.

These cosmic elements, human rituals, and memorial gestures become vessels of Christ's saving actions. At liturgy notice the rich texture of signs: The WORDS of Scripture, prayers, and homilies. The DEEDS of hands upraised in prayer, processions, reverential kneeling, silence, bowed heads, and signs of the Cross. The ARTS of colored glass, sculpture, architecture, music, songs, statuary. These liturgical symbols form a coherent symphony that appeal to the senses, the heart and the soul, as well as the mind. They reflect a divine artistry.

When do we celebrate? One liturgical musician put it this way. She played the organ at three consecutive Masses on Sundays. She wanted to make sure that her work did not become routine. The organ happened to be in the sanctuary area. Just as she left the sacristy she removed her watch, which tells human, clock time so that she could remind herself that she was entering God's "time," liturgical time.

At the heart of liturgy lies the Christian Sunday. It recalls the resurrection of Jesus and summons the Christian people to worship. Ideally it should be a family day and a time of rest from our busy work. There is also the liturgical year — Advent, Christmas Season, Lent, Easter Season, Pentecost, Trinity and Corpus Christi, and Ordinary Time. This year of grace unfolds for us the mystery of Christ.

The most solemn part of the liturgical year is the Sacrum Triduum, Holy Thursday, Good Friday, and Easter Vigil. Chronologically these are three days. Liturgically they are One Day unfolding the unity of Christ's paschal mystery.

Next, we have the memorials and feasts of the Blessed Mother and the saints. These events hold before us their example of Christian living and also invite us to seek their intercession on our behalf.

Every day we can join the Church in the Liturgy of the Hours. Seven times each day we can join the universal Church in praising God at the Office of Readings, Morning Prayer, Daytime Prayer (three sessions), Evening Prayer, and Night Prayer. The Liturgy of the Hours prolongs the celebration of the Eucharist, flowing from the Mass and flowing back to it.

Thus liturgical time consecrates and sanctifies human time and opens us to the flood of divine graces available to us every hour, day, week, and year.

Where do we celebrate? Sacred acts make sacred places! We worship in our parish churches, our diocesan cathedrals, monastery chapels, and shrines of our Blessed Lady and the saints. These buildings are visible images of the heavenly Jerusalem to which we are journeying and where we:

1. Worship God
2. Hear Scripture
3. Sing God's praises
4. Pray to God
5. Offer Christ's sacrifice
6. Center ourselves in God's presence

Jesus is the true temple of God and by his love we are temples of the Holy Spirit and living stones of the Church. All the visible richness of the "things" associated with places of worship are meant to minister to the building up of the holy community of love and faith.

Liturgy is Eschatalogical. We will celebrate liturgy until Jesus Christ comes again. The Communion of Saints in heaven celebrates with us. Read the Book of Revelation and note how often St. John takes us right to heaven to hear the choirs of angels and saints praising and adoring God. He told his people to read these words at their liturgies and to sing those hymns so that they might realize the intimate connection between the worship in heaven and that which took place at their Sunday Eucharists. Sacraments refer to eternal life as well as life here.

In a way, time "collapses" at liturgy. The Eucharist celebrates the Passover of the Old Testament, the Christian Paschal Mystery, and the future coming of Jesus. All these joyful events are "made present" by the power of the Holy Spirit at each Mass and other sacramental celebrations. This is why the pulse of incredible happiness surges at liturgy, for the joy of heaven itself is present. And it is enjoyed by those who have eyes to see, ears to hear — a possibility given to us by the grace of faith.

1. What are the sacraments?

"The sacraments are efficacious signs of grace, instituted by Christ and entrusted to the Church, by which divine life is dispensed to us. The visible rites by which the sacraments are celebrated signify and make present the graces proper to each sacrament. They bear fruit in those who receive them with the required dispositions." (CCC 1131)

2. What does Sunday mean for us?

"Sunday, the 'Lord's Day,' is the principal day for the celebration of the Eucharist because it is the day of the Resurrection. It is the pre-eminent day of the liturgical assembly, the day of the Christian family, and the day of joy and rest from work. Sunday is the 'foundation and kernel of the whole liturgical year. [Sacrosanctum concilium 106]' " (CCC 1193)

3. How is unity maintained among varied liturgical traditions?

"The criterion that assures unity amid the diversity of liturgical traditions is fidelity to apostolic Tradition, i.e., the communion in the faith and sacraments received from the apostles, a communion that is both signified and guaranteed by apostolic succession." (CCC 1209)

Response to objections

We agree that religion has a vital role in developing and strengthening the moral character of individuals, families, communities, and the nation itself. The whole history of religion has been connected to articulating moral principles and practical applications and providing ways to acquire a life of virtue. The Catholic Church sees this as essential to her mission in the world.

We cannot agree, however, that liturgy and worship have no connection to morality. The covenant with God and the worship of the Lord precede the call to morality as a way to witness what our relationship to God means in daily life. First we are loved and saved by God and given graces to accept divine love and salvation. By God's will this remarkable relationship and fount of graces is given to us again and again in the liturgy.

Each liturgy makes present the dying and rising of Christ out of love for us and for our salvation from sin and the grace of divine life. Making available Christ's dying and rising sacramentally is what we call his paschal mystery. Without this remarkable gift of grace and the awesome invitation to be in a loving relationship with God we would have a call to morality without the basis for it nor the graces needed to become moral witnesses.

In love terms, the liturgy is a continuing relationship between ourselves and the Father, Son, and Spirit. Obedience to the commandments and other moral demands are ways in which we show our grateful love back to God. In a sense moral witness is a "proof" of our love for God, expressions of our boundless affection for the Lord.

Liturgy never arose from human need alone, such as needs for ritual or art or music or painting or other esthetic productions. Liturgy originated with God who summoned it into existence as a divine plan for sharing with us priceless gifts of love and grace.

The Church is as ready as anyone to support life-ennobling art, music, and drama and the social settings that have evolved over the centuries to present these creations. That is quite different, however, from the Christ-sanctioned celebrations of the sacraments, events of faith and mystery where God continues to touch and sanctify the human soul.

Yes, it is sometimes costly — and occasionally perhaps too costly — but do we not want to give the one we love the best we have? As people of faith we have no choice about liturgy. A loving God wants it. A loving people wants it too.

For dialog

1. How does your personal temperament react to liturgy? Do you lean toward "high church" elaborate ceremony? Or are you more content with simple ritual? What do you think moves you one way or the other? How helpful have you found liturgy to be a place where you experience a sense of community? If not, what would be needed? Does the liturgy you participate in communicate a sense of mystery to you? Why? Why not? How can you be made aware of God's presence at liturgy as well as the presence of the angels and saints?

2. How would you explain to someone that liturgy is a faith event where

covenant union with Christ is renewed, sinfulness healed, and graces received? How you would show that same person that the moral life is a graced response of love to the Christ who loves you?

What kind of liturgies move you the most?

3. If there were times in your life when you stopped participating in worship, what caused it and what brought you back? What do you hope for in homilies you hear? Who are the best kinds of homilists? How does your involvement in the liturgy relate to the way the celebrant's pastoral service touches you?

Prayer

Heavenly Father, thank you for the call to worship where we can renew our love covenant with you. Divine Son, we praise you for the ongoing communication of the graces of your dying and rising in every liturgy. Holy Spirit, we are grateful for the transforming power of your presence at liturgy. The way in which you shape our souls into a greater likeness of Jesus is a most precious gift. May our lives witness the gifts received at liturgy as we live out the moral demands of the kingdom of love, justice, and mercy.

Glossary

Heavenly Liturgy — The books of Hebrews and Revelation describe acts of worship in heaven by means of various images. This heavenly liturgy is invisibly present at our earthly one.

Liturgy — The term comes from the Greek word meaning "people's work." By baptism all the faithful are called to offer a sacrifice of praise. The ordained priest acts in the person of Christ to make Christ's saving action present by the power of the Spirit.

Paschal Mystery — Liturgy is a mystery because it is the divine act of the Father, Son, and Spirit. It is paschal because it makes present the dying and rising of Jesus Christ.

Liturgical Year — The Church's year which unfolds the mystery of Christ. It includes Advent, Christmas Season, Lent, Easter Season, Pentecost, Trinity, Corpus Christi, Ordinary Time, the feasts and memorials of the Blessed Virgin and the saints.

Liturgy of the Hours — Seven times a day the Church praises God at the Office of Readings, Morning Prayer, Three Daytime Hours, Evening Prayer, Night Prayer. These prayers prolong the celebration of the Eucharist, flowing from it and back to it.

"The Church is not a museum for saints. It is a hospital for sinners."
Bishop Timothy Harrington

Chapter 16

THE SACRAMENTS OF BAPTISM AND CONFIRMATON

CCC 1213-1321

"No one can enter the kingdom of God without being born of water and Spirit."

John 3:5

St. Augustine the Seeker

Augustine came late to the love of Christ. Born in Tagaste, North Africa in 354, of Monica and Patricius, he was raised a Christian though not baptized. When he was sixteen, his parents sent him to Carthage to study law. Augustine's tastes, however, ran to literature and girls. After several love affairs, he settled in with one woman with whom he lived for the next fifteen years and by whom he sired a son, Adeodatus.

He became a religious seeker. He investigated the Bible but he recoiled from what appeared to him a contradiction between a vengeful Old Testament God and a loving New Testament Christ. Moreover the Old Testament scriptural stories seemed too coarse and unreal for his intellectual tastes that were nourished by the refinement of the Latin classics.

He joined the Manichean religion, which held a low opinion of the goodness of human nature and called for an austerity that could lead its followers to membership in a godly elite. After ten years of teaching in Carthage he moved to Rome where he continued as a teacher. Influential friends obtained a better teaching position for him at the court of the emperor in Milan, then the capitol of the West.

In Milan, three elements combined to move Augustine to seek Christian Baptism: the sermons of Bishop Ambrose, the insights of the Neo-Platonists, and a stream of light from St. Paul's epistles.

Augustine loved to attend the cathedral services on Sunday morning and listen to Ambrose speak. The bishop cleared away his objections to the Old Testament and presented a challenging appeal for the Catholic faith.

In studying the Neo-Platonists, at the urging of Ambrose, Augustine became aware of the reality of the spiritual and an awakening of his soul.

Then one day in his garden he thought he heard a child playfully call out, "Take and read." He picked up a copy of the epistles of St. Paul and read, "Let us conduct ourselves properly as in the day, not in orgies and drunkenness, not in promiscuity and licentiousness, not in rivalry or jealousy. But put on the Lord Jesus Christ, and make no provision for the desires of the flesh." (Rom 13:13-14)

In that moment his doubts dissolved and his soul filled with light. He went to Bishop Ambrose to be baptized a Christian and began one of the most brilliant Christian careers ever lived. He ultimately became a bishop himself in Hippo where he served the spiritual needs of his people for thirty-five years. He has influenced Christian theology and spirituality ever since his baptism. In the Liturgy of the Hours his sermons are the ones most often read.

He came late to the love of Christ. Hardly anyone has ever loved Christ more.

Is Baptism Required for Salvation?

Some say... If Baptism were really required for salvation, then billions of people would never be saved. Half the world does not belong to Christ and has not been baptized. If God wants to save everyone, then a means should be sought that is less tied to baptism and more reasonably available to a major portion of the human race.

Or think of the thirty-six million unborn babies that have been aborted since Roe vs. Wade. These poor children never had a chance to be baptized. Is it possible they will not be saved, especially considering the tragic way in which their lives were terminated? Jesus was known for loving children. Does he not still love them? Would he refuse them salvation because they missed getting a sacrament?

In our view, too much emphasis is put on physical rituals. The greatest value of the Church is its spiritual nature. Liturgical ceremonies have their value. Baptism seems to be more of a membership rite. It is a colorful way to visibly symbolize a person's belonging to the Church. This is quite a different question from being saved.

When Jesus spoke to Nicodemus in John chapter three, and said we need to be born again of water and the spirit in order to be saved, he did not seem to be talking about a baptismal sacrament. It sounded more like a personal conversion caused by some interior spiritual change. Many Christians in fact think of it just that way. The Spirit has come upon them, with no benefit of sacrament, and they experience being born again in Christ.

The baptismal rite is best understood as a useful ceremony for initiating people into membership in the Church — and so not required for salvation.

The Catechism *teaches* ... "The Lord himself affirms that Baptism is necessary for salvation [cf. Jn 3:5] . . . Baptism is necessary for salvation for those to whom the Gospel has been proclaimed and who have had the possibility of asking for this sacrament [Cf. Mk 16:16]." (CCC 1257)

The *Catechism* tells us the Sacraments of Initiation are Baptism, Confirmation, and Eucharist. We will deal with the first two sacraments in this chapter and with Eucharist in the next one.

Just before his Ascension into heaven, Jesus gave the apostles the Great Commission to preach the Gospel and baptize the converts.

"Go therefore and make disciples of all nations, baptizing them in the name of the Father and of the Son and of the Holy Spirit." (Mt 28:19-20)

The word baptism comes from the Greek word that means to plunge into water. The immersion in water symbolizes our death to sin. We die with Christ and are reborn in him. Early Christians liked to call baptism the "enlightenment" because the revelatory teaching that accompanies the sacrament gives the light of Christ to our minds and hearts.

Jesus voluntarily submitted himself to the baptism of John the Baptist, intended for sinners, "to fulfill all righteousness" (Mt 3:15).

Jesus did this to manifest his self-emptying. (cf. Phil 2:7) The Spirit who had hovered over the waters at the first creation, descended on Christ as the prelude to the new creation, and the Father revealed Jesus as his "beloved Son" (Mt 3:16-17; see also CCC 1224).

Through his saving death and Resurrection, Jesus gave Baptism a new meaning. We still have a Baptism for the forgiveness of sins, but the repentance is now seen as a turning to Christ, and the forgiveness of sins proceeds from the authority of Christ and by his power through the ministry of the Church.

The Liturgy of Baptism. The Rite of Baptism has varied throughout history, but six essential elements have always been present: (1) the proclamation of the Word; (2) a religious conversion that includes acceptance of the gospel; (3) the profession of faith; (4) the Baptism itself; (5) the receiving of the Holy Spirit; (6) admission to Eucharist.

In the early Church the candidacy for adults involved a number of stages that included religious instruction and various rituals. In the case of babies such a process was impossible beforehand, so there was need for a catechetical explanation after the child was old enough to understand. Vatican II has restored the "catechumenate," the process for initiating converts into the Church. It is called the Rite of Christian Initiation of Adults (RCIA).

The meaning of Baptism is best seen through the ceremonies by which it is celebrated. There are six rituals that teach us Baptism's significance:

1. Sign of the Cross. The imprint of the Cross on the candidate reminds us of Christ's sacrifice by which he saved us. Baptism is a sacrament of salvation.

2. Readings from Scripture. God's revealed Word is spoken to the candidate with the purpose of asking for a faith response, a faith that implies conversion to Christ and obedience to his Word. Baptism is a sacrament of faith.

3. Exorcism and Anointing. Jesus is about to liberate the candidate from evil. An exorcism prayer is recited to loosen the candidate from the power of Satan. The celebrant anoints the candidate with the oil of catechumens. The candidate explicitly renounces Satan and professes the faith of the Church.

4. The Essential Rite of Baptism. The candidate is either immersed three times in water, or water is poured three times upon the head. The celebrant says, "N., I baptize you in the name of the Father and of the Son, and of the Holy Spirit." This brings about death to all sin, original and personal, and entry into the life of the Trinity through identity with Christ's paschal mystery.

5. Anointing with Chrism. The celebrant anoints the newly baptized with oil of chrism to symbolize the person's internal anointing and reception of the Holy Spirit.

6. White Garment and Candle. The white garment shows that the baptized has put on Jesus and risen with him. The candle symbolizes the light of Christ, which now shines in the baptized.

These ceremonies are teachers of the meaning of Baptism. Not just the words that are spoken, but also the non-verbal elements as indicated above. Now the newly baptized is an adopted child of God in union with Jesus and able to pray, "Our Father."

Who can be baptized? Adults who have not been baptized are welcome to the sacrament after the proper preparation. This is clear enough in mission countries, but also true in the United States where many millions have not been baptized.

Infants are also to be baptized. The custom of baptizing babies goes back to New Testament times when whole households were brought into the faith. (Acts 16:15) The newborn come into the world with a fallen nature and original sin. They need a new birth in Baptism.

The faith that brings us to Baptism must not stop there. Growth in faith should be a lifelong process. This should happen in one's personal relationship with Christ and also must involve lifelong development in understanding the teachings of Christ as proposed and understood by the Magisterium of the Church.

How necessary is Baptism? Jesus taught that Baptism is necessary for salvation. He commanded his apostles and disciples to proclaim the gospel to all nations so that everyone would hear the Word, respond in faith, and be baptized. But for those who have never heard of Christ, the *Catechism* makes a crucial distinction. "*God has bound salvation to the sacrament of Baptism, but he himself is not bound by his sacraments.*" (CCC 1257)

"Every man who is ignorant of the Gospel of Christ and his Church, but seeks the truth and does the will of God in accordance with his understanding of it, can be saved. It may be supposed that such persons would have *desired baptism explicitly* if they had known its necessity." (CCC 1260)

People who die for Christ, though not yet baptized, are baptized by their death for the sake of Christ. Candidates who desire Baptism, but die before actual reception are considered to be saved by their "Baptism of desire."

What about children, babies, and the unborn who die without Baptism? The Church entrusts them to the love and mercy of God. Since God wills that all people be saved and since Jesus said, "Let the little children come unto me," (Mk 10:14) we have a hope that there is a way of salvation for children who die without Baptism.

Effects of Baptism. In Baptism all sins are forgiven, original sin and all personal sins as well as any punishment due to sin. But, consequences of sin remain in the baptized, such as illness, death, character weaknesses, and an inclination to sin.

Baptism welcomes us into membership in the Church — the Body of Christ, the Temple of the Spirit, and the People of God. This brings with it the responsibilities and rights of communion with the Church. By Word and sacrament and prayers and the witness of the believing community, each new member is nourished, strengthened, and sustained for the journey of faith. Baptism also unites us with other baptized people who are not yet in full communion with the Catholic Church. This serves as a bond with them as we work toward the unity of all believers desired by Christ.

Baptism confers on us a "seal," an indelible spiritual "mark or character" that signifies our belonging to Christ. No sin can annul this. Once we are baptized we stay baptized. The sacrament cannot be repeated.

1. What are the major effects of Baptism?

"The fruit of Baptism, or baptismal grace, is a rich reality that includes forgiveness of original sin and all personal sins, birth into the new life by which man becomes an adoptive son of the Father, a member of Christ and a temple of the Holy Spirit. By this very fact the person baptized is incorporated into the Church, the Body of Christ, and made a sharer in the priesthood of Christ." (CCC 1279)

2. How necessary is Baptism?

"Baptism is birth into the new life in Christ. In accordance with the Lord's will, it is necessary for salvation, as is the Church herself, which we enter by Baptism." (CCC 1277)

The Sacrament of Confirmation

(Please reflect on this section in conjunction with our chapter eleven on the Holy Spirit.)

The second sacrament of initiation is Confirmation.

The Old Testament prophets foretold that the Spirit of God would rest upon the future Messiah. Jesus was conceived by the Spirit in the womb of Mary. At his Baptism in the Jordan, the Spirit descended upon him to testify he was the expected Messiah. Jesus promised the Spirit to his followers. This happened first on Easter night and then most dramatically at Pentecost (Jn 20:22; Acts 2:1-4). The Spirit once given to the Messiah now is poured out upon the messianic people.

The apostles, after baptizing the new converts, laid hands upon them to impart the gift of the Spirit who completes the grace of Baptism. This imposition of hands is recognized by Catholic Tradition as the origin of the sacrament of Confirmation. Early in the life of the Church an anointing with perfumed oil (chrism) was added to the laying on of hands.

Anointing connects the person with the title "Christian" because the word Christ actually means the "anointed one." In Scripture oil is a sign of abundance and joy. It was used as a cleansing agent at one's bath and was employed by athletes to limber up their muscles. Doctors used oil to heal and soothe wounds. Kings, priests, and prophets were anointed with oil as a sign of their consecration to God.

All these symbols explain the use of oil at Confirmation and the effects of the sacrament. The oil marks the person with the seal of the Spirit signifying one's belonging radically and permanently to God. Hence Confirmation cannot be received again. We are enrolled in Christ's service forever. While we may reject our covenant with Christ, he never withdraws his commitment to us while we live.

The essential rite of Confirmation is conferred by the anointing with chrism on the forehead, which is done by the laying on of the hand along with the words, "Be sealed with the gift of the Holy Spirit."

1. What are the effects of Confirmation?

The effect of the sacrament of Confirmation is the full outpouring of the Holy Spirit as once granted to the apostles on the day of Pentecost.

"From this fact, Confirmation brings an increase and deepening of baptismal grace:
- it roots us more deeply in the divine filiation which makes us cry, 'Abba! Father!' [Rom 8:15];
- it unites us more firmly to Christ;
- it increases the gifts of the Holy Spirit in us;
- it renders our bond with the Church more perfect [cf. LG 11];
- it gives us a special strength of the Holy Spirit to spread and defend the faith by word and action as true witnesses of Christ, to confess the name of Christ boldly, and never to be ashamed of the Cross" [cf. Council of Florence (1439); DS 1319; LG 11;12;]. (CCC 1303)

2. Who may be confirmed?

"A candidate for Confirmation who has attained the age of reason must profess the faith, be in the state of grace, have the intention of receiving the sacrament, and be prepared to assume the role of disciple and witness to Christ, both within the ecclesial community and in temporal affairs." (CCC 1319).

3. How is Confirmation celebrated in the Eastern Church?

"In the East this sacrament is administered immediately after Baptism and is followed by participation in the Eucharist; this tradition highlights the unity of the three sacraments of Christian initiation." (CCC 1318)

Response to objections

"God has bound salvation to the sacrament of Baptism, but he himself is not bound by his sacraments." (CCC 1257)

Jesus Christ wants the salvation of every person. To make this salvation available he commanded the apostles and their successors to bring the gospel to every man and woman on earth. The case for Christ should be made and the hearers invited to faith, Baptism, and active, witnessing membership in the Church. Baptism is necessary for those who have heard the Word of God and have the possibility of asking for it.

This Baptism is more than a membership initiation rite; it is a sacrament of salvation from original and actual sin as well as an effective sign of membership in the Church.

What then of those who have heard and believed the gospel but were unable to be baptized?

The Church teaches that those who died for the faith before they were able to be baptized are in fact baptized by the sacrifice of their lives for Christ. This is commonly called *Baptism of blood*.

Candidates for Baptism who die before being able to receive the sacrament are saved by reason of their desire for the sacrament, repentance for their sins, and the love of Christ. This is often called *Baptism of desire*.

For the billions of men and women who have not yet heard the call of the Gospel and the Church, salvation is available to those who seek the truth and do God's will according to their understanding. This happens in a manner known to God alone. The *Catechism* teaches that God normally works through the sacraments, but is not bound by them. We believe the Holy Spirit offers to these people, in a manner known only to God, the possibility of salvation.

In the case of unborn babies — or born children — who were unable to be baptized — the Church entrusts them to the mercy of God. Since Christ died and rose to save everyone and showed special tenderness to children, we are moved to hope there is a way of salvation for children who died without Baptism.

For dialog

1. Share experiences you may have had attending a Baptism. Do you know the date of your Baptism? How might one celebrate a Baptism anniversary, given that we are usually ready and willing to celebrate our birthdays? How would you benefit from the intercession of the saint whose name you received at Baptism? If you are called to be a godparent at a Baptism, what responsibilities will you assume?

2. What is the relationship between Baptism and Confirmation? Why were you confirmed? From homilies and faith testimonies you have heard, what have you gleaned about the presence and power of the Holy Spirit? If Confirmation offers you graces of courage to witness your faith, what opportunities have arisen where you have exercised this witness?

3. What experiences have you had of people who are unbaptized? What kind of process would you follow to awaken in them the value of belonging to Christ and his Church? Why are some Catholics reluctant to share their faith with others?

Prayer

Dear Jesus, at our Baptism, we promised to renounce the devil and all his allurements. We pledged to live the Christian life according to the tenets of the faith. At our Confirmation, we were sealed with the Holy Spirit of courage and commitment and we promised to stand up for our faith. Give us the graces we need to keep these promises and remain firm in our love for you and all peoples.

Glossary

Baptism — The first of the sacraments of initiation whereby we are immersed in water three times in the name of the Father, Son, and Holy Spirit. We are freed from all sin, original and personal, and the temporal punishment due to sin. We are filled with divine life and enlightened by Christ's revelation.

Confirmation — The second of the sacraments of initiation. Confirmation perfects the grace of Baptism. We receive the Holy Spirit who roots us more profoundly in the divine filiation, incorporates us more deeply into Christ, renders us more solidly linked with the Church, associates us with the Church's mission, and helps us witness Christ by words and deeds.

RCIA — The initials for the Rite of Christian Initiation of Adults. This is a process for bringing converts into full communion with the Catholic Church through the sacraments of Baptism, Confirmation, and Eucharist.

Catechumenate — Another name for the RCIA process.

Indelible Character — A spiritual mark of identity with Christ received in the sacraments of Baptism, Confirmation, and Holy Orders. The character signifies the permanence of our covenant with Christ and means these sacraments can only be received once.

"The Church is not about satisfying expectations, but celebrating the mysteries."

Cardinal Carlo Maria Martini

Chapter 17

EAT THIS BREAD — DRINK THIS CUP
CCC 1322-1419

"For as often as you eat this bread and drink the cup, you proclaim the death of the Lord until he comes."

I Cor 11:26

You Will Enchant the Angels

Isak Dinesen's short story, "Babette's Feast," made into a film, illustrates the sacrificial and healing love of a feast. The setting is a fishing village in nineteenth-century Denmark. The story centers on Martine and Phillipa, daughters of a devout Lutheran pastor who has founded a small religious sect. The sisters rejected marriage and chose to continue their father's religious work after his death.

They have welcomed Babette, a Parisian refugee from the civil war of 1871, into their home. Babette cooks and keeps house for the sisters in return for room and board. She observes the twelve aging members of the sect becoming increasingly querulous and drifting away from the ideals of their founder.

One day Babette receives news that she has won ten thousand francs in a lottery. She asks Martine and Phillipa of she can use the prize money to prepare a feast to celebrate the one-hundredth anniversary of the founder's death.

The sisters agree, but are dismayed when the supplies arrive from Paris: cases of wine, a live turtle for the soup, live pheasants for the entree. Compared to their simple fare this seems like a "witches' sabbath." They share their misgivings with the sect. All decide they will partake of the meal but make no comments about it.

But as they eat and drink by candlelight they are warmed. They begin to talk animatedly, especially telling stories of their founder. With the wine they repent of their bad moods and words. They see one another with renewed affection and embrace with kindness.

Dinesen writes, "The room seemed filled with a heavenly light. Taciturn old people received the gift of tongues; ears that for years had been almost deaf were opened to it. The windows of the house shone like gold, and golden song flowed out into the winter air."

After the dinner the sisters went to the kitchen to thank Babette. She looked exhausted amid the greasy pots and pans. To their astonishment they discovered that she has spent all her prize money on the meal.

"You will be poor," they tell her.

"A great artist, my friends, is never poor," she replies.

Phillipa embraces her, "In paradise you will be the great artist that God meant you to be. Ah, how you will enchant the angels."

Babette's sacrificial act of love, expressed in a meal, brought joy to the little old group and healed them so they could forgive one another. Her story evokes the meaning and mystery of the Holy Eucharist, which we will reflect upon here.

How Is Jesus Present in the Eucharist?

Some say... Jesus is present in the Eucharist in a symbolic manner. The bread is a symbol that reminds us of Jesus and moves us to think of him and enter into a prayerful conversation with him. The Communion bread is like the flag of our country. When we see the stars and stripes, we think of America and are often filled with patriotic feelings. The Communion bread is associated with the Last Supper and helps us remember how much Jesus loved us to the point of going to the Cross on our behalf.

Symbols are like signs that point to something else. For example, a road sign tells us that a certain city is five miles away. The sign is neither the city nor the expanse of road that must be traveled to get there.

The Catechism teaches ... Jesus instituted the Eucharistic at the Last Supper. In a mysterious manner it contained the sacrifice of his Body and Blood and enables that sacrifice to continue in history until he comes again. He entrusted the Eucharist to his Church. It remembers and makes present his saving death and resurrection for our salvation. The Eucharist is a sacrament of love, a sign of unity, a paschal meal in which we consume Jesus, have our minds filled with grace and receive the pledge of eternal life. What are the names we use for this sacrament? The *Catechism* gives us ten names traditionally associated with this sacrament.

1. We call it *Eucharist* because it is act of *thanking* God for creation, salvation, and sanctification.

2. We name it the *Last Supper* because that is when Jesus instituted the Eucharist.

3. We recall it as the *Breaking of the Bread* because that is what Jesus did in the Upper Room, how he revealed himself to the disciples at Emmaus, and the name the early Christians used for Eucharist.

4. We view it as the *Eucharistic Assembly* since we celebrate it in community as a visible expression of the Church.

5. We know it as the *memorial* of Christ's passion, death, and resurrection. Not just a memory of the past, but a making it present by the power of the Spirit and the ministry of the priest.

6. We celebrate it as the *Holy Sacrifice of the Mass* because it makes present the one sacrifice of Jesus Christ.

7. We participate in it as the *Holy and Divine Liturgy* because it is the center and most intense expression of all Christian worship.

8. We adore the Eucharist as the *Most Blessed Sacrament*, reserved in the tabernacle for our continued worship and devotion.

9. We take the Eucharist as *Holy Communion* wherein we are united to Christ and shaped by him into the Body of Christ, the Church.

10. We witness Eucharist as *Holy Mass* a word that comes from the Latin "to send." At the end of Eucharist the priest sends us forth to love and serve the Lord and one another and do God's will in our daily lives. (See CCC 1328-1332 for a fuller coverage of these names.)

No one of these ten names says it all about the Eucharist, but taken together they give us a tapestry of the broad richness of what the Eucharist means.

Scriptural Background. The origins of the principal elements of Eucharistic celebration lie deep in the mists of Israelite history. The key may be found in the celebrations that followed three harvests: wheat, wine, and lambs. People naturally thanked God for the harvests and went on to have a party.

When the wheat was gathered they thanked God and celebrated the feast of the *Unleavened Bread*.

As the bushels of grapes filled their yards they made wine, danced for joy before God, and celebrated the *Feast of Tents*, in which they lived while harvesting the grapes.

When they saw their flocks of new lambs, they praised God and rejoiced in the feast of *Passover*.

In the beginning these were mainly agricultural holidays associated with pagan worship. In Israel they took on a new religious meaning as they were associated with their historical experience of the true God's mighty works of salvation, especially in the Exodus from Egypt, the pilgrimage in the desert, the covenant at Sinai, and the entry into the Promised Land.

Their most solemn annual feast was Passover, which combined unleavened bread, ceremonial wine, and the sacrificial lamb. Jesus transformed the old Passover into the new pasch. Jesus himself became the Lamb of sacrifice and changed the bread and wine into his Body and Blood.

In the gospels the wine miracle and the bread miracle (occurring five times) foreshadowed the Eucharist. The gospels of Matthew, Mark, and Luke, and Paul's first letter to Corinth recount Christ's institution of the Eucharist. While John does not contain this narrative, he devotes chapter six to a Eucharistic explanation of the multiplication of the loaves.

The scriptural narratives of the Last Supper, the words of institution of the Eucharist, the Breaking of the Bread at Emmaus, and the other references to the Breaking of the Bread by the early Christian community provide abundant revelatory testimony about the Eucharist.

The Essential Elements of Eucharistic Celebration. In the second century, St. Justin Martyr wrote to the pagan emperor, Anoninus Pius, around the year 155, to explain what Christians did at Eucharist. His description contained the outline of celebration that we use today in all our great liturgical families. There are five essential movements in all Eucharists.

1. THE GATHERING. Christians gather in one place for the worship. Jesus, our high priest, presides invisibly over the celebration. The bishop or priest is the visible presider, acting in the person of Christ, preaching the homily, receiving the offerings and saying the Eucharistic prayer. All the worshipers actively participate: readers, those who bring the offerings, the extraordinary Eucharistic ministers — and the whole assembly whose "Amen" signifies their participation.

2. LITURGY OF THE WORD. There are readings from the Old Testament, Letters of the Apostles, the Acts, the Apocalypse and the Gospels. This is followed by the homily and the intercessory prayers. This proclamation and explanation of the Word is meant to call us to a deeper faith and prepare us for the next part of the Mass.

3. THE PRESENTATION OF THE OFFERINGS. Normally on Sundays there is a procession with the bread and wine to the altar. This remembers Christ "taking the bread and wine," and changing it into his Body and Blood. From the beginning there have always been gifts for those in need. Hence the collection for the parish needs happens at this time.

4. THE EUCHARISTIC PRAYER. This part of the Mass has six parts:

a. *Preface*. We thank the father through Christ in the Spirit for the gifts of creation, salvation, and sanctification.

b. *Epiclesis.* (Invocation) We ask the father to send the Spirit to change the bread and wine into Christ's Body and Blood.

c. *Institution Narrative.* The acts of Christ and the Spirit give power to the words spoken by the priest to transform the bread and wine into Christ's Body and Blood. Only validly ordained bishops and priests may do this.

d. *The Remembrance.* We remember the passion, resurrection, and glorious return of Christ.

e. *Intercessions.* We celebrate with the whole Communion of Saints in heaven and on earth — with all of God's people.

f. *Communion.* After the Lord's Prayer, the breaking of the bread, we receive the Body and Blood of Christ.

Real Presence — Holy Communion. The Mass is both a holy sacrifice and a holy meal. The Eucharist is a sacrifice because it makes present the sacrificial act of Jesus at Calvary. The same Jesus who once offered himself in a bloody manner on the Cross to save us from our sins and give us divine life now offers himself on our altars in an unbloody manner. This sacrifice becomes the offering of the whole Church. At Mass, we unite ourselves with Jesus and identify with his Cross — an act that leads us to his resurrection where we rise with him.

The Mass is also a holy meal, a sacred banquet where we partake of the Body and Blood of Christ. We speak here also of the Real Presence of Jesus. Jesus is present to us in many ways: in the Scriptures, in the Eucharistic assembly, in the poor and the sick and those in prison, in the sacraments, in the priest, but above all in the Eucharist.

"This presence is called real — by which is not intended to exclude other types of presence as if they could not be real too, but because it is presence in the fullest sense: that is to say, it is a substantial presence, by which Christ, God and man, makes himself wholly and entirely present."[1]

At Mass we adore the real presence of Jesus in the Eucharist by genuflecting or by bowing deeply. And we adore the reserved presence of Christ in our tabernacles. "Because Christ is present in the sacrament of the altar, he is to be honored with the worship of adoration. 'To visit the Blessed Sacrament is . . . proof of gratitude, an expression of love, and a duty of adoration toward Christ our Lord.'"[2]

The celebration and reception of the Eucharist should have an impact on our lives. As we finish Mass we always hear the priest tell us to love and serve the Lord. This is done practically by acts of love, justice, and mercy to one another, especially the poor.

"You have tasted the Blood of the Lord, yet you do not recognize your brother. . . You dishonor this table when you do not judge worthy of sharing your food someone judged worthy to take part in this meal. . . God freed you from all your sins and invited you here, but you have not become more merciful."[3]

1. What happens at the consecration in the Mass?

"By the consecration the transubstantiation of the bread and wine into the Body and Blood of Christ is brought about. Under the consecrated species of bread and wine Christ himself, living and glorious, is present in a true, real, and substantial manner: his Body and Blood, with his soul and his divinity (cf. Council of Trent: DS 1640; 1651)." (CCC 1413)

2. What is an essential preparation for Communion?

"Anyone who desires to receive Christ in Eucharistic communion must be in the state of grace. Anyone aware of having sinned mortally must not receive communion without having received absolution in the sacrament of penance." (CCC 1415)

3. What are the benefits of Holy Communion?

"Communion with the Body and Blood of Christ increases the communicant's union with the Lord, forgives his venial sins, and preserves him from grave sins. Since receiving this sacrament strengthens the bonds of charity between the communicant and Christ, it also reinforces the unity of the Church as the Mystical Body of Christ.

"The Church warmly recommends that the faithful receive Holy Communion each time they participate in the celebration of the Eucharist; she obliges them to do so at least once a year." (CCC 1416-1417)

Glossary

Eucharist — The sacramental celebration in which the Word of God is proclaimed and responded to in faith; the priest consecrates the bread and wine which is turned into the Body and Blood of Christ by the power of the Spirit; the assembly in union with the priest, offers this sacrifice to the Father to thank him for creation, salvation, and sanctification; the worshippers receive Communion at the sacred banquet.

Sacrifice of the Mass — The Holy Eucharist makes present the redeeming sacrifice of Jesus at Calvary and his saving Resurrection at Easter.

Real Presence — After the bread and wine are consecrated at Mass, they become the Body, Blood, Soul, and Divinity of Christ. We know this with faith. The Real Presence of Jesus is reserved in the tabernacles of our parish churches for our adoration, devotion, and Communion for the sick.

Transubstantiation — Refers to the process of changes of substances that takes place in the bread and wine at Mass when they become the Real Presence of Jesus.

"O sacrament of devotion! O sign of unity! O bond of charity!"

St. Augustine

Endnotes

1. Paul VI, *Mysterium Fidei* (Mystery of Faith), 39.
2. Ibid., 66.
3. John Chrysostom, Homily on 1 Cor 21:40, CCC 1397.

Chapter 18

GOD, FORGIVE ME
CCC 1420-1532

Forgiveness is not rubbing it in; it's rubbing it out.

Forgiveness Stories

A little girl in a small town once claimed she had a vision of Jesus. Her case was reported to the bishop. He questioned her at length, but was unable to shake her story. He sent her to a therapist who concluded she was a normal little girl with no psychological problems. The bishop tried another approach.

"The next time you see Jesus, ask him what I told him in confession."

One month later she saw Jesus again and posed the bishop's question.

"What did Jesus say?" asked the bishop.

"Jesus said, 'I forget,'" replied the little girl.

A six-year-old boy was using a super-adhesive glue on an airplane he was building. Accidentally his right index finger was bonded to the wing of the plane. Frantically, he tried to free his finger but couldn't budge it. His father found a solvent and released the boy's finger.

The father recalled the incident two weeks later when he visited a new family in the neighborhood. The father of the family introduced his children this way: "This is Pete. He's the clumsy one."

"That's Kathy, coming in with mud on her shoes. She's the sloppy one."

"Here comes Suzy, always last. She'll be late for her own funeral."

That father did a fine job of gluing his children to their faults. People do this to us all the time. They stick us with our shortcomings and won't let it go.

When we don't let people forget their past, we glue them to their sins.

When we forgive them we gently pry the doer from the hurtful deed. We say the past is past — done forever.

God does this for us all the time. When we accept his forgiveness, he separates us from our sins. We don't need to be glued to our sins. God's healing power can always fix that.

Why Not Confess Our Sins to God Directly?

Some say... Since God is everywhere, knows everything — even the deepest secrets of our heart — it seems a simple matter to tell God directly our sins and our sorrow for them. God knows our sins before we tell him. Our verbalizing of our sinfulness reminds us of what wrongs we have done. We are not confessing to God matters of which he is unaware. We are making ourselves conscious of our misbehavior. We bring this confession to God in order to seek his forgiveness.

There is no need to use a priest as an intermediary. For one thing, the priest is also a sinner who must bring his sins to the mercy chamber of God. The priest is just a human being like the rest of us, in need of redemption like all other people. The priest can't forgive our sins; only God can do that. Even if the priest has the reputation of being a saint, he is still a creature, confined by the same rules as the rest of us.

No matter how good a priest may be, he bears the imperfections, frailties, moods, and shortcomings that are the common lot of all people. Why should we be bringing our sins to him? There were no confessional "boxes" in New Testament times. There were no confessional rooms for face-to-face confessions. This is an invention that developed in later history. The practice just gets in the way of the real face-to-face admission of sins to God. The custom clutters up the point of the whole exercise, which is to get into God's presence, tell him our sins, and beg forgiveness.

While most priests are capable of giving a sensitive hearing to the penitents, there are times when this fails to happen. This is yet another argument in favor of dispensing with a confessor and putting our souls directly into God's hands and merciful heart.

This is not to say we should avoid going to priests as spiritual counselors. That is a useful and profitable role for a priest and can frequently be a benefit to people in need of guidance. It seems to us that priests can be of far better help to us as spiritual directors than as confessors to whom we tell our sins. After all, God alone can take our sins away. We should go "right to the top" in such matters.

The Catechism *teaches ...* Only God can forgive our sins. But Jesus willed that the Church should be the instrument of divine forgiveness. On Easter night the risen Christ imparted to the apostles his own power to forgive sins. Bishops who are their successors, and priests, the bishops' collaborators, continue to exercise this ministry. Bishops and priests, by the sacrament of Holy Orders, have the power to forgive all sins, "in the name of the Father, and of the Son and of the Holy Spirit." Priests must receive the faculty of absolving from sins from a church authority.

The sacraments of initiation bring us new life in Christ. But we carry this life in earthen vessels and are inclined to sin again. Just as Jesus forgave the sins of the paralytic and healed his body, so the Church continues Christ's ministry of healing. The sacraments of healing are Confession and Anointing. We will deal with Confession first and then with Anointing.

The *Catechism* gives us five ways to speak of the sacrament that forgives our sins.

1. *Sacrament of Conversion*, which is the first step we take back to God after we have sinned.

2. *Sacrament of Penance*, since we are expected to atone for our sins and resolve to avoid them in the future.

3. *Sacrament of Confession*, for we are required to tell our sins to a priest and praise the mercy of God who will forgive us.

4. *Sacrament of Forgiveness*, in which God grants us pardon and peace through the absolution of the priest.

5. *Sacrament of Reconciliation*, because we are again at peace with God and the Church.

Interior conversion is an essential step in any approach to this sacrament. We like to hear stories of conversion, such as that of St. Peter, who denied Christ three times, or St. Augustine, who waited many years before turning to Christ. We admire those who join the Church. We forget they must continue their conversion after Baptism, just like ourselves. We should continually turn away from sin and turn towards God.

Real conversion is a grace from God. It is God who pulls our hearts away from sin and draws us longingly to him. All converts testify that their conversion belongs to God. To the Lord alone be the glory.

The major forms of conversion and penance are fasting, prayer, and charitable giving. Spiritual writers give us many paths to conversion: Reconcile yourselves with your enemies. Take care of the poor. Defend what is just and right. Admit your faults honestly like the prodigal son. Examine your conscience. Correct others in a humble and kind manner. Seek spiritual direction. Accept pain and persecution for the sake of the kingdom. Use the seasons of Advent and Lent for spiritual renewal. Deny yourself. Take up your cross. Follow Jesus.

Sin and Forgiveness. Sin breaks our relationship with God and damages our communion with the Church. Conversion brings us back to God and the Church. This is accomplished liturgically in the Sacrament of Reconciliation.

Over the centuries there have been different concrete forms by which the Church has exercised this power. But beneath the changes the same fundamental structure has remained. There have always been two essential elements: the acts of the penitent and God's action through the intervention of the Church.

The penitent is required to perform three acts.

First Is Contrition. This involves regret for the sin committed and the resolution not to do it again. Our motives for sorrow should arise from our faith. We may speak of perfect contrition that proceeds from loving God above all else. Such loving sorrow remits venial sins and even mortal sins so long as we resolve to confess them as soon as possible. Imperfect contrition, motivated by fear of damnation and the ugliness of sin, begins the process of withdrawing from sin, a process that, with God's grace, will be completed in confession.

Second Is Confession. Confession of our sins opens us to reconciliation. We look directly at our sins and take responsibility for them. Confession of sins to a priest is an essential act of the Sacrament of Reconciliation. After a diligent examination of our consciences, we must confess all our mortal sins. The Church recommends confessing venial sins too even though this is not strictly necessary. After the age of discretion, we are required to confess serious sins at least once a year. Children must go to confession before receiving Holy Communion for the first time.

Third Is Satisfaction. Many of our sins injure other people. We should do all we can to repair the harm. For example this could mean returning stolen goods, restoring the reputation of someone we have undermined, or paying compensation for injuries. Our sins also have a negative effect on our own souls. Absolution takes away the sin, but does not repair the damage done to us. We need to work on recovering our full spiritual health. The penance we receive from the priest is meant to be the first step in our self-improvement. Our return to spiritual health can include: prayer, acts of love and service for others, sacrifices, and patient acceptance of the cross we must carry.

After we have confessed our sins to the priest, we are given some encouragement by the priest for our moral and spiritual lives. The priest gives us a penance and asks us to make an act of contrition. Then the priest absolves us from our sins with these words:

God the Father of mercies,
through the death and resurrection of his Son
has reconciled the world to himself
and sent the Holy Spirit among us for the forgiveness of sins;
through the ministry of the Church may God give you
pardon and peace, and I absolve you from your sins
in the name of the Father and of the Son and of the Holy Spirit.

The *Catechism* has this to say about the forgiveness of sins and the remission of temporal punishment due to sin by indulgences. "Individual and integral confession of grave sins followed by absolution remains the only ordinary means of reconciliation with God and the Church.

"Through indulgences the faithful can obtain remission of the temporal punishment resulting from sin for themselves and also for the souls in Purgatory." (CCC 1497-1498)

Parishes offer confession face-to-face with the priest or in an anonymous manner when the penitent confesses behind a screen. There are also penance services from time to time during the year where there is a Proclamation of the Word, a homily, prayers, and music to help people appreciate the sacrament's purpose. These services are accompanied by individual confession to a priest. In emergency situations, general absolution may be given. If the penitent was in mortal sin, that sin should be confessed at a later time to a priest.

All sacraments bring the participants divine joy and peace. The special happiness received here arises from lifting the burden of sin and guilt. We are released to the freedom of grace. We are restored to the friendship of God, others, and self.

1. What are the main elements of the Sacrament of Reconciliation?

"The sacrament of Penance is a whole consisting in three actions of the penitent and the priest's absolution. The penitent's acts are repentance, confession or disclosure of sins to the priest, and the intention to make reparation and do works of reparation." (CCC 1491)

2. What are the spiritual effects of the Sacrament of Penance?

"The spiritual effects of the sacrament of Penance are:
- reconciliation with God by which the penitent recovers grace;
- reconciliation with the Church;
- remission of the eternal punishment incurred by mortal sins;
- remission, at least in part, of temporal punishments resulting from sin;
- peace and serenity of conscience, and spiritual consolation;
- an increase of spiritual strength for the Christian battle." (CCC 1496)

The Sacrament of the Anointing of the Sick

The second sacrament of healing is the sacrament of the Anointing of the Sick. The problem of pain, experienced in old age and illness, is one that bothers all of us eventually. Serious illness makes us think of our deaths. We feel powerless. We experience our limits. Sickness makes some people angry — even with God. They turn in upon themselves and tend to despair. For others, being ill matures them and draws them to God.

Jesus had a preferential love for sick people and even identified himself with the suffering. "I was sick and you visited me." (Mt 25:36 RSV) Jesus healed the whole person, body, mind, and soul. He cured the paralytic's physical disability as well as his moral one when he forgave him his sins. Jesus often touched people when he healed them. In the sacrament of anointing, Jesus touches the sick to heal them — always from sin, but sometimes even from the physical ailment.

Jesus did not heal all sick people. His cures were signs of the arrival of the kingdom of God. They were meant to tell us of a more basic healing, the conquest of sin and death by his death and resurrection. In the sufferings of the Cross, Jesus assumed the full weight of evil and took away the sin of the world, of which illness is an effect. He gave a new meaning to pain. We are now able to unite our suffering to his redemptive Passion.

The Church continues Christ's compassion for the sick and a healing ministry in three ways:

(1) Most frequently this is seen in the many religious orders that were founded to provide hospital care, originally for the indigent poor and then for others. Church-sponsored hospice care is a new form of this ministry of healing. We also think here of all the relatives and friends who show compassion for the sick.

(2) Then there are examples of singular people who have the "charism" or gift of healing. They manifest the power of the risen Lord. We know, however, that prayer does not always heal the sick. Sometimes Jesus calls us to unite our sufferings to his. St. Paul says, "In my flesh I complete what is lacking in Christ's afflictions for the sake of his Body, that is, the Church." (Col 1:24 RSV)

(3) Finally there is the sacrament of Anointing. St. James tells of this. "Is anyone sick among you? Let him call for the elders (presbyters) of the Church and let them pray over him, anointing him with oil in the name of the Lord; and the prayer of faith will save the sick man, and the Lord will raise him up; and if he has committed sins, he will be forgiven." (Jas 5:14-15)

Who may receive this sacrament? Anyone who is danger of death from sickness or old age may receive the sacrament. If the person recovers and then has another serious illness, he can receive the sacrament again. We may receive this sacrament before a serious operation. Only bishops and priests may minister this sacrament. The sick person receives a special grace to cope with the problems that attend grave illness or old age.

For those sick people who are on their final journey to the next life, this is an anointing unto glory, a sacrament of departure. Baptism began conforming them to the death and resurrection of Christ. This sacrament completes that work. The sick may also receive the Eucharist, which we call "Viaticum." The word means "Christ is with us on the way," through his Eucharistic presence and power.

It is often said that the dying go through stages of denial, anger, bargaining, depression, and acceptance. The Anointing of the Sick helps loved ones release the dying to God and assist the gravely ill to accept death should it be God's will for them at this time.

1. How do we celebrate the Anointing of the Sick?

"The celebration of the Anointing of the Sick consists essentially in the anointing of the forehead and hands of the sick person (in the Roman Rite) or of other parts of the body (in the Eastern Rite), the anointing being accompanied by the liturgical prayer of the celebrant asking for the special grace of this sacrament." (CCC 1531)

2. What are the effects of this sacrament?

• The special grace of the sacrament of the Anointing of the Sick has as its effects:

• the uniting of the sick person to the passion of Christ, for his own good and that of the whole Church;

• the strengthening, peace, and courage to endure in a Christian manner the sufferings of illness or old age;

• the forgiveness of sins, if the sick person was not able to obtain it through the sacrament of Penance;

• the restoration of health if it is conducive to the salvation of his soul;

• the preparation for passing over to eternal life." (CCC 1532)

Response to objections

We have only posed objections to confessing to a priest in the sacrament of Reconciliation, since these are the ones most frequently raised. The principle reason for bringing our sins to the priest in the sacrament of Reconciliation is that only Jesus Christ can forgive our sins and he willed that we should do so in this sacrament. On Easter night he appeared to the apostles and breathed the Holy Spirit upon them and told them that they were now able to forgive sins. (Cf. Jn 20:19-22)

They passed this power on to the bishops and their associates, the priests.

It is a power given to the Church and expressed through the ministry of priests and bishops.

Objections based upon the frailties and sins of priests and bishops do not stand. The power to forgive sins is not tied to the given moral perfection of the confessor, but rather connected to his ordination and the gifts of the Spirit to make this possible. Of course this does not excuse him from being an authentic witness to Christ.

Another reason we confess to a priest is that we are members of the Church. When we sin we not only harm our relationship with God, but also our relationship with the Church. It is therefore entirely fitting that we beg God to heal our connection with the Church as well as with him. Since the priest is an authorized representative of the Church, he is able, by the power of Christ, to reconcile us both to God and the Church.

Finally, every time we sin we diminish ourselves. But we also affect the Body of Christ negatively. "No man is an island," wrote the poet John Donne. He argued that we are part of the mainland, members of one another in a planetary community. "Do not go to see for whom the bell tolls. It tolls for thee."[3] Again, we need to be reconciled with God's people and that is done by confession to the Church's representative, the bishop or priest.

For dialog

1. How often do you go to confession? In general, what principles determine your participation in this sacrament? What do you expect from the sacrament? Why is the sacrament of Reconciliation necessary for spiritual growth and moral health? Do you prefer private auricular confession or the face-to-face type? Why? Do you find that confession is a time for spiritual direction?

2. What do you find appealing about a Penance Service that includes going to confession? Satisfaction for sin is necessary both to signify your sorrow for sin and overcome, with the Spirit's help, the residual damage due to sin. What spiritual practices help you in this regard? What examples from everyday life can you think of where you have made a mistake or need to apologize but sense you have to work on the matter to undo the damage?

3. What experience have you had of the Sacrament of Anointing? If you were seriously injured in an accident, how would the Anointing be important for you? If Jesus healed physical ailments during his ministry in Galilee, why would he not be able to do the same today?

Prayer

Jesus, healer of our minds, bodies, souls, and emotions, we are grateful for the sacraments of Reconciliation and Anointing. We know we need to be reconciled to God, the Church, and others. We realize there will be times in our lives when we will need the Anointing both for our spiritual and physical health — the latter if profitable for our salvation. Give us the graces we need for lifelong conversion. Remind us to have compassion for the sick as well as those who need reconciliation with God, the Church, and others. May our hearts be homes of faith, hope, and love.

Glossary

Sacrament of Reconciliation — Also called the sacrament of Confession, Penance, Conversion and Forgiveness, the sacrament of Reconciliation is the sacrament in which the sins committed after Baptism are forgiven. It results in reconciliation with God and the Church.

Acts of the Penitent in Confession — The acts of the penitent in confession are contrition, confession of sins, and satisfaction for sins.

Perfect and Imperfect Contrition — Perfect contrition means sorrow for sins based on love for God. Imperfect contrition is based on fear of damnation and disgust for sin. The Holy Spirit motivates us in both instances.

Ministers of Confession — Bishops, and their collaborators, priests, are the ministers of the sacrament of Reconciliation.

Sacrament of Anointing — The Church, through anointing with oil and the power of the Spirit, prepares a gravely ill person for the passage to eternal life. Sometimes physical health is restored if it is God's will.

"It is in pardoning that we are pardoned."

Prayer of St. Francis of Assisi

Chapter 19

CALLED TO BE A PRIEST
CCC 1536-1600

"I have never found anything in life more attractive to me than the priesthood."

Father Walter Burghardt, S.J.

I Always Wanted to Be a Priest

We offer here a testimony of a remarkable priest, Archbishop Helder Camara, retired bishop of Refice, Brazil. He has become world famous for his love of the poor and his efforts to help them find social and economic justice through prayer, community, and social action. Archbishop Camara is equally known for his contagious holiness and enthusiasm for the treasures of spirituality. This is what he has to say about being a priest:

"I can't imagine being anything but a priest. Just think, I consider the lack of imagination to be a crime and yet I haven't the imagination to see myself as not a priest. For me, being a priest isn't just a choice; it's a way of life. It's what water is for a fish, the sky for a bird. I really believe in Christ. Jesus for me is not an abstract idea — he's a personal friend.

"Being a priest has never disappointed me nor given me regrets. Celibacy, chastity, the absence of a family in the way laymen understand it, all this has never been a burden to me. If I've missed certain joys, I have others much more sublime. If you only knew what I feel when I say Mass, how I become one with it! The Mass for me is truly Calvary, and the Resurrection: it's a mad joy!

"Look, there are those born to sing, those born to write, those born to play soccer, and those who are born to be priests. I was born to be a priest. I started saying so at the age of eight and certainly not because my parents put the idea in my head. My father was a Mason, and my mother went to Church once a year.

"I even remember that one day my father got frightened and said: "My son, you're always saying you want to be a priest. But do you know what that means? A priest is someone who doesn't belong to himself, because he belongs to God and to his people, someone who must dispense only love and faith and charity.

"And I said, 'I know. That's why I want to be a priest.' "[1]

Is Every Catholic a Priest?

Some say... All Catholics by their Baptism belong to the common priesthood of the faithful. As the People of God, Catholics are called by Christ to be a holy people, a priestly people. "You are a chosen race, a royal priesthood, a holy nation." (1 Pt 2:9)

What is the nature of this calling? God expects his people to be priests according to the meaning of priesthood — a mediator or bridge between earth and heaven. A priest stands between God and people and facilitates the relationship between them. Catholics as a priestly people are expected to fulfill this very mission.

It has already been noted that Vatican II teaches that the Church is the Sacrament of Salvation. This is another way of describing the priestly role of the Catholic people. This is why each Catholic should be aware of the priestly calling to connect the world with Christ. All this is given to Catholics at their Baptism. It is the origin of the missionary impulse implanted in Catholics by the Spirit in this sacrament.

What then are we to say of men who are officially called bishops, priests, and deacons in the Church? The best way to think of them is that they are called and chosen from the priestly community to minister on their behalf. Their legitimacy derives from the Catholic community that calls them, trains them, and supports them in their ministry of service within the Church.

These priests are not substantially different from the priesthood of all the faithful. Holy Orders does not produce an essentially different priest. The ordained priest is distinguished from the baptismal priesthood only in terms of function, not because of some radical change in being by the Holy Spirit. It is a matter of organizational need and convenience. Whatever authority or status the ordained bishop or priest may have derives from the permission and consent of the Catholic priestly people.

Generally, the ordained priests have been endowed with a permanent role. But this is not an absolute state. It is a custom that has grown up in the Church's history because it is helpful for the continuity and stability of the community, not due to some intrinsic quality given at ordination.

Yes, every Catholic is a priest. Some Catholics are ordained or "ordered" for a special function in the Church community.

The Catechism teaches ...

By Baptism all Catholics are initiated into the common priesthood of the faithful. By Holy Orders, certain men are called to an ordained priesthood, which is essentially different from the baptismal priesthood.

The *Catechism* groups Holy Orders and Marriage under the Sacraments of Communion *because they minister to the salvation of others*. If they help us with our personal salvation it is through our service to others. We will devote our attention to Holy Orders in this chapter and Marriage in the next one.

"Holy Orders is the sacrament through which the mission entrusted by Christ to his apostles continues to be exercised in the Church until the end of time: thus it is the sacrament of apostolic ministry. It includes three degrees: episcopate, presbyterate, and diaconate." (CCC 1536) Without the bishops, priests, and deacons one cannot speak of Church, for these three orders are organically connected to the Church.

The Church borrowed the word *order* from the Roman empire which used the term to designate a governing body. In this sacrament there are three orders: bishop, priest, and deacon. The rite that makes this possible is called ordination. In the Old Covenant God's people were called a priestly people. But God chose the tribe of Levi to serve as priests for them. They offered gifts and sacrifices to God on behalf of the people. They prefigured the ordained priesthood of the New Covenant.

The former priesthood finds its perfect fulfillment in Jesus Christ, the one mediator between God and ourselves. Christ's priesthood is made present in the ordained priesthood.

The whole Church is a priestly people. The baptized believers share in the common priesthood of the faithful. The Sacrament of Holy Orders confers a special spiritual ministry. Only the ordained priest and bishop may celebrate Eucharist and the Sacrament of Reconciliation. Only the bishop can ordain priests and deacons. Only bishops can ordain other bishops.

There are two ways to share in the one priesthood of Christ. The two priesthoods (of Baptism and Orders) differ from each other but are ordered to one another. "Though they differ essentially and not only in degree, the common priesthood of the faithful and the ministerial . . . priesthood . . . are ordered one to another."[2] Christ calls the common priesthood of the baptized to share in the Spirit's work of *sanctifying the world*. Christ calls the ordained priesthood to share in the Spirit's work of *sanctifying the faithful*. Because of his sacred responsibility, the ordained priest has a special obligation to continually and consciously deepen his spiritual life and union with Christ.

The ordained priest acts in the *person of Christ* as head of the Church: teaching, shepherding, and sanctifying God's people. The priest also acts in the *name of the Church*, offering the sacrifice of the Body of Christ to the Father for the salvation of God's people and of the world itself. Because the priest represents Christ at worship, he can represent the Church there.

Bishop, Priest, Deacon. The bishop has the fullness of the Sacrament of Holy Orders. By it he belongs to the college of bishops and becomes the visible head of the local Church entrusted to him. Bishops are successors of the apostles. As a college, bishops have responsibility for mission of the whole Church under the authority of the Pope, the successor of St. Peter.

Priests are united with the bishops in sacerdotal dignity. They depend on bishops for the exercise of their pastoral ministry. With the bishop they form a presbyteral community and assume with him the responsibility for the local Church. The bishop appoints priests to parishes or other diocesan ministries.

Deacons receive the Sacrament of Holy Orders, but not ministerial priesthood. The deacon is conformed to Christ the servant. Deacons may baptize, preach, impart liturgical blessings such as at marriages, and participate in pastoral governance. They exercise their ministries under the pastoral authority of the bishop.

"The *essential rite* of the Sacrament of Holy Orders . . . consists in the bishop's imposition of hands on the head of the ordinand and in the bishop's specific consecratory prayer asking God for the outpouring of the Holy Spirit and his gifts proper to the ministry to which the candidate is being ordained" [cf. Pius XII, apostolic constitution, *Sacramentum Ordinis:* DS 3858]. (CCC 1573)

Only a baptized man may be ordained. Jesus chose only men to be apostles. In turn the apostles picked only men to succeed them in ministry. The Church believes that it is bound by the choice made by the Lord himself. For this reason the ordination of women is not possible. (Cf. CCC 1577)

Ordination is not a right; it is a call from God. The man who believes he has a call to priesthood must submit his desire to the Church, which has the responsibility to discern whether this call is genuine or not. Normally it is the role of seminaries to determine this discernment through admissions and screening procedures, followed by a number of years of priestly formation. This process involves human, theological, pastoral, and spiritual training. The seminary presents the candidate to the bishop who must make the final determination about the suitability of the candidate.

In the Latin Church ordained ministers, with the exception of married deacons, are chosen from the ranks of men of faith who live the celibate life for the sake of the kingdom. Their commitment to celibacy signifies they have resolved to love God and be dedicated to pastoral ministry with an undivided heart. In some cases, married clergy of the Anglican and Lutheran communions, who have converted to Catholicism, have asked to become Catholic priests. After a discernment process, some of them have been admitted to Catholic priesthood and must be re-ordained.

In the Eastern Church only the bishops must be celibate. Priests and deacons may be married. Still many of their priests also practice celibacy. In both the East and the West, once a man is ordained, he may no longer marry.

The ordained priest receives an indelible character, similar to the one received in Baptism and Confirmation. This means both that this sacrament cannot be received again and also teaches us that Christ is absolutely loyal to the covenant he makes with the priest. It is expected that the priest returns this loyalty to Jesus by making a permanent covenant promise to serve God's people and love them with all his heart, mind, and soul.

The graces of the sacrament of Holy Orders are rich and abundant to help the priest keep this commitment. The Holy Spirit offers the priest an ocean of divine love and strength to accomplish this pastoral mission. The Blessed Sacrament is the burning heart of his priesthood giving him the strength to persevere throughout all his days.

1. What are two ways God's people participate in the one priesthood of Christ?

"The whole Church is a priestly people. Through Baptism all the faithful share in the priesthood of Christ. This participation is called the 'common priesthood of the faithful.' Based on this common priesthood and ordered to its service, there exists another participation in the mission of Christ: the ministry conferred by the sacrament of Holy Orders, where the task is to serve in the name and the person of Christ the Head in the midst of community." (CCC 1591)

2. What are the three degrees of ordained priesthood?

"Since the beginning, the ordained ministry has been conferred and exercised in three degrees: that of bishops, that of presbyters, and that of deacons. The ministries conferred by ordination are irreplaceable for the organic structure of the Church: without the bishop, presbyters, and deacons, one cannot speak of the Church (cf. St. Ignatius of Antioch, *Ad Trall* 3,1)." (CCC 1593)

Response to objections

All Catholics by their Baptism are initiated into the common priesthood of the faithful. Christ calls them to share in the Spirit's work of sanctifying the world.

Certain men are called to Holy Orders to become bishops, priests, and deacons. The priesthood of bishops and priests is different from baptismal priesthood, not just in degree but in kind. It is an essentially different priesthood with a distinguishing purpose. Christ calls bishops and priests to share in the Spirit's work of sanctifying the faithful.

The selection of a bishop or a priest for ordination is not a democratic procedure; it is a hierarchical one. This does not mean that counsel and advice is not sought about the suitability of the candidates. Prior to any ordination there are years of screening, training, and evaluation. From the beginning of the process the sponsorship of a bishop is required.

At an ordination of a priest the judgment of a seminary rector is solicited about the worthiness of the candidate. The positive support of the assembly is also asked for. But the final decision is in the hands of the bishop speaking in the name of Christ and the Church.

The difference between the baptismal and Holy Orders priesthood is not just based on function. By the power of the Spirit the ordained priest is substantially changed. He receives an indelible, sacramental character by which he is expected to imitate the special and permanent covenant that Christ establishes with him in the sacrament.

The ordained priest's capacity to celebrate the Eucharist and hear Confessions is not just an organizational convenience or specialized function that any Catholic could perform. It is a gift and Spirit-awarded power for the ordained priest and bishop alone.

The sacrament of Holy Orders does not make the recipients automatically holy, nor place them in a prideful position in the Church. Bishops, priests, and deacons have a grave responsibility to develop a deep union with Jesus. They are expected to live a holy life and to cultivate humility. They are called to be servants of God's people.

For dialog

1. What do you admire in priests that have impressed you? What do you hope for from any priest or bishop? It has been said that the witness of faithful celibacy in priests encourages the fidelity of husbands and wives — and fidelity among married people supports the celibate witness of priests. What experiences have you had of this observation?

2. We are often encouraged to see the humanity of a priest alongside his office. Why is this of value? Why are priests asked to invite the parishioners to collaborate in the building up of the local parish? What is the best

way to make this happen? What can you do to strengthen priests in their calling?

3. What can you do to promote vocations to the priesthood? How would you react if your son told you he would like to be a priest?

Prayer Christ, our high priest, we thank you for calling priests to help us achieve our sanctification, to celebrate the Eucharist and the Sacrament of Reconciliation and the other sacraments. We need good pastors to be stewards of God's mysteries and doctors for our souls. We ask you to awaken the call to priesthood in a whole new generation. We pray for our bishops and priests that they may always be led by the Spirit, be filled with compassion, and be enthusiastic about their calling.

Glossary **Sacrament of Holy Orders** — By the bishop's imposition of hands and a prayer of consecration, the Holy Spirit is invoked to ordain bishops, priests, and deacons for the sanctification of God's people.

Common Priesthood — The baptized share in Christ's priesthood and become the common priesthood of the faithful for the sanctification of the world.

Ministerial Priesthood — Those ordained for Holy Orders share in Christ's priesthood in a uniquely different way and become the ministerial priesthood to serve the Communion of the Church and the sanctification of her members.

"Young people ask me what it takes to be a priest. I tell them: You need two things, a funny bone and a backbone. If you don't have a sense of humor, you won't be able to preach the Good News. You also need a backbone; if you don't, you will soon fall in line with the surrounding culture."

Father Arnold Weber, O.S.B.[3]

Endnotes

1. Adapted from "A Prophet's Vision and Grace: The Life of Archbishop Helder Camara" by Vicky Kemper and Larry Engel, in *Sojourner's Magazine*, December 1987, pp. 12-15.

2. *Lumen Gentium* (LG) ("The Church"), 10. Flannery, O.P., General Editor, *Vatican II* (Northport, NY: Costello Publishing, 1975).

3. *Extraordinary Lives: 34 Priests Tell their Stories*, Francis Friedl and Rex Reynolds, Editors (Notre Dame: Ave Marie, 1987), p. 95.

Chapter 20

THE RING OF FIDELITY — THE EMBRACE OF LOVE

CCC 1601-1666

"Marriage is like twirling a baton, turning handsprings, or eating with chopsticks. It looks easy until you try it."

Helen Roland

The Colors of Marriage

Father George F. O'Neill likes to give the bride and groom a box of crayons, accompanied by the following words:

"First I give you the brown crayon. Brown is the color of the earth, from which God created you and to which one day you will return. Today God calls you to build a home on this earth. Be sure it is on rock and not sand.

"I give you this green crayon because green is the color of hope. I encourage you to take every dream you have for your marriage and go for it.

"Now here is a blue crayon for those days when you need to say, "I'm sorry. I love you today more than ever before." Be quick to forgive. Be even faster to accept forgiveness. Nothing kills love more than holding grudges and bad feelings.

"Next I have a yellow crayon for you just to remind you of this wonderful day God gives you for your marriage. Think of this day when you need to put a smile back on your face and cheer in your heart.

"I give you this orange crayon that catches the mellow rays of the sunset. Don't grow too old too fast. Never let your love become stale with the passing years. Stay young in love. Dance together. Play together. Sing together. Stay close to the dream that made you fall in love in the first place.

"Here's a purple crayon, a royal color to remind you that soon you will not be just another man and woman. God calls you to be husband and wife, the world's most honored union. It is the highest dignity he can bestow on a man and woman. With it comes the wonderful responsibility to care for each other. Handle each other's hearts carefully. A heart is easily broken.

"Finally, a red crayon. It is the color of the Holy Spirit. The Spirit brought you together and to this altar. Make yours a holy marriage with prayer, worship, fidelity, and growth in virtues with the Spirit's graces.

"These crayons are no good if kept in a box. Love is useless if it is locked in your heart. Take out the love and give it to each other. Do it every hour of every day until God calls you home."

What Is the Purpose of Marriage?

Some say... The purpose of Marriage is the love and fulfillment of the spouses. A man and a woman who enter a romantic relationship may reach the point where they determine they are meant for each other and want to conserve what has begun. All cultures have found that a formal Marriage is the best structure for making this possible. Customs, laws, and community support converge to help them preserve the love they have found in one another.

This arrangement may or may not include the decision to have children. The begetting and nurturing of children is an option. Some like having children because they are temperamentally suited to this or because they need children for some other personal reason.

Science has made it possible to prevent conception and so relieve the anxieties of those who may not wish children or who wish to limit the number of those they may want to have. With amniocentesis the prospective parents can see whether the unborn child has a birth defect or not and so could plan whether or not to have the baby.

The point here is that children are not a purpose for getting married. The love and careers of the spouses are the primary intentions of the institution of Marriage. Older cultures needed many children for the economic well being of the family. The state preferred large birth rates. In our modern world with large populations, there is not the same urgency about replenishment of a nation's population.

Emotional and financial pressures have changed couples' views about children but have not obscured the age-old goal of a flourishing love between man and woman. Today society provides the financial means and social approval for a husband and wife to seek careers and obtain the security they need to be there for one another. Social and political support is needed for this. A happy nation is one that has happy and fulfilled spouses. Adding children to this bond may be desirable but not necessary.

The evolution of Marriage styles contributes to this state of affairs. Liberalizing divorce and remarriage laws has provided couples with the ability to correct mistakes made in marital choices and allows them to get a fresh start with a new spouse. The goal of being happy spouses determined to grow ever more deeply in love with each other is both worthwhile and commendable. It may take several marriages to fine the right partner, but the goal is the same: a joy-filled and maturing love life between the spouses.

The Catechism *teaches* ...

God is the author of Marriage. In God's plan Marriage has two goals: (1) Unitive Love, in which the spouses pledge everlasting love and fidelity to one another; (2) Procreative Love, in which the spouses are open to the possibility of children whom they will beget, nurture, and raise.

The Bible's teaching about Marriage begins with the Lord's creation of man and woman who become two in one flesh and ends with a vision of the Marriage feast of the Lamb. Scripture constantly speaks of Marriage, its "mystery," its history, its problems, and its renewal in the covenant Jesus made with the Church.

God created Marriage. It is not a purely human institution, despite the changes it has experienced in different cultures and social situations. We should be more aware of the common and permanent features of Marriage. All cultures sense the greatness of Marriage, even if not with the same perceptiveness. Most of the world's peoples believe that a healthy Marriage is important for a wholesome society and the human and Christian good of the individual.

Marital love should be an image of the absolute and unfailing love God has for every human being. Scripture teaches that man and woman were created for one another. "It is not good that the man should be alone." (Gen 2:18) The woman is his counterpart and his equal. Jesus repeated the teaching of Genesis when he declared that Marriage ought to be an unbreakable union, for man and woman are no longer two, but one flesh. (Cf. Mt 19:6)

But all of us experience the impact of original sin. We are radically flawed — and radically redeemed. We all suffer tendencies to infidelity, disorder, jealousy, and conflicts that can cause hatred and separation. The first sin ruptured our relation with God and negatively affected the original communion of man and woman. Domination and lust can spoil and ruin a Marriage. God offers his grace to married couples to overcome these wounds of sin.

The Old Testament describes the evolution of people's consciences toward the ideal of the unity and indissolubility of Marriage under God's guidance. God's covenant with Israel taught the people about permanent commitment and love. The books of Ruth and Tobit witness the ideals of Marriage, describing the fidelity and tenderness that should exist between the spouses. The Song of Solomon pictures a human love that mirrors God's love, a love as strong as death which "many waters cannot quench." (Cf. Song 8:6-7)

Jesus brought this divine plan for Marriage to full awareness. At the beginning of his public ministry, Jesus performed his first sign-miracle at a wedding in Cana of Galilee. Jesus confirmed the goodness of Marriage and made the sacrament of Marriage an efficacious sign of his presence.

Jesus unequivocally taught the indissolubility of Marriage. (Mt 19:3-12) Many today think this is an impossible ideal. Even his first disciples thought so too. "If that is the case of a man with his wife, then it is better not to marry." (Mt. 19:10) But Jesus argued that he has come to restore the original order of creation disturbed by sin. He will offer couples the graces they need in the new world of the reign of God to stay faithful to each other until death.

In the Latin Church, the celebration of Marriage normally takes place at Mass because all sacraments have a connection to the paschal mystery of Christ. Moreover, all Christian life reflects the spousal love of Jesus for the Church. In Marriage, the couple witness this truth in the most vivid manner. St. Paul writes, "Husbands love your wives as Christ loved the Church. . . This is a great mystery, and I mean in reference to Christ and the Church." (Eph 5:25,32)

In the Latin Church the spouses, as ministers of Christ's grace, confer on each other the sacrament of Marriage by expressing their consent before the Church. In the Eastern liturgies the minister is the priest or bishop who "crowns" the bride and groom after receiving their vows.

The sacrament of Marriage bonds the man and woman to each other forever. A Church Father, Tertullian, dwelt on this joy of Marriage:
"How can I ever express the happiness of a marriage joined
by the Church, strengthened by an offering, sealed by a
blessing, announced by angels and ratified by the Father. . .
How wonderful the BOND between two believers, now one
in hope, one in desire, one in discipline, one in the same
service! They are both children of the same Father and
servants of the same Master, undivided in spirit and flesh,
truly two in one flesh. Where the flesh is one, one also
is the spirit."[1]

The Goods of Marriage. The *Catechism* teaches that Christ's graces in the sacrament of Marriage protects three blessings or goods: (1) unity and indissolubility; (2) the fidelity of conjugal love; (3) openness to fecundity and the welfare of the children.

Unity and Indissolubility. The unitive aspect of Marriage deals with all that conjugal love between the spouses implies. This involves the mutual attractiveness of the bodies of the spouses, their emotional lives, their spiritual growth, and their wills. All of these elements go into the whole gift of the persons of the spouses to one another. Love includes it all. They are to form one heart, mind, soul, and body with one another. While these elements are part of all natural conjugal love, they are elevated by the sacrament to the expression of Christian values.

Because of the sacrament, the spouses not only enter into communion with each other, but also with Jesus Christ, who deepens their common faith, and in the Eucharist, nourishes and perfects their profound love for one another. The indissolubility of their union affects their whole married life because they are forever two in one flesh.

Fidelity of Conjugal Love. The second good of Marriage, which the sacrament protects, is their marital fidelity to one another. This human covenant is raised to a divine level by the sacrament where it shares in the power of Christ's covenant. By this he enables husband and wife to participate in his powerful fidelity to the Church. Just as Jesus is the bridegroom of the Church and will never let her down, so the spouses gain entrance into a similar covenant because of Christ's graces to them. Marital love is meant to be forever, not just "until further notice."

The goods of unity and fidelity are destroyed by divorce. In obedience to the sixth and ninth commandments, and to the very nature of Marriage itself, the Church teaches that these goods require that sexuality be confined to the married state. Hence adultery and fornication and homosexual acts are forbidden. The bond between unitive-faithful love and procreative love is meant to be unbreakable.

Openness to Children and Their Welfare. "Children are the supreme gift of marriage and contribute greatly to the good of the parents themselves. . .True married love and the structure of family life that results from it, without diminishment of the other ends of marriage, are directed to disposing the spouses to cooperate valiantly with the love of the Creator and Savior, who through them will increase and enrich his family from day to day."[2]

By its nature, Marriage is directed to the procreation and education of children. Parents should oversee the moral, spiritual, and supernatural growth of their children, as well as to their physical, intellectual, and emotional development. Parents are the principal and first educators of their children.

"The home is the first school of Christian life and a school for human enrichment." In this domestic Church, the members learn love, the joy of work, perseverance, how to forgive, how to pray, and to participate actively in divine worship.

Once again, we should say that the bond between the unitive-faitfhul aspect of Marriage and the procreative one is meant to be unbreakable. At the same time, it should be noted that spouses who have not received a gift of children from God can still have a married life full of meaning in human and Christian terms.

Jesus obviously has blessed married life. He also blessed virginity. Consecrated virginity and celibacy do not devalue married life. The fidelity of married people encourages those with a celibate commitment. Conversely the faithful celibate witness enriches marital commitment.

Pastors should have a special solicitude for single people, many of whom have no opportunity to marry and some of whom have no family to whom they can turn. The Christian community should open its heart to these folks and welcome them to a circle of friendship.

1. What are the graces of the sacrament of Marriage?

"The sacrament of Matrimony signifies the union of Christ and the Church. It gives spouses the grace to love each other with the love with which Christ has loved his Church; the grace of the sacrament thus perfects the human love of the spouses, strengthens their indissoluble unity, and sanctifies them on the way to eternal life (cf. Council of Trent: DS 1799)." (CCC 1661)

2. What is the role of public consent and celebration for marriage?

"Marriage is based on the consent of the contracting parties, that is, on their will to give themselves, each to the other, mutually and definitively, in order to live a covenant of faithful and fruitful love.

"Since marriage establishes the couple in a state of public life in the Church, it is fitting that the celebration be public, in the framework of a liturgical celebration, before the priest (or a witness authorized by the Church), the witnesses, and the assembly of the faithful." (CCC 1662-1663)

3. What is the status of divorced and remarried Catholics?

"The remarriage of persons divorced from a living, lawful spouse contravenes the plan and law of God as taught by Christ. They are not separated from the Church, but they cannot receive Eucharistic communion. They will lead Christian lives especially by educating their children in the faith." (CCC 1665)

Response to objections

How one sees the purpose of Marriage depends on who one considers is the creator of Marriage. Modern society tends to think that Marriage is a purely secular institution controlled and developed by common custom, cultural preferences, and public law. The Church argues that God is the author of Marriage and God's purpose for this sacred institution should be honored.

That couples get married in order to protect, honor, and advance the love and development of the spouses is a perfectly legitimate goal. This love should be so strong that it is accompanied by a fidelity that lasts the entire life of the spouses. It should be a love that is as strong as death. The two are meant to become one flesh.

However, this is not the exclusive purpose of Marriage. It is expected that the couple be open to the possibility of children whom they will welcome, love, support, and educate. Children are meant to be the fruit of marital love and are gifts from God. Even in the case of some couples who are unable to have their own children, they could adopt some and so experience the fruitfulness of marital love in that manner.

The Church supports responsible parenthood through natural family planning. This process has proven to be a special way of bringing husband and wife closer together and integrating their sexuality with their love. Diocesan offices for family life are prepared to help local parishes and individual couples learn about natural family planning. Numerous testimonies from couples who have used it declare that the unitive purpose of Marriage – their love for each other – is increased all the more.

The Church teaches that the unitive and procreative purposes of Marriage ought to be kept together in an inseparable bond. When the bond is broken, then the dream of the full potential of Marriage is broken. The graces of the sacrament of Marriage are meant to preserve the marital bonding of the unitive and procreative purpose.

For dialog   1. What would you say are the ideals and expectations of Marriage promoted by the secular culture? What is your evaluation of the vision of Marriage as found in the media, the government, and other social forces affecting Marriage? When you look at successful Marriages what would you say are the qualities that made them work? What behaviors, attitudes, and practices contribute to the failure of Marriages?

2. Why is it important to be open to the possibility of children? What is the impact of divorce upon children? When you hear the expression, "dysfunctional families," how do you react? What are the practical ways you would use to make a Marriage work? How can we change the culture's adverse effects on Marriage?

3. What do you believe to be the best age for getting married? Why is living together before Marriage destructive to marital fidelity and success?

How do religion, faith, prayer, and Church contribute to the stability and success of Marriage?

Prayer   Jesus, Mary, and Joseph, you formed a holy family at Nazareth and gave all families the ideals of love, faith, prayer, meditation, and responsible work as models for Christian families. Surround all our families with your ideals and example and protection that they may be filled with the hope and idealism which foster family growth. Help us all to face with courage and faith the challenges that contemporary life presents to families today. Let each family be truly a domestic church, a haven in a heartless world and a light of welcome to all around us.

Glossary   **Unitive Aspect of Marriage** — God willed that husband and wife be committed permanently to one another in a communion of love. This communion of persons reflects the community of the Trinity.

Procreative Aspect of Marriage — God willed that Marriage have a parental dimension in which husband and wife procreate and educate children. The bond between the procreative and unitive aspects of Marriage may not be broken.

Goods of Marriage — The three goods or blessings of Marriage are: (1) unity and indissolubility; (2) fidelity to conjugal love; (3) openness to fecundity and the welfare of children.

Virginity and Celibacy — Consecrated virginity and celibacy, normally lived in the priesthood and religious life, is a call from God to witness the reality of the kingdom of heaven and our supernatural life and destiny.

"Don't be annoyed when your children ask you impossible questions. Be proud that they think you know the answers."

Illustrations Unlimited[3]

Endnotes

1. GS, 50,1.
2. Ibid., 48.
3. *Illustrations Unlimited*, James Hewett, Editor (Wheaton, IL: Tyndale House, 1990).

Chapter 21

MORALITY BEGINS WITH LOVE FOR JESUS

CCC 1691-2051

"When people speak ill of you, so live that nobody will believe them."

Plato

The Miracle of a Brother's Song

When Karen found out she was to have another baby, she did what she could to help her three-year-old son, Michael, prepare for a new sibling. They found out the new baby was going to be a girl. Day after day Michael sang to his sister in his mommy's tummy. He was building a bond of love with his little sister before he even met her.

The pregnancy progressed normally for Karen until complications arose during delivery. After hours of labor it was decided there should be a c-section. Michael's little sister was born. However the baby was gravely ill and had to be placed in intensive care.

The days inched by. The little girl got worse. The pediatric specialist regretfully had to tell the parents, "There is very little hope. Be prepared for the worst." Karen and her husband contacted a local cemetery about a burial plot.

Michael, however, kept begging his parents to let him see his sister. "I want to sing to her," he kept saying. Week two in intensive care looked as if a funeral would happen soon. Michael kept nagging about singing to his sister, but kids are never allowed in intensive care.

Karen made up her mind to smuggle Michael in to see his sister. She dressed in an oversized scrub suit and marched him into ICU. A nurse recognized him as a child and bellowed, "Get that kid out of here!" Karen remained firm and said, "He is not leaving until he sings to his sister."

Karen towed Michael to his sister's bedside. He gazed at her. In the pure-hearted voice of a three-year-old, Michael sang, "You are my sunshine, my only sunshine, you make me happy when skies are gray. . ." Instantly the baby girl responded. Her pulse rate calmed down and became steady.

"Keep on singing, Michael," urged Karen.

"You never know dear, how much I love you. Please don't take my sunshine away."

The baby's strained breathing became as smooth as a kitten's purr.

"The other night dear, as I lay sleeping, I dreamed I held you in my arms. . ."

His sister began to relax. A healing rest swept over her. Even the bossy head nurse began to weep. Karen glowed.

"You are my sunshine, my only sunshine. Please don't take my sunshine away."

The next day, the very next day, the little girl was well enough to go home! *Women's Day* magazine called it "The Miracle of a Brother's Song."

Karen called it a miracle of God's love!

Deep love for God, such as this, is the basis of the moral life.[1]

Are Rules the Basis of Morality?

Some say... Love is the only sure basis of the moral order. We know an act is moral if it does no harm to people. Love is all we need in order to know whether an act is good or bad. Without love there would be moral chaos. The golden rule says that we should do unto others as we would have them do unto us. What else is this but the practical application of love to every situation?

Those who would say that rules and laws are the substance of moral thinking and behavior put abstract ideas above the needs of persons. This is legalism, not love. It is a harsh view of morality and does more harm than good. It is also a simplistic way of doing ethics. Love is the more complex and difficult road to righteousness, but its results are more creative and long lasting.

People who put their ethical trust in the "Thou shalt nots" produce a restrictive moral life that tightens up the users and spreads gloom in the family and community. To substitute the warmth of love with the coldness of rules is to empty morality of all its meaning and purpose. All the great sages and philosophers of history have made love the norm for the virtuous life. St. Augustine wrote, "Love, and do what you will."

Look at all the times in the gospels where Jesus criticizes the Pharisees for their rule-centered morality. When they attacked Jesus for curing on a sabbath day, thus "breaking" the rule about sabbath work, they heard Jesus reply that the sabbath was made for man, not man for the sabbath. In other words people are more important than rules. Laws were made to serve people, not to control them.

This is but another way of saying that the love of people is the sure and effective norm for morality.

The Catechism *teaches ...* Love as a covenant with God is the basis of morality. But rules and laws are needed to understand how love should be practiced. The Ten Commandments are ways to express the love relationship established by the Sinai covenant. The total picture of morality leads to happiness.

The World Database on Happiness lists 2,475 titles — books, journal articles, dissertations, conference papers — on the topic of happiness. Among their findings, they conclude: (1) Close relationships, including a happy marriage and religion, are the most important elements in achieving happiness; (2) Physical attractiveness doesn't guarantee subjective well-being; (3) Happiness is more desired by people than are cherished social goals such as peace and equality.

Book three of the *Catechism* is about the Catholic moral life, which it calls Life in Christ. Part one lays down the foundations of the moral life. Part two deals with each of the Ten Commandments. It is clear from the text that living morally brings the much-desired human fulfillment and happiness that we all hunger for. In this chapter we explore the basics of the moral life. Subsequent chapters will deal with each of the Ten Commandments.

The *Catechism* lays out nine basic "building blocks" which form the conditions for the moral life and the happiness which results from it.

Images of God. The building blocks of morality begin with understanding ourselves as images of God. What does it mean to be an image of God?

• I have a mind that can know the truth, including the ultimate truth of God and the faith-realization that God is truth.

• I have a will that can love the good in the world and the absolute good that is God.

• I have received the gift of freedom. I am free to do what I should and not just whatever I please.

• I have been wounded by original sin. This means I have a difficult time knowing the truth and must struggle for it. I notice a conflict in my will. I often choose what I shouldn't — and fail to choose what I should. I am inclined to evil in the exercise of my freedom.

- I have new life in the Holy Spirit, due to my Baptism and my participation in the sacraments. These graces help me not just to "be" an image of God, but also to "act" as God's image and overcome the difficulties posed by original and actual sin.
- I am destined for the life of glory in heaven.

It is because I am an image of God that I even have the possibility of happiness. The capacity to know and love in a properly free manner opens me to the only permanent source of joy, an enduring relationship with God.

I am called to happiness. The second building block is found in the beatitudes. In his eight beatitudes, Jesus calls me to be happy and shows me the way to it. True happiness, following the beatitudes, is the best motivator for being moral. God has planted in me a natural desire to be happy. I should discover that God alone will satisfy me. "How is it then that I seek you, Lord? Since in seeking you, my God, I seek a happy life, let me seek you so that my soul may live, for my body draws life from my soul, and my soul draws life from you." (St. Augustine, Confessions, 10, 20)

"The Beatitudes teach us the final end to which God calls us: the Kingdom, the vision of God, participation in the divine nature, eternal life, filiation, rest in God." (CCC 1726)

God has put us in this world to know, love, and serve him and to be with him in paradise. The beatitudes help us to live this vocation. The Ten Commandments, the Sermon on the Mount, and the Church's teaching office (the Magisterium) show us how to live the life of the beatitudes. Because of our sinful inclinations, we cannot be completely happy on earth. But in heaven we will have perfect joy.

Responsible use of freedom. The third building block of Christian morality is the responsible use of our freedom. God made us rational beings. Our human dignity as persons means we can initiate and control our own acts. We are not robots, determined by some outside force or inner compulsion. It is true there are outer social pressures and, in some cases, inner psychological drives that sometimes overwhelm us. Normally, we are basically free to act. Our freedom is rooted in our intelligence and will.

"The imputability or responsibility for an action can be diminished or nullified by ignorance, duress, fear, and other psychological or social factors." (CCC 1746)

The more we do the good, the more free we become. The more we do evil, we become slaves of sin, and lose our freedom. Freedom makes us responsible for our behavior. The right exercise of our freedom, especially in moral and religious matters, is an inalienable part of our dignity as a human person. Freedom does not mean the right to say or do anything we please — only what we should, according to God's will.

People, who are truly free, in the sense meant here, have the best chance for happiness.

The morality of human acts. How can we tell what goes into a truly moral act? Our fourth building block addresses this question. There are three parts to the moral act: (1) The act itself, (2) The subjective motive, (3) The situation or circumstances. All three parts must be good for the act to be good. Moral laws can help us tell whether the act is good or bad. Rape is wrong. So is abortion. Some acts are clearly always wrong — intrinsically evil. This is the objective part of a moral act.

The second part of the moral act is the intention. What are some morally wrong intentions? Hate, greed, lust, envy, sloth, malice, despair. This is the subjective side of a moral act.

The third part of a moral act is the situation or the circumstance surrounding the act. Circumstances contribute to increasing or diminishing the moral goodness or badness of the act (such as the amount of a theft). The circumstances diminish or increase the moral responsibility of the agent (such as acting out of a fear of death).

To have a morally good act, all the parts must be good: the act itself, the intention of the doer, and the circumstances.

Lastly, the end does not justify the means. We may not do evil so that good may come of it.

A proper moral conscience. The fifth building block of Christian moral teaching is the development of a proper moral conscience. What is conscience?

• Conscience is judgment of reason by which the human person recognizes the moral quality of a concrete act." (CCC 1796)

A good conscience requires lifelong training and formation. The Word of God is a major light for informing our consciences. We must assimilate it in faith and prayer and put it into practice. Our consciences are also enlightened by the prudent advice of others, their good behavior, and the authoritative teaching of the Church. Regular examination of conscience, aided by the gifts of the Spirit, will help us develop a morally sensitive conscience.

A well-formed conscience makes judgments that conform to reason and the real good willed by the wisdom of God. Any time we face a moral choice, our consciences can make a correct judgment according to reason and God's law, or, on the contrary, make an erroneous judgment that contradicts reason and divine law.

• A human being must always obey the certain judgment of his conscience.

"Conscience can remain in ignorance or make erroneous judgments. Such ignorance and errors are not always free of guilt." (CCC 1800-1801)

Read the *Catechism*, 1790-1794.

Practice virtues. If we want to be happy, we must be moral. If we want to be moral, we must practice the human and theological virtues. This is our sixth building block. Human virtues are habits of mind and will that govern our behavior and control our passions. These virtues guide our conduct according to faith and reason. What are some of these virtues? They include self-discipline, compassion, responsibility, friendship, work, courage, perseverance, honesty, and loyalty. Traditionally we group them around the "cardinal" virtues of prudence, justice, temperance, and fortitude.

How do we acquire these virtues? First, by hearing stories of virtuous people that inspire us to practice them. Second, by the good example of others who motivate us to imitate them. Third, by education in the value of virtues and ways to acquire them. Fourth, by formal, repetitive acts, doing them over and over until they are grooved into our character and behavior. Fifth, by determination to have them and perseverance in their quest. Sixth by prayer, especially to the Holy Spirit for the seven gifts to help us: wisdom, knowledge, understanding, courage, counsel, piety, and fear of the Lord.

We also should practice the theological virtues of faith, hope, and charity. They are direct gifts from God and dispose us to have a vital relationship with the persons of the Trinity. They are called theological because they explicitly direct us to faith and hope in God and a loving surrender to his divine plan for us. Theological virtues affect all the moral virtues, elevating them to the divine level and increasing their stability and effectiveness in our lives.

Understanding sin. To talk about morality and avoid a discussion of sin would be absurd. An understanding of sin is the seventh building block of the *Catechism's* teaching about morality. For a long time there was a denial of sin in our culture. This led psychiatrist Karl Menninger to write a book, *Whatever Became of Sin?* He wrote that there was a time when people admitted their sins, went to a priest, and obtained absolution. Then sin became a crime, which was presented to the judge and punished by imprisonment or execution. Finally, sin became a neurosis or psychosis, which we "confessed" to a psychologist and received therapy.

He exploded this myth and argued that this confusion should be clarified. Yes, mentally ill people should see a therapist and criminals should go to a courtroom. But sinners should admit their spiritual guilt to a proper authority and receive absolution and forgiveness.

The *Catechism* couldn't agree more. The recovery of a sense of sin is an act of moral realism that both gives us an honest assessment of self, as well as the opportunity for redemption. If there is no sin, then why would Jesus be called a Savior and why did he suffer so much for us on the Cross? Why did he rise from the dead to give us new life and the graces that would help us avoid sin?

What is sin? It is any word, thought, deed, or desire that is against God's law and breaks our relationship with him as well as other people. It is an act of disobedience to God. Sin is an act that is opposed to reason. Sin corrupts our nature and harms our communion with people.

When we commit a mortal sin, we knowingly and willingly do something that is gravely contrary to the divine law and opposed to our ultimate destiny. Mortal sin destroys the love that we need for eternal happiness. If we do not repent of a mortal sin, we will suffer eternal death.

A venial sin is a moral disorder that can be overcome by the charity that it allows to remain in us. Repeated sins, even venial ones, open us to vices, especially the capital ones: pride, envy, lust, anger, sloth, gluttony, and greed. (Read again our chapter on the Sacrament of Reconciliation as well as the material on original sin to supplement what is said here. Read also the *Catechism* itself, 1846-1876.)

A sense of community and social justice. The eighth building block for a Christian moral life is an appreciation of our human community with all peoples and our call to work for Christ's kingdom of love, justice, and mercy. The Holy Trinity is a communion of persons, bound by absolute love. On earth we are called to form a community among all human beings, a communion of love that, in a certain manner, reflects the inner life of God.

Connected to this should be a profound respect for the dignity of each human person. All governments and other social institutions should serve and enhance the integrity and dignity of persons. It is the responsibility of society to create a situation that favors the growth of virtue and a hierarchy of values that give the primacy of spiritual values over physical and instinctual ones.

The state and its authority is based on human nature and so belongs to an order established by God. Political authority must be used for the common good of society. To reach such a goal this authority should use morally acceptable means. This will involve establishing the social conditions that allow the citizens the proper exercise of their freedom. All of this is meant to promote the common good.

"The common good comprises 'the sum total of social conditions which allow people, either as groups or as individuals, to reach their fulfillment more fully and more easily' (GS 26,1)." (CCC 1924)

Social justice demands that people be allowed to form associations to achieve their goals. This will include genuine human rights and human equality that flow from an understanding of the dignity of the human person. Each of us should consider the other as "another self." The quest for social justice will seek to reduce excessive social and economic inequalities. Solidarity with all people is a form of communion of persons and is a Christian virtue. God calls us to share both spiritual and materials goods with one another.

Law and grace. God's plan of salvation through law and grace constitutes the ninth building block of the Christian moral life. In the divine law, God teaches us the way to heavenly happiness and the ways of evil that must be avoided. The natural law is our way of participating in God's goodness and wisdom. It expresses our human dignity and forms the basis for rights and duties. Because it is a participation in divine law, the natural law is a changeless presence in history. It continues to serve as the bedrock of moral and civil law.

The Old Testament contains the first stage of revealed law, and this is summarized in the Ten Commandments. This law prepared the world for the gospel. We call the new law the grace of the Holy Spirit, which is received by us through faith in Jesus Christ. Its major expression is found in Christ's Sermon on the Mount. We receive these graces by active participation in the sacraments.

Because of the salvation won for us by Jesus Christ in his death and resurrection, the Holy Spirit makes us sharers in the life of God. In the application of Christ's saving work, the Spirit can move us away from sin and toward God. This salvation is also called justification, which includes the forgiveness of sins and the sanctification of our inner lives.

We cannot stress enough that our salvation and justification has been won for us by the paschal mystery, the death and resurrection of Jesus Christ. Our Christian moral lives are made possible by this supreme act of love and mercy, willed by the Father, accomplished in Christ and made available to us by the activity of the Spirit in the Church and sacraments.

The popular hymn "Amazing Grace" touchingly reminds us that sin is not the primary focus of the moral life despite its powerful and unfortunate presence and influence in the world. The *Catechism* correctly raises our eyes to the throne of divine mercy from which flows sanctifying grace. This grace enfolds us, precedes, prepares, and elicits our free response to God's love. God gives us this grace in total freedom because he loves us.

Hence, we merit salvation only because God decided to involve us in this work of grace. Merit belongs in the first place to the grace of God and secondly to our collaboration with it. At the same time it must be said that we do not merit the initial grace of conversion. This is a gracious and free act of the Holy Spirit.

1. How does the Church give us assured moral guidance?

"The Roman Pontiff and the bishops, as authentic teachers, preach to the People of God the faith which is to be believed and applied in moral life. It is also incumbent on them to pronounce on moral questions that fall within the natural law and reason.

"The infallibility of the Magisterium of the Pastors extends to all the elements of doctrine, including moral doctrine, without which the saving truths of faith cannot be preserved, expounded, or observed." (CCC 2050-2051)

2. Why are correct moral decisions necessary for salvation?

"The way of Christ 'leads to life'; a contrary way 'leads to destruction' [Mt 7:13; cf. Deut 30:15-20]. The Gospel parable of the *two ways* remains ever present in the catechesis of the Church; it shows the importance of moral decisions for our salvation: 'There are two ways, the one of life, the other of death; but between the two, there is a great difference [Didache 1,1: SCh 248, 140].'" (CCC 1696)

3. What are major elements that help us form our consciences?

"The conscience of each person should avoid confining itself to individualistic considerations in its moral judgments of the person's own acts. As far as possible the conscience should take account of the good of all, as expressed in the moral law, natural and revealed, and consequently in the law of the Church and in the authoritative teaching of the Magisterium on moral questions. Personal conscience and reason should not be set in opposition to the moral law or the Magisterium of the Church." (CCC 2039)

Response to objections

Here on earth love is one of the two essential components of morality. The other is rules and laws that spell out the practical application of love in a given situation. In heaven we will only need love, but here we must have moral guidance to see how love works. Love alone, absent moral guidance, can be vague, sentimental, and at the mercy of feelings. Popular songs and films romanticize morality and often mislead people, with lines like these: "Love means never having to say you're sorry;" and "It can't be bad if it feels so good."

The problem with making love alone the criterion of morality is that the term love has many meanings. Most often love is equated with feelings and emotions, an unsound basis for morality, since they come and go and are an uncertain foundation for action. If I only want to do the right thing when I feel like it, then my moral life will be abrupt, unpredictable, and based on the equivalent of sand. The pervasive impact of the media has promoted the romantic idea of love that is mostly emotional and often tied to giving into sexual feelings regardless of the divine law that sex should only occur within marriage.

The correct vision of morality is like a mosaic in which love and law are supported by principles, norms, rules, the practice of virtue, the quest for ideals like the beatitudes, the inner help of the graces of the Holy Spirit, the power that comes from prayer, worship, the good example of others, and the general support of an ecclesial community.

The love that should govern Christian morality is *agape*, a self-giving, sacrificial love that is a gift from God. This is the love that comes to us with the gift of the Holy Spirit: God as pure, always giving love. In an ideal world this would be all we would need. But we live with the energies left over from the effects of original sin as well as the impact of our own personal sins. Hence our mind is darkened and our will is weak and our passions want to dominate us.

So, we need graces to help us be moral, and we need light from rules and laws. We need inspiration and encouragement from the ecclesial community, and strength from the acquisition of virtues. This is the total package that forms the vision of the Christian moral life.

For dialog 1. Some people say they want to be moral but they are weak and can't help themselves. How would you counsel them? How does family life and training affect people's ability to be moral? If you heard someone say that love is all you need to be moral, what would your response be? On the other hand, if someone told you that keeping the rules is the secret of being moral, what would be your reaction?

2. Name three people whom you consider to be outstanding examples of living Christian morality. Why have you chosen them?

3. Since virtues are needed to stay moral, what would you do to acquire such virtues? How do you see the role of prayer and the help of the Holy Spirit in seeking the moral life? Why do we tend to admire people whom we perceive to be persons of moral principles?

Prayer Lord Jesus, you were a great moral teacher, but you were also the perfect witness to how to live the moral life. Help us to understand your teachings and follow your example. Beyond this, we believe that your sacrificial love manifested in your death and resurrection provided us with the salvation we need that makes possible our moral life. Open our hearts to receive your saving powers so that we may become authentic moral persons.

Glossary

Human Virtues — Human virtues are habits of mind and will that govern our behavior and control our passions.

Cardinal Virtues — These are prudence, justice, temperance, and fortitude. These human virtues guide our conduct according to faith and reason.

Theological Virtues — The theological virtues are faith, hope, and charity. They are gifts of the Holy Spirit. They are directed to believing and hoping in God and our loving surrender to him. They elevate and perfect the cardinal virtues.

"The trouble with most of us is that we would rather be ruined by praise than be saved by criticism."

Norman Vincent Peale

Endnote

1. Story from a Web site: http://www.cybermom.com.

Chapter 22

MY SOUL THIRSTS
FOR THE LIVING GOD

CCC 2052-2141

"There never was found in any age of the world, either philosopher or sect, or law or discipline, which did so highly exalt the public good as the Christian faith."

Francis Bacon

Patrick Maguire Meets Cardinal Hume

My family and myself were all arrested in 1974. I was thirteen years old at the time. After a trial at the Old Bailey, which lasted for more than seven weeks, we were all sent to prison for many years.

As a boy I had always gone to church, and I did so even when I was in prison. I would always ask God why he had let this happen to us. I felt let down by my faith. So I gave up.

Some years after I was released from jail, I received a phone call from Cardinal Basil Hume, Archbishop of Westminster. He wanted to see me. I knew he had played a big part in helping us to prove our innocence. He had put his name at the top of our fight for justice. What a man to have at our side! But my faith had gone.

When I entered his room and saw him stand up to greet me, the room lit up as though a thousand lights had been turned on. With open arms he welcomed me. We had some tea and talked — well, I did the talking while he listened. He winced as I relived my story, sharing the pain with me.

He asked me if I would like to go to Lourdes with him. I said yes. With him and 300 others, we traveled to Mary's shrine. It was there for the first time in years I felt at peace with myself and with all that had happened to me.

Toward the end of our week at Lourdes, just after dinner, the Cardinal drew me aside and asked me how things were going. I told him how happy I was, and now I knew that God had not let me down. A great big smile appeared on his face. He was happy.

I also told him I was afraid that when I returned home I would lose all that I had found. He told me that my peace would never leave me. "Hold onto the peace you have found with one hand, and with the other go through life as best you can."

To this day, over ten years later, I have never forgotten the week in Lourdes or the man who took me there. I saw him many times in those years and we would have a laugh and a joke. He was my friend. Though he has died and gone to God, I shall never forget him. If wealth were judged by the friends we have made, then I am the richest of men.[1]

How Helpful Are the Ten Commandments?

Some say... It is about time that Christianity leave aside the Ten Commandments as a major component in moral teaching. They had their place in the evolution of moral development, serving as a discipline for people of faith in the early stages of spiritual growth. The commandments were needed when people were more rough-hewn and required stern black and white rules to stay on the straight and narrow path. They worked best in the "childhood" of our race.

It was fitting that they were delivered in Old Testament times when God was experienced as a God of justice. People were thus saved by laws delivered in awesome and scary circumstances at Sinai. Moreover, these laws were not just for the Hebrew peoples. Similar lists of commandments have been found in other cultures of those ancient times – such as in the Code of Hammurabi. This suggests that they were largely meant for primitive mentalities, well-suited then, but hardly applicable for today's more advanced cultures.

One of the principal problems of the commandments is their negative, "Thou shalt not," tone. Negative rules that forbid certain acts tend to make the person fearful and legalistic. They restrict the range of moral behavior and seem to rob the soul of its inherent desire for expansiveness. The God of justice, appearing so threatening, does not seem very appealing.

Far better is the New Testament approach where God is presented as Love personified, where the pursuit of virtue is preferred to the narrow vision of keeping commandments. No wonder St. Paul became so appealing in his letter to the Romans where he extolled the Spirit over the law. He says quite clearly we are not saved by keeping the law, but by a gracious act of love and the gift of the Spirit.

It is, therefore, difficult to agree with some people today who hearken back nostalgically to the days when children were drilled in the commandments. Such moralists imagine that this will save today's youth from the values crisis in modern society. This is not likely to help anyone, since rote memory of rules and unthinking keeping of them will scarcely prepare the young for the numbing complexity of contemporary life, let alone solve the intractable moral dilemmas that face modern people.

Love, combined with a positive approach to morality, along with trust in rational processes, is the best way to deal with moral issues today.

The Catechism *teaches* ...

Jesus himself taught the Ten Commandments in his Sermon on the Mount. When asked by the rich young man what was needed to gain eternal life, Jesus immediately said, "Keep the commandments."

Any discussion of the commandments should begin with the scene at Sinai where God gave them to us. (Read Exodus 19:16-25; 20:1-17) The scene begins with a covenant experience. God tells Moses how much he has loved the Israelites, delivering them from slavery and "raising them up on eagles' wings," bringing them to freedom. God then offers them a binding covenant of love. He will be their only God and they will be his chosen people. It's like a marriage experience, an exchange of vows between God and Israel.

The next section shows God telling them how to live out the love they have pledged. He gives them the Ten Commandments as a means to live the covenant, to express the love they have promised. The *Catechism* points out that the Ten Commandments are privileged expressions of the natural law, made known to us by reason as well as divine revelation. We are obliged in obedience to observe these laws of love, both in serious and light matters. Love is in the details as well as the large matters. We must remember that what God has commanded, he makes possible by his grace.

Jesus set the tone for understanding the importance of the commandments. When a rich young man came to him and asked him what he should do to enter eternal life, Jesus replied, "If you would enter eternal life, keep the commandments." (Cf. Mt 19:16-19) In another case, someone asked him which were the greatest commandments, Jesus replied, "You shall love the Lord, your God with all your heart, with all your soul and with all your mind. This is the greatest and first commandment, and the second is like it: you shall love your neighbor as yourself." (Mt 22:37-40)

The first three commandments deal with Christ's call to love God with all our being. The last seven commandments show us how to love our neighbor as we love ourselves.

First Commandment. The first commandment summons us to have faith in the true God, to hope in him and love him enthusiastically with mind, heart, soul, and will. This is our response to the God who has revealed himself to us, created and redeemed us, and looks after us caringly in his providence.

Every commandment calls us to a virtue and forbids certain kinds of behavior. The commandments are not uniformly negative, even the ones that begin with a "Thou shalt not." There is always a twofold aspect to them, the positive value and the negative injunction. The positive invitation of the first commandment deals with faith, hope, love, and the virtue of religion. In the virtue of religion we respond to God's generosity with acts of adoration, prayer, and fidelity in keeping our promises to God.

The negative injunction of the first commandment forbids superstition, idolatry, magic (not the entertainment kind), sacrilege, simony (sale of church position), and atheism.

Faith. Social observers such as George Gallup, Jr., report that most Americans believe in God. The majority believe they will face God on judgment day and confess that they sometimes feel very aware of God's presence. Generally, Americans have a religious worldview.

But there are many who do not believe in God, or seriously doubt his existence. Some hesitate to believe because they cannot overcome objections to faith, or do not know how to handle the mystery. Some baptized Catholics lapse into heresy when they formally and consciously deny a truth that is held as a matter of faith by the Church. We use the term "apostasy" to describe those baptized who repudiate the faith. "Schismatics" are those Christians who refuse to acknowledge the authority of the pope.

Hope. When God revealed his plan to save us, he offered us the gift of hope, which gives us confidence that God will bless us here and give us heaven hereafter. When we refuse this gift, we lapse into either the sin of presumption or the sin of despair. Those who practice the sin of presumption think they can be saved by their own efforts without grace, or they simply expect God's grace without their taking the trouble to live a moral life. Those who presume do not need to hope, or so they think. Those who fall into the sin of despair think they are so evil that God cannot forgive them. They have lost hope in God's mercy. Those who despair do not think they have any reason to hope.

Love. God loves us with an everlasting love. He invites us to respond with love in return. The *Catechism* teaches that we sin against this call to love by: indifference, ingratitude, lukewarmness, sloth, or outright hatred. Read CCC, 2093-2094.

What Is Rejected by the First Commandment?

Idolatry. Scripture teaches that idolatry is the worship of false gods, who have eyes that do not see, ears that do not hear and feet that do not walk. Today idolatry takes new forms. We have discovered fresh ways to adore creatures instead of God. Many today are willing to worship Satan — i.e. in satanic cults, money, power, pleasure, race, even the state. Many martyrs died rather than worship the "beast." (Cf. Rev 13-14)

Belief in God is weakened by taking seriously the promises of those involved in astrology, palm reading, interpretation of omens, clairvoyants, mediums, and others who claim to know the future and to have control over time and history.

Atheism. Atheists deny the existence of God. Atheism comes in different forms. Some atheists put all their hope in materialism. Some are called atheistic humanists because they place man in absolute control of himself, his history, and the world. Others look for human liberation through radical economic and social reform. They reject religion because they argue it gets in the way of such improvement of the social and economic order.

The guilt of these atheists may be significantly diminished by their intentions and the circumstances. "Believers can have more than a little to do with the rise of atheism. To the extent that they are careless about their instruction in the faith, or present its teaching falsely, or even fail in their religious, moral, or social life, they must be said to conceal rather than reveal the true nature of God and religion."[2]

Another form of evading the call of the first commandment is agnosticism, a word that means, "I don't know." Some admit there is a God, but we cannot know anything about him. Others say it is impossible to know whether there is a God. Some honest agnostics are looking for God. Others are merely too lazy to try developing a moral conscience, or they are indifferent to ultimate questions. Many are practical atheists.

Is Religious Art Permissible? When God gave the first commandment, he included the injunction not to make "graven images." The point was that God is greater and more mysterious than any artistic representation of him. The rule also was meant to keep the Israelites from carving idols like the pagans. Nonetheless, God did permit Israel to make images that symbolically pointed to the coming Incarnate Word. Hence they did have the bronze serpent, the ark of the covenant, and the golden cherubim.

In early Church history some of the Christians of the East decided that religious icons were against God's law. They proceeded to smash them and eliminate them from their churches. They were called iconoclasts. To correct them, the seventh Council of Nicaea (787) justified the veneration of icons using the doctrine of the Incarnate Word. The Fathers judged we could venerate images of Jesus, the Mother of God, angels, and saints.

When the Son of God became a visible human being, he introduced the basis for making such images for fostering faith. Whoever venerates a holy image, honors the person portrayed. This honor is a respectful veneration, not the adoration due to God alone. We do not venerate the things (statues, paintings, stained glass windows), but the holy persons portrayed by these images.

1. What are the acts of the virtue of religion?

"Adoring God, praying to him, offering him the worship that belongs to him, fulfilling the promises and vows made to him are acts of the virtue of religion which fall under obedience to the first commandment." (CCC 2135)

2. How are covenant and commandments related?

"The Commandments take on their full meaning within the covenant. According to Scripture, man's moral life has all its meaning in and through the covenant. The first of the 'ten words' recalls that God loved his people first...

"The Commandments properly so-called come in the second place: they express the implications of belonging to God through the establishment of the covenant. Moral existence is a *response* to the Lord's loving initiative." (CCC 2061-2062)

3. What is the call of the first commandment?

"The first commandment summons man to believe in God, to hope in him, and to love him above all else." (CCC 2134)

Response to objections

God's commandments should be understood in connection with God's creation of human nature. God created us out of love. God redeemed us because he loved us and wanted us to join the communion of the Trinity both here and hereafer. The author of human nature knows us better than we know ourselves.

The creator of our souls and bodies – our personhood – wants this creation to flower according to the inner dynamic and potential of human nature. No one wants our human perfection more ardently that the God who made us for union with him in absolute love.

If we are aware that we want to be humanly fulfilled, we can be sure the one who made us put that desire within us and provides the tools to make that possible. One of the main reasons that the Son of God became man was to show us how greatly he regarded humanity – his greatest masterpiece. The incarnate Christ shows us how much he has honored the human and, even more, shows us what it ultimately means to be human.

Therefore, the commandments given us by God are designed to work with — not against — human nature. They are more than external guidelines, they are conformed to the interior structure of human nature itself. That is why all the commandments contain a positive, soul expanding, self transcending aspect — virtues that cause us to grow spiritually. This true of the, "Thou shalt nots," as well as the, "Thou shalls."

No one wants us to be more perfectly human than the God who made us this way, the God who himself assumed humanity. Jesus both obeyed and taught the commandments and witnessed their marvelous value for ennobling what is human about us.

There is nothing primitive about the commandments. They are as relevant today as they were at Sinai. Human nature was whole and entire then; it remains so today. When St. Paul contrasted Law and Spirit, he was not denying the value of the Law, but putting it into the proper context. He was arguing that a saving covenant comes first, a salvation truly achieved in Jesus Christ. The keeping of the Law is our loving expression of what it means to be saved.

For dialog   1. The positive thrust of the first commandment is faith in a real God, not a false one. What do you think is needed to help people appreciate this primary meaning of the first commandment? How would you help someone who was experiencing a crisis of faith? Why do some people lose their faith? When you see deep faith in a person, how do you recognize it?

2. The first commandment is against idolatry, giving honor to someone or something that belongs to God alone. What are examples of this from your own experience? Why do you think there has always been idolatry from early biblical times to the present day? What motivates people to adore a created being instead of the Creator?

3. Why do some people become atheists or agnostics? Have you met any? What are they like? Do you think you could persuade them to come to faith in a real God? How would you do it? If you become argumentative with an unbeliever what is likely to happen? What is the better approach to the unbeliever?

Prayer   Loving Father, you revealed yourself to us for the purpose of helping us believe in a real God who loves us and wants us to have communion with him. You have planted this faith and desire in us. We pray that we shall receive these gifts with gratitude and the will to live by them all our days. Enable us to be loving witnesses of your presence and existence in our lives and in all creation. By this may we be able, with your grace, to bring many others to such joy and peace.

Glossary

Sacrilege — Disrespect in word and act toward the sacraments and liturgical actions as well as to persons, things, or places consecrated to God.

Simony — The buying or selling of spiritual things. Cf. Acts 8: 9-24.

Agnostic — The agnostic says one cannot know whether God exists.

Atheist — The atheist denies God's existence.

Secularist — The secularist appears not to care whether God exists.

"God gently leads his children along. Me? He yanks!"

Bob Pierce[3]

Endnotes

1. This story is adapted from a series of memories published on the occasion of Cardinal Hume's death in *The Tablet*, June 26, 1999. Patrick Maguire II was one of the "Maguire Seven" who were cleared of supplying explosives for the Guilford pub bombings in 1974.
2. GS 19,3. Flannery, O.P., General Editor. *Vatican II* (Northport, NY: Costello, 1975).
3. *Illustrations Unlimited*, James Hewett, Editor. (Wheaton, IL: Tyndale House, 1990), p. 205.

SING A NEW SONG TO THE LORD

Chapter 23

RESTORE THE SACRED TO A SECULAR CULTURE

CCC 2142-2167

"Whoever wrestles with God in prayer puts his whole life at stake."
Jacques Ellul[1]

The Culture of Disbelief

For a long time various movements in American society have contributed to what has come to be known as secular culture. It is a vision of life that excludes the influence of faith and religion in public life. Secular thought argues that religion is a purely private matter and should not intrude on the public square. The secular is public and the sacred should be personal and private.

In his book, *The Culture of Disbelief: How American Law and Politics Trivialize Religious Devotion*, Stephen Carter[2] has written a provocative summons to rethink the role of religion in American law, politics, and culture.

America, it is often noted, is the most religious nation in the Western world. At the same time, many political leaders and opinion makers have come to suspect any religious element in public discourse that tries to reshape American society.

In our zeal to keep religion from dominating our politics, Stephen L. Carter argues, we have constructed political and legal cultures that force the religiously devout to act as if their faith doesn't really matter.

His book explains how we can preserve the vital separation of church and state while embracing rather than trivializing the faith of millions of citizens or treating religious believers with disdain. What makes Carter's work so intriguing is that he uses the ideals of democracy to arrive at fairness for the role of religion in American society.

Carter explains how preserving a special role for religious communities can strengthen our democracy. The book recovers the long tradition of religious witness in public life (for example, the antislavery and the civil rights movements).

Carter's voice is a refreshing return to fairness and balance in treating the relationship of religion and society. The second commandment, which we address here, calls for a personal and social morality that is based on reverence for the sacred, the holy, and the spiritual dimension of all life. If we authentically reverence God's name, we shall extend that reverence for all persons and their dignity.

Is Nothing Sacred?

Some say... Nothing should be so sacred that it is beyond criticism. The history of religion is full of events where the sacred was used to cover up scandalous behavior. The Crusades of the Middle Ages were cloaked in language about the desirability of liberating the Holy Land from infidels. It was "God's will." But was it God's will that Jews were massacred or that the Great Church of Hagia Sophia in Constantinople was desecrated and plundered by the Christian crusaders?

Or take the case of Galileo. There was a great scientist defending scientific truth about the real relationship of the earth to the sun, but forced to back down for religious reasons. Who would say that the world of the sacred was justified in doing this?

Other similar examples could be cited. But there is another aspect that should be noted. People in our modern society have reached their level of prosperity and personal fulfillment in an atmosphere of academic, political, and economic freedom. The marketplace of ideas and money has proven to be beneficial for human development. Secularity has proven to be a wonderful stimulus for human growth, comfort, and stability.

The intrusion of the sacred into this process, a religious worldview that is filled with absolutes, intolerance, and a closed system of thought, would be a disaster. While secular freedoms must allow the sacred a certain voice, there should be a strict and watchful eye kept upon it and there should be no deference paid to it on grounds of some special dignity it presumably deserves.

In this sense there is "nothing sacred" in a secular culture. Religion should know its place, be simply one of many competing voices, and not be allowed special privileges because of some imagined mysteries to which it could appeal. Scientific reason and logic ought to prevail over faith.

The sacred is bound to be at odds with the secular. Given the opportunity, the believers in the sacred would seek control over education, television, films, popular music, and even contemporary art. The secular culture must remain vigilant and do all it can to maintain its ascendancy.

The Catechism *teaches* ... There is a distinction between the divine and the human, the creator and the creature. Though God and man and woman are distinct from one another, they are also intimately related. Today many speak of the distinction between the sacred and the secular in such a way that an intimate relationship is denied.

But throughout most of history the sacred and the secular, though distinct, worked together in harmony for the good of people. This is not to deny that sins and mistakes have been made by representatives of both the secular and the sacred, but in the long view a working relationship was the most beneficial for the destiny of the human soul. The second commandment specifically addresses this tension between the sacred and the secular.

The positive value upheld by the second commandment is the virtue of reverence for the holiness of God and the God-given sacredness of people, places, and things. In our culture, we often hear, "Is there nothing sacred anymore?" The questions reflect an instinct people have that God has planted his holiness in the world and the human capacity to celebrate it.

The commandment says we should respect God's name. His name reveals his personhood, who he is and what he plans to do in creation. When we meet new people, we ask them their names. The name reveals the humanity of the person. We admire people who remember our names, because that is a sign they respected us enough to take the trouble to remember. As we hear someone's name, we notice distinguishing characteristics about the person: height, hair color, the look in their eyes, posture, weight, sound of the voice, quality of the handshake, clothing style and so on. The name leads us to the person.

This is just as true of God's name. We could not know God's name unless he told us. We would never know about God's thoughts, plans, and attitudes toward us if he had not revealed these secrets of his inner, mysterious life. God respected us enough to tell us his name. God expects our respect in return, both to himself and to one another, and to creation itself.

In any introduction between us there is usually a process that goes from fear to love. Meeting a new person has elements of apprehension. Will he or she like me, accept me for who I am, treat me respectfully, enjoy my presence, and be friendly to me? So the opening moments of a new relationship has elements of unease, uncertainty, yes, even fear.

If the new acquaintance is a powerful authority figure, a famous celebrity, a person of great wealth — a president, pope, actor, billionaire — then the fear of rejection or clumsy self-presentation on our part enters the picture. "Will I be loved?" That causes our initial fears. If acceptance and affection are offered, we relax and feel at home with this new person who has entered our lives.

It is the same with relating to God. The first encounter causes us fear, mixed with awe. God always puts us at ease. Think of how often God the Father in the Old Testament and Jesus in the New Testament says to frightened people, "Do not be afraid — I love you. I accept you. I respect you." When we move from fear to love of God, we spontaneously break out into words of praise and glory for God. We both kneel and bow our heads in adoration and stand, throwing up our arms and exclaiming, "Then sing my soul to my savior God — How great thou art!" Adoration of God, exultation in his presence, becomes customary for us.

The more we respect God, the more we will reverence us. The reason our culture is so coarse and tawdry is the loss of the practice of adoration and reverence for God. Once we undermine the source of the sacred, we vulgarize the rest of life. The "word pollution" in our conversations, TV and films, talk radio, and novels is an inevitable outcome of losing touch with the fountain of holiness. It used to be said, that "All that is, is holy." That dream is gone. We now say, "All that is — *should* be holy."

Sins Against the Second Commandment. The second commandment forbids the wrong use of God's name. In times past in our parishes, the Holy Name society was founded to spread reverence for God's name and to eliminate curses and blasphemies that use the names of God and Jesus Christ in a callous, scornful, and improper way.

Blasphemy is an act that speaks against God in words of hatred and defiance. It is blasphemous to use God's name to justify criminal practices, the enslavement of peoples, torture, and murder.

We are also forbidden to use God's name to witness a perjury or a false oath and thus use God to approve our lie.

Wrong use of God's name has been used to justify wars, slaughter enemies, and impose unlawful power over others. Tragically, many have used the God of love to impose hatred, the God of trust to enhance betrayal, and the God of mercy to support acts of cruelty. Critics of religion have a field day dramatizing the sins of hypocritical Christians who have made the wrong use of God's name.

At our Baptism we were initiated into the Church, "in the name of the Father and of the Son and of the Holy Spirit." God's name sanctified us and we were given a personal name, one taken from a canonized saint. The Church names us after a disciple of Christ who has led an exemplary life. This model of Christian love will also be a special saint to intercede for our needs. God calls us by name. Our name is sacred, a revelation of our personal dignity. We deserve respect and we are obliged to respect others.

1. What is the positive call of the second commandment?

"The second commandment enjoins respect for the Lord's name. The name of the Lord is holy." (CCC 2161)

"Like the first commandment, it belongs to the virtue of religion and more particularly it governs the use of speech in sacred matters." (CCC 2161, 2142)

2. What are some deeds forbidden by the second commandment?

"The second commandment forbids every improper use of God's name. Blasphemy is the use of the name of God, of Jesus Christ, of the Virgin Mary, and of the saints in an offensive way.

"False oaths call on God to be witness to a lie. Perjury is a grave offense against the Lord who is always faithful to his promises." (CCC 2162-2163)

3. What is the value of our baptismal name?

"In Baptism, the Christian receives his name in the Church. Parents, godparents, and the pastor are to see that he be given a Christian name. The patron saint provides a model of charity and the assurance of his prayer." (CCC 2165)

Response to objections

Every human being possesses a spiritual soul whose need for the sacred will always be around. The hunger for God, to which religion and faith minister, is present in all cultures all the time. Any systematic denial of this truth goes against reality and ultimately fails.

The split between the sacred and the secular may be traced to a long history of battles between religion and science, or between religion and emerging democracies, or between religion and the totalitarian states of the twentieth century. The industrial and technological revolutions also have played a role, especially when they produced widespread social dislocation. Some of the division was due to the ill-advised behavior, hypocrisy, and policies of members of the Church.

While secular progress has produced many undeniable benefits for people, it has also provided the means for human self-destructiveness on a hitherto unimaginable scale as the brutal wars of the twentieth and twenty-first centuries can testify. In their zeal to eliminate the influence of religion from society, the advocates of secularity have created schools that suffer from a values vacuum, laws which accelerate the divorce rate and weaken families and a popular culture that tolerates and even promotes a public, dehumanizing language and sexuality.

There is plenty of blame to spread around. What is needed are repentance and forgiveness. Religion and secular culture should seek a reconciliation and work together for the common good of humanity. In recognizing one another's strengths, an attitude of trust and respect ought to be restored. Religion can rightly ask that the sacred be honored and that public displays of offensive speech and behavior be curtailed. Religion and culture should be a partnership for the nourishing of the human soul. It has happened before and it can happen again.

For dialog

1. How do you perceive secular culture having an impact on your faith in the sacred? How is your spirituality helping you stay in touch with the sacred? What is your reaction to the prevalence of blasphemy and vulgar speech in today's popular culture? How might it affect your spiritual and moral life?

2. Some places today have laws and rules against "hate speech." In what way might this be a re-emergence of the spirit of the second commandment? Curbing sexual harassment includes eliminating speech that causes degrading one gender or another. Again, how could this be seen as a modern application of the second commandment?

3. Why do we connect reverence for God to reverence for persons? In seeking practical ways to preserve respect for one another, what would be the value of good manners, rules of politeness, and social customs that alleviate tensions among people? A person likes to hear the sound of one's name spoken correctly and with honor. Why is this so? Why then is this all the more true for God's name?

Prayer

God, Father, Son, and Spirit, we praise your holy name. In praying your name, we adore your mystery and majesty. In respecting you, we learn to respect one another. In glorifying your name, we acquire a sense of the sacred, which we begin to experience in the midst of this world. As we reverence you and one another here on earth, we pray for the graces needed to discover constantly your holy presence in all creation.

Glossary

Awe and Wonder — Awe and wonder are attitudes that draw us to God and cause us to reverence his holiness. This respect for God then flows into our reverence for the dignity of people and the sacredness of creation.

Blasphemy — Blasphemy is a wrong use of God's name, a disdain for

God, and a rejection of God's love for us. We make wrong use of God's name when we perjure ourselves, take a false oath, or justify cruelty, torture, enslavement, or all forms of injustice in the name of God.

"Millions long for immortality who do not know what to do with themselves on a rainy Sunday afternoon."

Susan Ertz[3]

Endnotes

1. *Illustrations Unlimited*, James Hewett, Editor. (Wheaton, IL: Tyndale House, 1990).
2. Stephen Carter, *The Culture of Disbelief: How American Law and Politics Trivialize Religious Devotion*
3. *Illustrations Unlimited*, James Hewett, Editor. (Wheaton, IL: Tyndale House, 1990).

Chapter 24

I TASTE IN YOU MY LIVING BREAD
CCC 2168-2195

"The charity of truth seeks holy leisure. The necessity of charity accepts just work."

St. Augustine

Let's Go to Mass

"An anguished cry arises from many of our students today, expressed openly and without fear right in the classroom: 'Father, I go to Mass and I don't get anything out of it. Why should I keep going?'

" 'I haven't gone in ten years. It's so boring. Since God loves me, I won't go to hell, so why bother?' 'Every time I go it's the same old thing. You can see a movie and enjoy it. But how many times can you see the same old movie? Father, tell us what you think. What do we do?' "[1]

Father Tripole is a professor of theology at St. Joseph's University in Philadelphia, Pennsylvania. He had heard the above questions often and finally felt the need to respond. He said to himself, "Please God, help me to do this," and plunged in, not knowing exactly what he was going to say. In his warm and pastoral response, he made the following points that are summarized here:

(1) Come to Mass with faith which is a form of knowledge and a lot like love. Faith is a love encounter with Jesus, an experience that occurs most profoundly at Mass.

(2) Try to understand the Mass. Appreciate what is happening. This requires study, prayer, and attentiveness. Faith should move you to understanding.

(3) Frankly admit your sinfulness. You cannot save yourselves and seem

unable even to be the kind of persons you would like to be. Become aware of the destructive power of sin that can ruin your life and impede your ability to commune with God.

(4) Joyfully realize that redemption from sin and its effects is offered to you when you experience the life, death, and resurrection of Jesus in the Mass. Value the sense of the sacred at Mass where eternity enters time and God actually touches you with saving power.

(5) Participate in the Mass as a member of the believing community. Faith is a personal act and also a communal one. It is difficult to believe all by yourself. We all need the witness and prayerful presence of other believers to remain firm in faith. The living Jesus comes to us in the living community of faith.

What this good priest shared with his college students can be a lucid guide to all of us struggling to enter into the celebration the Eucharist with greater awareness, energy, and faith.

Where Should I Worship?

Some say... In chapter fifteen we offered several reasons why church buildings are not necessary as places of worship. Here we extend that argument by noting what many people have appreciated, namely, that natural settings, created by God, are the best locales for adoration.

The ancients saw the world itself as God's Temple. The world is filled with the grandeur and presence of God. Mother nature provides settings for adoring God that are more beautiful and inspiring than any human-made building. What could surpass praising God at sunrise on a quiet beach where the beauty of God can be sensed with the emerging colors of the dawn and the restful rhythm of the waves?

What cathedral could match encountering God on a mountaintop? The valley rolls away from the lofty mountain grandeur. The birds are singing like a choir in the trees. One hears the brook and feels a gentle breeze. The solitude draws us to contemplate the clouds above and breathe in the life-giving fresh air. We are drawn to sense the mystery of God. Even Scripture places great moments of meeting God on mountains. Moses met God in a burning bush on Mount Sinai. Elijah communed with God in the silence of a gentle breeze on Mount Horeb.

Others have been able to worship God best when walking through the woods feeling the peace there that comes from the Lord. The gifts of God's creation appear on every side. Here is a natural chapel worthy of the name.

It would appear that God's creation was divinely designed to serve as a worship setting. The chapels, churches, and temples which man has built are often beautiful but not to be compared to the great worship space that God himself has given to us. We submit, then, that people would be far better advised to "go to church" in mother nature's domain.

The Catechism *teaches* ... The gospels tell us that Jesus worshiped at the Jerusalem Temple. When he cleansed the Temple of its commercial businesses, he told the people he did so because it was a holy place, a "house of prayer." The Acts of the Apostles show Peter and John going to the Temple to pray and St. Paul going to the Temple to renew a vow.

If Jesus and the apostles honored the setting of a house of God, it would seem that such a place is in accord with the will of God.

The third commandment calls us to keep holy the sabbath day. This is Sunday, the day Jesus rose from the dead. The Church asks us to keep Sunday holy by active participation in the Mass. Celebrating the Eucharist is an essential way of observing the Sunday.

At the Last Supper, Jesus instituted the Eucharistic sacrifice of his Body and Blood. By his divine power he made it possible for the sacrifice of the Cross and its saving graces to be present for us at every Mass. Not only the Cross, which saves us from our sins, but also the Resurrection which gives us divine life communicated to us in the active presence of the Holy Spirit. At the Eucharist we can experience a sacrament of perfect Love. In this paschal banquet, we consume Christ, are filled with grace, and receive a pledge of future glory.

In a magnificent passage, the Fathers of Vatican II tell us why we should celebrate Eucharist on Sunday (or its beginning on Saturday evening):

"The Church, therefore, earnestly desires that Christ's faithful, when present at this mystery of faith, should not be there as strangers or silent spectators. On the contrary, through a good understanding of the rites and prayers, they should participate knowingly, devoutly and actively. Offering the immaculate Victim, not only through the hands of the priest, but also with him, they should learn to offer themselves too. Through Christ the Mediator, they should be drawn day by day into ever closer union with God and each other, so that finally God may be all in all."[2]

Hence the Eucharist is more than a passive experience of the acts of the priest and the music of the choir. It should be an active event in which we pour out our love to God and to the members of the worshiping community. The more we concentrate on what we bring to it, the more we worship in spirit and truth and benefit from the ocean of graces that flow from the altar to our souls.

The *Catechism* begins its teaching about the third commandment with the biblical explanation of the sabbath. In Exodus 20:8-11, we read that the sabbath was the seventh day on which the Lord rested after the work of creation on the previous six days. Deuteronomy 5:12 stresses that the sabbath is a day to renew our covenant with God. In other words the sabbath is linked both to creation and covenant, two major events in the history of salvation.

The idea that God rested on the sabbath is more than a quaint picture of God being exhausted after a tough work week, just as we are after our weekday exertions. This is a faith insight. Creation is the first act of the process of salvation. Once the work of creation was over, God began his love affair with us.

If all we do is work, we shall have no time to love one another or love God. If God did nothing but work, he would (in a symbolic way of speaking) have no time to have a love relationship with us. We need a day off to nurture our love of God — and with the bonus result to renew ourselves and our love of our family and friends.

The biblical history of sabbath observance shows that it was a day of worship, joy, and relaxation with one's family. "Then [on the sabbath] you shall delight in the Lord, and I will make you ride on the heights of the earth." (Is 58:14) God intended that people enjoy their day off. They should include worship in their renewal process. God wanted some "love time" with them. At their liturgies, the people looked back on their history and family roots. They praised and thanked God for his love and renewed their covenant faith. They considered their whole day holy because it reminded them of God's gifts.

As time passed the religious leaders added numerous burdens to sabbath observance. The *Book of Jubilees* forbade the marital act, lighting a fire, or preparing food on this day. The *Mishna* listed thirty-nine kinds of forbidden activities. In Christ's time the Pharisees prohibited people to carry a bed, nurse a sick person, or pick a few ears of corn on the sabbath. Jesus rejected this legalism. He preached that care for people was more important than joyless rules. "The sabbath was made for man, not man for the sabbath." (Mk 2:27) Still, Jesus respected the holiness of the Jewish sabbath. He declared that the sabbath was a day to love and care for others. (Cf. Mk 3:4)

Sunday. Jesus rose from the dead on Sunday. That is why we make it the Christian sabbath. Because it is so special, Sunday is called the "eighth day" — a day signifying eternity. Sunday fulfills and completes the meaning of the sabbath because it signifies our eternal rest in God. The sabbath recalled the first creation. Sunday remembers the "new creation in Christ." Our Sunday celebration implements our inner moral drive to give God visible, public, and regular worship. It also carries forward the Old Testament tradition of sabbath worship. Only now we adore our Creator and Redeemer.

Sunday Eucharist is at the heart of the commemoration of the Lord's Day. The practice of the Christian assembly celebrating Sunday Eucharist dates from the beginning of the apostolic times. "We should not stay away from our assembly, as is the custom of some, but encourage one another." (Heb 10:25) The passage refers to the Sunday Eucharistic assembly.

The Catholic parish, shepherded by the priest under the authority of the diocesan bishop, is the ordinary setting for Sunday worship. Here we are initiated into the Church's liturgical life. We hear the saving teachings of Christ, offer Jesus to the Father, and take his saving Body and Blood into our bodies and souls. We are then missioned to love and serve the Lord and all peoples.

Not only is the Sunday a day to pray, it is also a day to "play." This means it should be a day that we take time to be with one another in meals, conversation, and the deepening of family life. We all need leisure, mental, and emotional refreshment. Our batteries need to be recharged. It is also a day to uplift the spirit by acts of generous service to the sick, the old, and the needy.

1. What does the Church require of us on Sunday?

" 'Sunday . . . is to be observed as the foremost holy day of obligation in the universal Church.' (CIC, can. 1246, 1) 'On Sundays and other holy days of obligation the faithful are bound to participate in the Mass.' (CIC, canon 1247)" (CCC 2192)

2. What about work on Sundays?

" 'On Sundays and other holy days of obligation the faithful are bound. to abstain from those labors and business concerns which impede the worship to be rendered to God, the joy which is proper to the Lord's Day, or the proper relaxation of mind and body.' (CIC, canon 1247)" (CCC 2193)

3. How should Sunday be a day of personal renewal?

"The institution of Sunday helps all 'to be allowed sufficient rest and leisure to cultivate their familial, cultural, social, and religious lives' (GS 67, 3).

"Every Christian should avoid making unnecessary demands on others that would hinder them from observing the Lord's Day." (CCC 2194-2195)

Response to objections

Jesus Christ left us the celebration of the Eucharist as the divinely appointed way to worship God. In the

Eucharist we received the graces of salvation that come from the making present of Christ's paschal mystery.

In the first centuries of the Church, when communities were small and the threat of persecution required that the visibility of a Church building would either be banned or be an occasion of unwanted hostility, the believers met to worship in each others' homes or in the catacombs.

After the liberation of the Church by the edict of the Roman emperor Constantine in 313 AD, the bishops were able to have public worship in church buildings. In many cases the emperor or other imperial officials provided existing basilicas – or law courts – for the worship use of the Christian community.

In time, the Christians began to construct their own chapels and churches, many of which still exist and date from the fourth and fifth centuries. There is always an ecclesial and Eucharistic aspect to the Church's life of worship. This means that Catholic worship must be both Eucharistic and enacted in the presence of the believing community with the bishop or priest celebrating the service. The first Eucharist was not a solitary act of worship. It took place with Jesus our high priest as celebrant and the apostles as the community.

The communal celebration of the Eucharist can occur in settings outside a Church building, but this is not normative. The pope has celebrated Masses in stadiums and large fields because the number of people wishing to participate far exceeds what any building can contain. In lands where the Church is persecuted, Masses are celebrated in homes or other secret places, but when liberation comes, the first thing they do is build their chapels and churches.

One can indeed worship God in a forest, a beach, or on a mountaintop. But if it is not a Eucharist **and is done all alone, it does** not represent the worship that Jesus commanded us to perform and participate in as the source of our salvation.

For dialog 1. How would you describe your usual Sunday? What is the attitude of your family and friends toward Sunday? How would you evaluate the depth of your active participation in Sunday Eucharist? How could you improve your participation in the Mass? What would you like to see improved in the Mass you attend?

2. Think back on Masses that stand out in your memory? What was different about these Masses? How would improved understanding of the Eucharist make your participation in Mass more meaningful? What is the connection between your sinfulness and the need for salvation provided by the Mass?

3. How aware are you of the presence of Jesus in the reserved Eucharist

in the tabernacle? How would prayer before the Blessed Sacrament be beneficial for your spiritual growth? When you return to your pew after receiving Communion, what is the appropriate thing to do?

Prayer
Eucharistic Lord, I love you for this great gift you have given me both in the Mass and in your reserved presence in the tabernacle. You fill my mind with love. I recall the gift of salvation you gained for me by your passion, death, and resurrection. I receive from you the pledge of eternal life and the hope that one day I shall be with you forever. Thank you for this grace. Never let me be parted from you.

Glossary
Sabbath — The biblical seventh day on which God's people were expected to rest from work and praise God for the gifts of creation and covenant.

Sunday — The Sunday carries forward and completes the meaning of Sabbath. Relaxation should be accompanied by participation in the Eucharist to praise and thank God for the gifts of creation and redemption and begin to savor the eternity prepared for us.

"We should not stay away from our assembly, as is the custom of some, but encourage one another."

Heb 10:25

Endnotes

1. "Why Go To Mass?" by Father Martin Tripole, S.J., "America" Magazine, May 9, 1998, p.15.
2. *Sacrosanctum Consilium* (Constitution on the Sacred Liturgy), 47-48. Flannery, O.P., General Editor, *Vatican II: The Conciliar and Post-Conciliar Documents* (Northport, NY: Costello Publishing, 1975).

Chapter 25

THE FAMILY AS A DOMESTIC CHURCH
CCC 2196-2257

"The most important thing a father can do for his children is to love their mother."

Rev. Theodore Hesburgh

What Mother Owes Johnnie

"Our little boy came up to his mother in the kitchen one evening while she was fixing supper, and he handed her a piece of paper that he had been writing on. After his mom dried her hands on an apron, she read it, and this is what it said:

For cutting the grass	$5.00
For cleaning up my room this week	$1.00
For going to the store for you	.50
Babysitting my kid brother while you went shopping	.25
Taking out the garbage	$1.00
For getting a good report card	$5.00
For cleaning up and raking the yard	$2.00
Total owed:	$14.75

"Well, I'll tell you, his mother looked at him standing there expectantly, and boy, could I see memories flashing through her mind. So she picked up the pen, turned over the paper he'd written on, and this is what she wrote:

For nine months I carried you while you were growing inside me: No charge.

For all the nights I've sat up with you, doctored and prayed for you: No charge.

For all the trying times, and all the tears that you've caused through the years: No charge.

When you add it all up, the cost of my love is: No Charge.

"When our son finished reading what his mother had written, there were great big, old tears in his eyes, and he looked straight up at his mother and said, 'Mom, I sure do love you.' And then he took the pen and in great big letters he wrote: 'PAID IN FULL.' "[1]

What Is the Point of the Fourth Commandment?

Some say... With the "graying" of our society, it would seem as though the focus of the fourth commandment should be on the care of the elderly. Because of better diet, health care, and exercise a far greater number of people are living longer than ever before in history. This means that adult children of older parents will have a responsibility to "honor their fathers and mothers" to an extent not known in earlier times.

The pubic discussions about the stability of Social Security and the financing of health care have become crucially important in this time of the aging of society. We are witnessing a smaller number of young people called upon to support a larger number of elderly. All citizens need to pay attention to the political and economic implications of an aging population and a diminished youthful workforce.

The burden on the young adults goes two ways, upward to their parents and downward to their children. This is why they have come to be called the "sandwich generation" — sandwiched in between their parents and their children. Nonetheless, there should be confidence that solutions can be found to solve this new demand on the filial and parental responsibilities.

In traditional societies the family setting was like a pyramid in which children formed a large base, parents constituted a middle track and grandparents were at the slender tip, often small because so many of them died soon after reaching their senior years. Today the pyramid is reversed. Fewer children per family means the slender part is at the bottom. Parents are still in the middle. And the bulk is at the top due to multiple ways of living longer.

The fourth commandment has always been seen in terms of filial responsibility. The interpretation of that role has been shifted to attention to the elderly since there are now so many of them, often needing expensive health care. This also places an emotional drain on the adult children, hence they need our sympathy and support. But the fact is the fourth commandment has changed its focus, and that is directed toward the care of elderly parents.

The Catechism *teaches* ...

The fourth commandment deals with all aspects of family life —filial and parental duties and responsibilities. It also speaks to the state and the society and what they need to do to foster authentic family values and strengthen the whole family in every way possible.

The first three commandments explain how to love God with all our minds, hearts, and strengths. The next seven commandments show us how to love our neighbors as we love ourselves.

The fourth commandment shows us that, after God, our parents are next, in the divine order of charity, to be the focus of our love. The following commandments deal with other aspects of family life as well as relationships to our neighbor: respect for life, the role of marriage, attitudes to material goods, and the proper use of speech. Taken together these establish the foundation of the Church's social teachings.

The fourth commandment lays out the duties of children to their parents as well as the responsibilities of adult children toward their older parents. It also refers to all those who exercise authority: teachers, leaders, judges, and all those who govern the community.

A man and a woman, bound by their marriage vows, together with their children, form a family. God is the author of marriage and the family. The institution of the family exists before any other institution. The family precedes the state, which is obliged to recognize and support it.

The Christian family is expected to be a community of faith, hope, and love. When these virtues are practiced by the parents and children, the family begins to realize its spiritual quality as a "domestic church." This family, becoming a community of love, is an image of the loving communion of the Father, Son, and Holy Spirit.

The Family and Society. The family is the basic unit of society. A healthy family means a healthy society. Family virtues, such as authority, stability, and loving relationships, are essential for a society that desires a life of freedom, security, and community awareness. Successful societies need citizens who are honest, respect one another, disciplined, trustworthy, peaceable, faithful, chaste, loyal, dependable, loving, just, and merciful and have faith in God. All these virtues can and should be taught and practiced in the family.

The family is the school of the virtues. Society can help families achieve these goals, but society needs families that already do so. Weakened family life is a threat to society. Hence society and the state should do everything possible to provide the family with the means to achieve what families have been designed by God to accomplish.

To guide governments and other institutions of society (media, business, education, etc.) the Church has outlined a Bill of Rights for the Family:

"The political community has a duty to honor the family, to assist it, and to ensure especially:

- the freedom to establish a family, have children, and bring them up in keeping with the family's own moral and religious convictions;
- the protection of the stability of marriage bond and the institution of the family;
- the freedom to profess one's faith, to hand it on, and raise one's children in it, with the necessary means and institutions;
- the right to private property, to free enterprise, to obtain work and housing, and the right to emigrate;
- in keeping with the country's institutions, the right to medical care, assistance for the aged, and family benefits;
- the protection of security and health, especially with respect to dangers like drugs, pornography, alcoholism, etc.;
- the freedom to form associations, with other families and so have representatives before civil authorities."[2]

Family Duties:

1. Respect your parents. They gave you life, loved you, worked for your well-being, and helped you grow to maturity. "With all your heart, honor your father and do not forget the birthpangs of your mother. Remember that through your parents you were born; what can you give back to them that equals their gift to you?" (Sir 7:27-28)

2. Children, obey your parents. During the years of growing up, children should obey parents and accede to what is for your good and that of the family. Anticipate your parents' wishes, seek their advice, and accept their just admonitions. When you are grown up your obligation to obey ceases, but your duty to respect and reverence your parents never stops. This attitude is rooted in one of the gifts of the Holy Spirit, the fear of the Lord — fear meaning reverence for the sacred bond that ties you to your parents.

3. Become responsible grown children. Do all you can to give your parents the support they will need in their old age, be that moral or material, especially when your parents are sick or lonely.

4. Promote family harmony. Be energetic in reducing rivalries, angers,

hostilities, and hurts among brothers and sisters. Fill your home with light and warmth. Establish the possibilities of the flow of love between the generations. Support one another with patience and charity. Draw strength from the graces of your Baptism, the Eucharist, your faith and your life in the Church.

Parental Duties:

1. Raise your children conscientiously. It is not enough simply to give birth to children. They need a lengthy nurture physically, spiritually, intellectually, emotionally, and morally. Care for their souls as well as their bodies. Give them every opportunity that you can for a wholesome education. Oversee their moral training with diligence. All this takes a great deal of personal time on the part of both father and mother. It means giving proper example to your children. Parental witness is a powerful form of child rearing.

2. Emphasize the virtues. It will be hard to keep the commandments without the acquisition of virtues, grooved habits that incline the person to virtuous behavior. Children need training in virtues, through storytelling that inspires them to virtue, through good parental example, and finally through repetitive acts of virtue which ingrain these acts into their behavior and attitudes. Virtues also become the source of self-fulfillment. Children need to acquire virtues such as self-discipline, compassion, responsibility, friendliness, work, courage, perseverance, honesty, loyalty, and faith.

3. Focus on faith. Teach your children to pray from the earliest years. Share with them the lives of the saints. Bring them to Church. Help them to feel at home in the liturgy. Encourage them to go to confession. Emphasize the positive side of faith and help them be forgiving of the weaknesses of the Church's members. Show them how to be in touch with the Blessed Mother, the angels, and the saints, and to have a personal relationship with Christ.

Civic Authorities. Civic authorities should consider their powers in terms of service to the people. Decisions should be in harmony with God's plan for humanity, the natural law, and the dignity of each person. Government leaders must do what they can to promote freedom and responsibility in the citizenry. They ought to be defenders and protectors of the family. They ought to dispense justice in a humane manner and be especially fair when dealing with the poor.

Citizens should collaborate with civic authorities for the common good of society. Submission to authority and co-responsibility for society make it morally obligatory to pay taxes, vote, and defend the country. When the governing authorities require behavior that is against the moral order, then the citizens have a moral obligation in conscience not to obey such a law. There is a distinction between serving God and the political community. "Render therefore unto Caesar the things that are Caesar's and to God the things that are God's." (Mt 22:21)

1. What is the basis of the fourth commandment?

"The conjugal community is established upon the covenant and consent of the spouses. Marriage and family are ordered to the good of the spouses, to the procreation and education of children.

"Children owe their parents respect, gratitude, just obedience, and assistance. Filial respect fosters harmony in all of family life." (CCC 2249, 2251)

2. What are the duties of parents?

"Parents have the first responsibility for the education of their children in the faith, prayer, and all the virtues. They have the duty to provide as far as possible for the spiritual and physical needs of their children.

"Parents should respect and encourage their children's vocations. They should remember and teach that the first calling of the Christian is to follow Jesus." (CCC 2252, 2253)

3. What are some principles that govern the relationship of citizens and society?

"Public authority is obliged to respect the fundamental rights of the human person and the conditions for the exercise of freedom.

"It is the duty of citizens to work with civil authority for building up society in a spirit of truth, justice, solidarity, and freedom."

" 'The well-being of the individual person and of both human and Christian society is closely bound up with the healthy state of conjugal and family life.' (GS 47, 1)" (CCC 2254, 2255, 2250)

Response to objections

The argument that the fourth commandment's contemporary focus should be the elderly parents of adult children is partially true. The other half, that children of young parents have filial responsibilities, is also true. Moreover, all parents have parental duties that cannot be ignored.

Nor should the state and the culture forget their duties to support family values and the stability of the household. Civil authorities at all levels should see that their behavior contributes to the advancement of the family. At the same time young adult parents as well as the elderly ones still have the duties of citizenship.

A given family unit needs to be as healthy as possible for the fostering of the human dignity of each member. A strong family is the basis of a strong society. Conversely, the state and the culture have a critical investment in a given family so that their role will remain creative and productive.

Seen in this way, the implications of the fourth commandment touch the vitality of a nation as well as the health of a whole family. Authority at all levels: parental in the home, political in the state, managerial in the economy, creative in the arts, is commanded to act responsibly for the good of children, citizens, employees, and the cultural community.

Still, it is at the family level that the power of the fourth commandment's truth comes alive most tellingly. In that coherent society, that domestic church, we can see all the dynamic relationships that go to make up the society at large. The interplay of the parental and the filial, of authority and obedience, of loving and reverent respect flowing in all directions – up, down, and lateral – signal to us what kind of a society we will produce.

It is here that the faith is born, raised, and nourished in communion with the Church. The fourth commandment is not constrained to one or another aspect of family life, but rather to the whole family.

For dialog

1. What are your expectations for family life? What principles and experiences govern your vision of the family? When you think of families you admire, what characteristics attract you the most? What could our culture and government do to make family life more stable and beneficial to the members?

2. What can the Church do to make family life flourish? Why are faith, prayer, and practice of virtues so important for the strengthening of the family? When you hear of the family being called a "domestic church," what do you understand by the term? Why is a strong family life essential for a healthy society and a good government?

3. What do you see in the culture that seems to prevent the healthy growth of family life? How should we help the media to take a responsible attitude toward family life? How does your local parish become a center of strength for the family? Why do we say that honoring father and mother includes filial obedience from the children and parental respect for the children?

Prayer

Jesus, Mary, and Joseph, help us to acquire a family life that is loving, forgiving, mutually supportive. May we witness the spirituality that can bond our family together at the inter-generational level, as well as with extended family members. Show us how to be a domestic church, a real *communio* in faith, hope, and love and all the other virtues that will make us reflect the life of the Trinity here on earth.

Glossary

Bill of Rights for Families — A list of rights for support of the family published by the Synod of Bishops in 1980. It dramatizes the highest priority the Church gives to defending and protecting the family.

Communion of Persons — The Trinity is the supreme model of the communion of persons where absolute unity and love exists. The family needs to be such a community, striving for the highest ideals of love among the members.

"Children will not remember you for the material things you provided, but for the feeling that you cherished them."

Richard I. Evans

Endnotes
1. M. Adams, in *Chicken Soup For the Soul*, Volume 3, pp. 100-101.
2. John Paul II, *Familiaris Consortio* (Letter to Families), 46.

Chapter 26

SUPPORT THE CULTURE OF LIFE
CCC 2258-2330

"Life must be protected with the utmost care from the moment of conception."[1]

Is There Life After Birth?

This story is by Father J. J. Mueller, S.J., from Gonzaga University, Spokane, Washington:

Imagine you are a baby in your mother's womb, warm, dark, cozy, at home in a place you are used to after nine months.

Mother: Are you awake? Good. I feel you kicking. I have great news for you. Today you are going to be born.

Baby: Mom, what's "born" mean?

Mother: That means you will become an individual apart from me. You will live out here with your brothers and sisters. You know me now from the inside. But soon you will know me face to face. By the way, your father is waiting here with open arms to greet you. I know it's time.

Baby: Is it hard to be born? IS THERE LIFE AFTER BIRTH?

Mother: Oh yes, but it is quite different and wonderful. You will have to breathe air, so the doctor will slap you on the back to clear the fluid from your lungs.

Baby: Breathe air? Is that possible? Isn't fluid good enough? Mom, are you sure about this?

Mother: Yes, trust me. I should tell you that you will be cold when you come forth. So we will have a nice blanket to wrap you in. You'll be a little bloody, so we'll have to wash that off.

Baby: Cold? Bloody? I like the temperature here just fine.

Mother: And we'll cut your nourishment line to me in order to have you eat with your own mouth.

Baby: Mom, are you sure there's really life after birth?

Mother: Yes, dear, trust me. Have I ever let you down?

Baby: No, but maybe I could stay here a couple more weeks to get used to the idea.

Mother: I'm sorry. That's not possible. Nine months is all you need. The time is up. You are ready to be born.

Baby: Okay. I don't really understand it but I believe you. Even if I'm not sure there's life after birth, I trust you. I trust my father's waiting. I'd like to meet him face to face. Here I come!

This parable of the mystery of life before birth speaks to our concern for the mystery of life after life on this earth.

Are There Exceptions to the Fifth Commandment?

Some say... While generally we should protect life, there are a number of times when we will be moved to kill. We will always do this in "a mournful mood," since we never do it with any sense of satisfaction. In self-defense a father will kill an assailant who threatens to murder his child. For centuries a theory of just war has legitimized the killing that goes on in warfare when a nation has been attacked by an unjust aggressor.

The laws of most nations permit abortion of an unborn child in cases of rape, incest, and threat to the life of the mother. To control a dangerous population increase, China has ordered its married citizens to have only one child. If an extra pregnancy occurs, the new child should be aborted. The self-preservation of a nation seems to justify these extreme measures.

Capital punishment for murderers seems justified. It can serve as a deterrent to other potential murderers. For some persons it is the only threat that stops them from further killing. Take the case of a convict who is serving a life term with no parole. What is to stop him from further murdering behind prison walls? What is to be done with a violent revolutionary when the government is in danger of being overthrown? Should not the state protect itself against the murderer and promise to kill him if he attempts further action against the government?

Our position is, "Let the punishment fit the crime." In the case of Murder One, the death penalty seems to be a suitable moral response.

The Catechism teaches ... "No one can arbitrarily choose to live or to die. The absolute master of such a decision is the Creator alone, in whom 'We live and move and have our being.'"2

The principal thrust of the fifth commandment is the sanctity of every human life. It calls us to love everyone in such a way that the world is made safe for life.

When Jesus was born, a choir of angels filled the sky over Bethlehem and sang praises to the glory of God. An angel proclaimed that Christ's birth was an event of great joy. The source of this joy was the birth of our Savior. Christmas also reveals the meaning of every human birth. The birth of the Messiah heralds the joy we have for every child born into the world.

Jesus preached the heart of his salvation message when he said, "I came so that they may have life and have it more abundantly." (Jn 10:10) He was referring to the eternal life to which we are called by the Father, won for us by the Son, and given to us by the power of the Spirit. This eternal life bestows meaning on all stages of human life.

The Father calls us to divine life, a vocation that reminds us how precious is our human, earthly life. Had we not received the gift of life here, we would not know the possibility of divine life hereafter. Our human lives are sacred. We must live them with responsibility and with a love for all people. With the light of reason and the hidden reality of grace, all people can come to know their personal dignity and final destiny in God.

Vatican II teaches that "By his incarnation, the Son of God has united himself in some fashion with every human being."3 Because of this our human lives are precious from beginning to end on earth, and we have the right to have our lives respected .

Threats to Human Life. This same council document listed threats to human life that are forbidden by the fifth commandment. Its powerful words deserve to be quoted in full:

"Whatever is opposed to life itself, such as any type of murder, genocide, abortion, ethanasia, or willful self-destruction, whatever violates the integrity of the human person, such as mutilation, torments inflicted on body or mind, attempts to coerce the will itself; whatever insults human dignity, such as subhuman living conditions, arbitrary imprisonment, deportation, slavery, prostitution, the selling of women and children; as well as disgraceful working conditions, where people are treated as mere instruments of gain rather than free and responsible persons; *all of these things and others like them are infamies indeed*."4

All of these acts are attacks on the dignity of human beings. Worse yet, public opinion often approves of such behavior and justifies crimes against life. Some governments have decided not to punish these practices against life — and have even made them legal. *Choices that were once considered criminal have become socially acceptable*. This is a serious sign of moral decline in our modern world. Connected to this is the gradual darkening of human conscience so that increasingly, people cannot tell the difference between good and evil.

In this brief chapter we can only underline the major life issues that confront us today. Study the *Catechism's* treatment of the fifth commandment and the superb exposition of the Church's teaching on life in Pope John Paul II's "Gospel of Life."

There are five life issues that command our attention: Murder, Abortion, Euthanasia, War, and the Death Penalty. Let us examine each of these in turn.

Murder. The biblical account of Cain's murder of Abel reveals the presence of anger and envy in all human beings. These negative attitudes have been the consequences of original sin from the dawn of human history and often lead to murder. Scripture forbids murder. "Do not slay the innocent and the righteous." (Ex 23:7) Jesus forbade murder and also inner attitudes of anger, hatred, and revenge that can lead to murder. He asked us to turn the other cheek and love our enemies. At the beginning of his Passion, he did not defend himself, and he told Peter to put away his sword.

The murder of a human being offends the dignity of the person and the holiness of the Creator. At the same time, self-defense against an unjust aggressor is permitted. In fact, self-defense is a moral duty for whoever is responsible for the lives of others and the common good.

Abortion. Ever since Roe vs. Wade, no moral issue has engaged our attention more than the legalization of abortion. From the very beginning of Christianity, the Church has condemned abortion. "You shall not kill the embryo by abortion." (Didache 2,2 — written around 60 AD) This teaching has never changed and it will not change. Abortion is ever and always contrary to the moral law. Formal cooperation in an abortion is morally wrong.

At the same time, the Church extends Christ's gift of mercy to those who have had an abortion. *Project Rachel* is a ministry extended to those mothers who have had abortions and mistakenly believe they have committed the unforgivable sin. Psychologically and spiritually, many such mothers believe they have no recourse to God's mercy. Project Rachel reaches out to them to restore their unity with God and to offer them whatever counseling that may be needed.

The pro-life movement has developed a range of services to pregnant women to help them save their children, offering them options for adoption or for raising the children themselves.

The Church teaches that the embryo should be treated as a person from conception, defended and cared for, and healed like any human being.

Euthanasia. Intentional euthanasia is murder. It is morally unacceptable. The publicity given to Dr. Jack Kervorkian's "Physician-Assisted Suicide" and to the experiments with euthanasia in Holland appear to justify this behavior. But many state and federal courts have been ruling against the constitutional right to die. Judge Noonan of the Ninth Circuit Court overruled a May 1994 decision of Judge Barbara Rothenstein in *Compassion in Dying vs. Washington State.* Judge Noonan cited five special reasons why this is wrong. Following is a paraphrased summary of his argument.

1. We should not have physicians in the role of killers of their patients. It would perversely affect their self-understanding and reduce their desire to look for cures for disease, if killing instead of curing were an option.

2. We should not subject the elderly and infirm to psychological pressures to consent to their own deaths.

3. We should protect the poor and minorities from exploitation. Pain is a significant factor in the desire for doctor-assisted suicide. The poor and minorities often do not have the resources for the alleviation of pain.

4. We should protect all the handicapped from societal indifference and antipathy and any bias against them.

5. We should prevent abuses similar to what has happened in the Netherlands, which now tolerates both voluntary and involuntary euthanasia.

Catholic moral tradition has always taught that we can discontinue medical procedures that are burdensome, extraordinary, or disproportionate to the outcome. The use of painkillers to alleviate the sufferings of the dying, even at the risk of shortening their lives, is morally permissible so long as death is not willed or intended.

Suicide is contrary to justice, hope, and charity and is forbidden by the fifth commandment. Serious psychological disturbances, anxiety, fear of suffering, or torture can diminish the responsibility of the one committing suicide. Can suicides achieve eternal salvation? Only God knows, the God who can provide the opportunity for repentance. The Church prays for those who have taken their lives.

War. The *Catechism* begins its treatment of war by emphasizing the need to safeguard peace. We must cherish peace in our hearts and abandon the anger and hatred that leads to wars. Peace is more than the absence of war. Peace is a process that eliminates the causes of war. Real peace is the work of justice and the effect of love. Peace can happen when we protect human rights and respect the dignity of all peoples. We need to disarm our hearts if we wish to disarm the world. "The arms race is one of the greatest curses on the human race and the harm it inflicts on the poor is more than can be endured." (CCC 2329)

Historically, the Church has tried to mitigate the evils and horrors of war. Just because a war has started does not mean that the moral law has stopped. Genocide and ethnic cleansing are evil. Destruction of cities and their inhabitants is wrong. Wounded soldiers and prisoners of war deserve humane treatment. In paragraph 2309, the *Catechism* outlines the strict conditions for legitimate defense by military force. It concludes by saying "The power of modern means of destruction weighs very heavily in evaluating this condition [for a just war]."

When Christ rose from the dead, his first words were about peace. "Peace be with you. As the Father has sent me, so I send you." (Jn 20:21) Ultimately, peace is a gift from God. Humanly speaking, we must do all we can to achieve it. Divinely speaking, we must never stop imploring God with fervent prayer for the gift of peace.

Death Penalty. The *Catechism* teaches that governmental authority has the right and duty to punish criminals by means of suitable penalties, not excluding, in cases of extreme gravity, the death penalty. (Cf. CCC 2267) Pope John Paul II, in his "Gospel of Life" gives this passage of the *Catechism* a very restrictive interpretation. He says the death penalty is an extreme solution that should only be used when it would be otherwise impossible to defend society. "Today, however, as a result of steady improvements in the penal system, such cases are very rare, if not practically nonexistent."[5]

The pope asks us not to dwell on a legal argument about the death penalty against the background of danger and revenge, but in the positive light of building a culture of life.

1. Why is human life sacred?

"Every human life, from the moment of conception until death, is sacred because the human person has been willed for its own sake in the image and likeness of the living and holy God.

"The murder of a human being is gravely contrary to the dignity of the person and the holiness of the Creator." (CCC 2319, 2320)

2. Why is abortion wrong?

"From its conception, the child has the right to life. Direct abortion, that is, abortion willed as an end or a means, is a 'criminal' practice (GS 27, 3), gravely contrary to the moral law. The Church imposes the canonical penalty of excommunication for this crime against human life.

"Because it should be treated as a person from conception, the embryo must be defended in its integrity, cared for, and healed like every other human being." (CCC 2322, 2323)

3. What is our teaching about euthanasia?

"Intentional euthanasia, whatever its forms or motives, is murder. It is gravely contrary to the dignity of the human person and to the respect due to the living God, his Creator." (CCC 2324)

Response to objections

We all ought to be people of life and for life. We are people of life because Jesus has saved us by the Cross and Resurrection, the source of all life. By our rebirth in Baptism we are called to be people for life. All of us, both as individuals and members of the Church community have the responsibility to proclaim, celebrate, and serve Christ's Gospel of Life.

The commandment, "You shall not kill," has absolute value when it refers to the innocent person. While this right to life is always precious, there are instances where it is not absolute. The Church teaches that we have the right to legitimate self-defense, a right based on the value of life and the duty to love one's self no less than others. Secondly, there is the remote possibility of legitimizing capital punishment — but there are few, if any, extreme cases where capital punishment can be justified.

In our review of some major points in the *Catechism*, we lay out the arguments against abortion, euthanasia, and war. However, no matter how strong our arguments are against these evils, they must be matched by an even more powerful and concerted effort to create a culture of life.

This demands a conscious effort to relate freedom to truth which is our best strategy of undermining relativism, a way of thinking that imperils the life and existence of the weak and helpless. Second, we need to do all we can to witness the existence and presence of God toward all creation and every human being. "Where God is denied, and people live as though he did not exist, or his commandments are not taken into account, the dignity of the human person and the inviolability of human life also end up being rejected or compromised."[6]

Last, we need to confront the darkening of conscience in modern society. Too many people find it difficult to distinguish between good and evil when facing the value of human life. They are confused about the basic goodness of life and so are led to make choices that desecrate the dignity of life. This eclipse of conscience needs to be countered by the Church's authentic position of conscience as a reflection of God's eternal law imprinted on the human soul and designed to foster the integrity of human nature. God is the author of our nature and knows what will really bring it fulfillment.

For dialog

1. Why do you think our opening story about the birth of a baby was used to introduce a reflection on the fifth commandment? Why does relativism pose a threat to the value of innocent life? When the culture decides to do business both financially and politically with no reference to God, what effect will this have on human dignity and life? If conscience is darkened, people will become confused about the issues of good and evil when faced with the

protection of a given human life. Why do you think this would happen?

2. We constantly hear about the forthcoming execution of prisoners in our country and the stories of appeals to governors and courts for a "stay of execution." These are "Dead Men Walking," as the book and film dramatized. Where do you find yourself on this issue, especially in the light of John Paul II's "Gospel of Life?" Why is the Church taking such a powerful, public stand against abortion and doctor-assisted suicide? How would you defend the Church's Pro-Life teachings and witness?

3. In the film, "Saving Private Ryan," a detachment of American soldiers set out to rescue one man, even though this meant certain death for some of them. What is your reaction to this story? What do you think will happen to America if the culture of death prevails over the Gospel of Life?

Prayer

God, you are pure Life. Every impulse that flows from your divine life is filled with life for each human being. By sin death entered the world. By the death of the Son of God, life returned to the world and the promise of eternal life was made possible for us. When the angel announced the conception and birth of God's Son to Mary, the promise of life was established once and for all in this world. Fill us with love and respect for the life and human dignity of all human beings.

Glossary

Abortion — Abortion is the intended destruction of an unborn child and is gravely contrary to the moral law and the holiness of the Creator.

Euthanasia — Direct euthanasia is the intended killing of the sick, the dying, or the elderly or those with disabilities. It is morally unacceptable.

Suicide — Suicide, the taking of one's own life, is contrary to justice, hope, and love. Grave psychological disturbances, anxiety, fear of pain, or torture may diminish the responsibility of the one committing suicide. The Church prays for the salvation of their souls.

"God loved us not because we were lovable, but because he is love."
C. S. Lewis

Endnotes

1. GS 51, 3. Flannery, O.P., General Editor. *Vatican II* (Northport, NY: Costello Publishing, 1975).
2. John Paul II, *Evangelium Vitae* ("The Gospel of Life").
3. GS 22.
4. Ibid., 27.
5. *Evangelium Vitae*, 56.
6. Ibid., 96, 3.

Chapter 27

GOD'S PLAN FOR
MARRIAGE AND SEXUALITY

CCC 2331-2400

"A deaf husband and a blind wife are a happy couple."

Danish Proverb

Scenes from a Marriage

In Thornton Wilder's *The Skin of Our Teeth*, Mrs. Antrobus says to her husband, "I didn't marry you because you were perfect, George. I didn't even marry you because I loved you. I married you because you gave me a promise. That promise made up for your faults. And the promise I gave you made up for mine. Two imperfect people got married and it was the promise that made the difference."

Kept promises produce the kind of union sensed by the author of a *New Yorker* article: "Their enjoyment of each other was arresting — sharp as pepper, golden. I have seen other happy old couples, but this picture of the Joneses, renewed many times, came to represent to me the essence of human exchange. It showed me something indescribably moving and precious, which comes to fruition only after a lifelong marriage. It has struck me as one of the greatest possibilities life has to offer."

Some years ago in London a host of British VIP's, including Prime Minister Sir Winston Churchill and his wife, lady Clementine, attended a banquet. It was a tradition at this particular banquet to play a little game before the main address by the guest speaker. The game that night was, "If you couldn't be who you are, who would you like to be?"

The honored guests answered the question in their own way, but all waited with immense curiosity for Churchill's answer. Who else would he want to be? As the last speaker, he rose and said, "If I can't be who I am, I would most like to be," seventy-eight-year-old Winston turned to his wife and took her hand, "Lady Churchill's second husband."

These three tales of marriage promises kept, of marital fidelity, form the mental background of the sixth commandment.

Is the Sixth Commandment Any Longer Relevant?

Some say... In survival societies before the industrial revolution, stable marriages were essential. Marital fidelity was needed for economic reasons. Marital promises had to be kept because the alternatives were too destructive. Furthermore, life spans were relatively short. Most people died in middle age. The itch to change spouses did not have much time to develop.

But in today's culture the relevance of the sixth commandment seems diminished. One teacher recently asked his students, "If you were asked to downsize the ten commandments, which ones would you remove?" Most of the class said the one about adultery should go. It was outdated. Nobody obeyed it. Why have it?

The culture asks us to relax our judgment about many kinds of behavior, especially sexual acts. Society is accepting adultery, divorce, infidelity (but oddly not when it is done by one's spouse). It is just part of "human nature." Even clergy today are unwilling to condemn adultery or fornication. Just like everyone else, they are reluctant to make judgments about what used to be thought of as immoral sexual behavior. People refuse to make much of sexual misconduct because so many of them are engaged in it themselves.

The culture today defends, promotes, and romanticizes adultery. Novels, films, songs, and stories have created a tolerance for adultery by removing the sting of infidelity and broken promises that goes with it. Having an "affair" has become acceptable because it will recharge worn-out sex and relationships in a marriage.

It's a new world out there. People are becoming more at ease with their sexuality. Rigid relationships, once confined by the customs of marriage, are melting. In the light of all this, it seems fair to say that the sixth commandment is now irrelevant.

The Catechism teaches ...

God is the author of marriage and sexuality. God has a plan for sex and marriage that is meant to correspond to our human nature's proper development, peace, and fulfillment. The sacrament of Marriage along with the sixth and ninth commandments are specific ways in which this divine plan is implemented.

The sixth commandment forbids adultery, which is a sexual act performed by a married person with someone other than one's spouse. The commandment prohibits infidelity.

On the positive side, the sixth commandment summons the spouses to practice fidelity to each other. Fidelity is the marital value that is essential for the success of the marriage. God established marriage and intended that the solemn promises made by husband and wife to be faithful to one another forever should reflect the very covenant that God has made with us.

Just as God is always faithful to his promises, so must the spouses be faithful to one another. The sacrament of Marriage enables the spouses to share in Christ's fidelity to his Church. By their marital chastity, the spouses witness this mystery to the world.

St. John Chrysostom suggests that young husbands say this to their wives:

"I have taken you in my arms and I love you, and I prefer you to my life itself. For the present life is nothing, and my most ardent dream is to spend it with you in such a way that we may be assured of not being separated in the life that is reserved for us. . . . I place your love above all things, and nothing would be more bitter or painful to me than to be of a different mind than you."[1]

Chastity. Related to fidelity is the virtue of chastity that is the process by which the spouses integrate their sexuality into their persons. As everyone knows, chastity demands self-mastery, especially in a culture that too often idealizes promiscuity. Chastity brings bodily sex within the broader human reality. It unites bodily sexuality with our spiritual natures so that sex is seen as more than a purely physical act. Sexuality affects every aspect of the person because of the unity of body and soul. In particular it is bonded to our emotional life and our capacity to love and procreate. Jesus is the model of chastity. Every baptized person is called to chastity according to one's state in life.

In this section, the *Catechism* places the unitive and procreative aspects of Marriage under the topic of chastity. The unitive nature of Marriage refers to the bond of love between the spouses. The procreative side of Marriage speaks of the openness to having children and raising them spiritually in the faith as well as looking after their physical, emotional, and intellectual development.

The bond between the unitive and procreative should be inseparable and unbreakable. Sexual acts should take place only within the context of Marriage. Chaste and faithful spouses will not commit adultery. Similarly, men and women religious, vowed to celibacy and consecrated virginity must also practice chastity, meaning they must abstain from all sexual acts. Unmarried people observe chastity by continence, that is, abstinence from sexual acts.

The *Catechism* lists the following acts as opposed to chastity:

1. Lust. This is the fostering of disordered desire for sex. Jesus teaches, "You have heard it said, 'You shall not commit adultery.' But I say to you, everyone who looks at a woman with lust has already committed adultery with her in his heart." (Mt 5:27)

2. Masturbation. This is a deliberate stimulation of the genital organs to derive sexual pleasure. The explicit use of a sexual organ outside the marital act, for whatever reason, is morally unacceptable.

Moral culpability should take into account immaturity, anxiety, habit, or other factors that may diminish responsibility.

3. Fornication. This is sexual union between unmarried men and women. It is wrong because it violates the dignity of the persons and the unbreakable bond between the unitive and procreative aspects of Marriage.

4. Pornography. This is the display of sexual acts or fantasies in pictures, films, videos, stories, and other imagery — disconnected from the intimacy of the marriage act. It engenders lust and immoral sexual behavior. It corrupts the participants. Civil authorities should prevent the production and distribution of pornography.

5. Prostitution. Prostitutes sell their bodies for sex. The act degrades both the seller and the buyer.

6. Rape. Rapists and child molesters force sex on unwilling partners. This is always gravely evil and never permitted. Those who rape children (especially in cases of incest) can cause irreparable psychological harm.

7. Homosexuality. This is a case of sexual relations between persons of the same sex. Homosexual acts are intrinsically disordered and never permitted. The *Catechism* gives the following guideline for the attitude toward homosexual persons: "They must be accepted with respect, compassion, and sensitivity. Every sign of unjust discrimination in their regard should be avoided." (CCC 2358)

Adultery, divorce, polygamy, and "free union" break the promises of fidelity. Some biblical scholars note that the Hebrew word for adultery is similar to the word for idolatry. Since pagan temples in biblical times employed prostitutes, they were havens for adultery. To engage in immoral sexual acts under the sign of a false god was also to enter into a false relationship with another person. Covenant acts take place in the sight of a living and true God. Unfaithful acts occur under the sign of delusion. (Read the *Catechism* 2382-2386 for its teaching on divorce.)

The late Archbishop Fulton J. Sheen had this to say about marriage in his book *Three to Get Married*: "Fidelity in marriage means much more than abstaining from adultery. All religious ideas are positive — not negative. Husband and wife are pledges of eternal love. Their union in the flesh has a grace which prepares them for union with God. The passing of time wears out bodies, but nothing can make a soul vanish or diminish its eternal value. Nothing on earth is stronger than the fidelity of hearts fortified by the Sacrament of Marriage."[2]

1. What did God intend in creating man and woman?

"By creating the human being woman and man, God gives personal dignity to the one and the other. Each of them, man and woman, should acknowledge and accept his sexual identity." (CCC 2393)

2. What is our teaching about birth control?

"The regulation of births represents one of the aspects of responsible fatherhood and motherhood. Legitimate intentions on the part of spouses do not justify recourse to morally unacceptable means (for example, direct sterilization or contraception)." (CCC 2399) (Also read CCC 2366-2379.)

3. What is implied by the marital covenant?

"The covenant which spouses enter into entails faithful love. It imposes on them the obligation to keep their marriage indissoluble." (CCC 2397)

Response to objections

The culture should not be the standard by which we understand sex and marriage. This is especially so when there is a radical divide between Christ's gospel and the culture — a situation in which we find ourselves today. The culture did not invent sex and marriage. God did. The purposes for sex and marriage should be discovered in the intentions of the author.

There was a time, of course, not all that long ago, when marital infidelity in all its forms was frowned on by the culture and reflected in the customs and laws of the nation. Politicians, civic leaders, parents, and clergy were generally of one mind about sex and marriage — and that mind was far more in accord with God's laws than is evident today.

The wisdom of the sixth commandment is more relevant than ever before. All around us we see that broken promises lead to broken lives. Despite the seductive teachings of the culture, it is the sixth commandment that really protects and enhances sexuality. It proscribes sexual activity outside of Marriage because fidelity is not the foundation stone of such acts. Moreover, the human dignity of persons engaged in immoral acts is assaulted, as is clearly evident in rape.

The great experiment, termed sexual liberation, is actually a sexual enslavement. Instead of being in charge of one's sexual life, it is sex that leads people around in a series of chance encounters and loveless exchanges. Confusion abounds as moral leaders fail to heal by sound teaching and personal witness.

The risen Christ, however, as alive now as he was in Galilee, still loves us, wants to heal us, and call us to our real destiny. He still teaches the splendor of truth and his witness is incomparable. He told the rich young man to keep the commandments. That same message comes to us. We are not supposed to downsize the commandments. We have a better goal, to upgrade our lives with the moral standards set by them.

In a time of sexual and marital chaos, we argue that the sixth commandment is more relevant than ever.

For dialog

1. What would you consider to be three successful strategies for preserving fidelity in Marriage? What could our culture do to foster stronger marital fidelity? What spiritual means does the church provide to help couples remain faithful to each other? What tempts spouses to infidelity?

2. Why is marital fidelity so important for the stability of your children? What do you notice about the children of divorce? What can be done to stem the tide of divorce in our country?

3. What are five positive possibilities for helping married couples stay together and grow in fidelity to one another? Who are some couples you admire for their fidelity? Why is it working for them? What could you gain from their witness?

Prayer

Father in heaven, you are the author of Marriage and willed that the covenant of husband and wife should reflect the covenant you have established with us. Your beloved Son willed that the covenant of Marriage should reflect his own union with the Church. In these events the virtues of fidelity and chastity are paramount, Christian ideals that assure the stability of the family and look to the welfare of children. We ask for all the virtues, gifts, and blessings we need to fulfill these Christian ideals of Marriage and the family. Amen.

Glossary

Adultery — Sex outside of marriage involving a married person.

Fornication — Sex outside of marriage involving two unmarried persons.

Incest — Sex between a parent and a child.

Natural Family Planning — A permissible regulation of births within certain conditions. Cf. CCC 2366-2372.

Artificial Contraception — The use of a pill or other device to prevent conception in the marital act.

"An archaeologist is the best husband a woman can have. The older she gets, the more interested he is in her."

Agatha Christie[3]

Endnotes

1. Chrysostom, "Homily on Ephesians," 20.
2. Fulton J. Sheen, *Three to Get Married* (Scepter, 1996).
3. See *Agatha Christie: An Autobiography* (Boulevard [Mars Market], 1996).

Chapter 28

REMOVE THE SYMPTOMS AND CAUSES OF INJUSTICE

CCC 2401-2463

"It is the duty of all God's people, with the bishops giving a lead by word and example, to do all in their power to relieve the sufferings of our time."[1]

The Dorothy Day Story

Dorothy Day was born in Brooklyn on November 8, 1897. Her father was a newspaperman and a permanent influence on her life. She chose journalism as a profession. She attended the University of Chicago on a scholarship for two years and enrolled in the Socialist Party because she was greatly troubled by the widespread poverty caused by the Great Depression.

She moved to New York where she continued her efforts to alleviate the appalling poverty she saw and the conditions that caused it. She took her first job on the Socialist daily paper, *The Call*, where she worked for $5.00 a week writing a column emphasizing the sordidness of slum living.

During this period of her life, she discussed revolution with her friends, walked in picket lines, went on hunger strikes, and was jailed. In order to make a more positive contribution, she worked for a year as a probationer nurse. Disturbed and frustrated by all she saw, Dorothy wandered through Europe, back to Chicago, to New Orleans and, finally, to New York. Here, two important events happened. She joined the Catholic Church and met Peter Maurin. She and Peter formed the basis of the Catholic Worker Movement.

They founded *The Catholic Worker* newspaper to spread the vision of a society where justice and love were possible. In three years, its circulation increased to 150,000. They also established "houses of hospitality" so that mutual aid could supplant state aid. Peter Maurin believed that charity should be personal and should not be confined to the duties of the government. Third, they created farming communes to provide land and homes for the unemployed.

Peter Maurin died in 1947. He has been called the St. Francis of Assisi of modern times, for he chose to live in poverty all his life.

Under the leadership of Dorothy Day, the Catholic Worker Movement continued to do good for those in need, to give a vision to the working class, and create a meaningful synthesis of the gospel and social values.

Her story relates to that aspect of the seventh commandment which deals with the Church's social teachings.

What Is the Import of the Seventh Commandment for Us?

Some say... While it is obvious that the seventh commandment cautions us against stealing, it is less clear to many that it also points to the deeper issue of justice in the world. Most people know that stealing is wrong. Yet the majority of people are less aware of the issue of justice for the poor and helpless and its relationship with peace. Individuals, indeed, become exercised about justice when they themselves have been mistreated. But they can be blind to the problem of injustice when it touches the lives of millions of people beyond and "below" their social class. We would argue that it is better to concentrate on the issues of poverty and social justice rather than matters of stealing when reflecting on the seventh commandment.

Of children who die before their fifth birthday, ninety-eight percent are in the poor nations of the world. Of those who die prematurely of tuberculosis, malaria, measles, tetanus, and whooping cough, all but a few thousand live in the poor world. The gap is rising between the very richest and very poorest nations of the world. In forty-two countries with the highest indebtedness, there are seven hundred million people whom Mother Teresa called the "poorest of the poor."

While the poor are getting poorer, the rich are getting richer. On Park Avenue in New York City, a new forty-three-story condominium has apartments that sell for $8 million apiece. The penthouse goes for $15 million. The owners will pay $450,000 for servants' suites, $25,000 to store one thousand bottles of their wine, and pay $4,000 in monthly fees. Prospective owners of these properties will have to prove they have $100 million in assets so they can take care of the costs of living in this condo.

The Church teaches the doctrine of the universal destination of the goods of the earth, meaning that God meant the goods of the earth to be for the benefit, support, and human dignity of all human beings. It is the moral and social responsibility of the "haves" to address the symptoms and causes of a poverty in the world that causes millions of children to die before they are five and hundreds of millions of people to go to be hungry and hopeless every night.

This is the "hidden agenda" of the seventh commandment, a call to acquire a social conscience.

The Catechism *teaches* ...

Dorothy Day put into practice the social teachings of the Church. She exemplified the Church's teaching that God intended the goods of the earth to be for the benefit of all people. The *Catechism* calls this principle: the universal destination of the goods of the earth. God made human beings the stewards of the earth's goods. We also have the right to private property, which supports our dignity and freedom and helps families meet their basic needs. This right to private property does not abolish the universal destination of goods.

The *Catechism's* treatment of the seventh commandment deals with the question of stealing and then the broader issue of the Church's social teaching.

It is well known that the seventh commandment forbids stealing. Theft is taking someone's money or property against the reasonable will of the owner. We should acquire the virtues of moderation, justice, and solidarity in order to keep this commandment. Moderation curbs our attachment to worldly goods. Justice helps us respect our neighbor's rights. Solidarity is another name for the Golden Rule, "Do unto others as you would have them do unto you."

In a special way we should have solidarity with the poor, the alien, the widow, and the orphan. The helpless need us and deserve our compassion. Helping the poor is a witness of love and a work of justice pleasing to God.

We should not steal from one another, cheat in business, pay unfair salaries, or exploit people's weaknesses or distress to make money. Promises and contracts should be made and kept in good faith and with fairness.

Social Teachings. The *Catechism* explains the Church's social teachings in two major sections, first in part one of book three, and second, here under the seventh commandment. Its first treatment may be found in paragraphs 1877-1948, where it reflects on the person and society, the common good, and social justice.

The second coverage is in paragraphs 2419-2449. Here it teaches that

Christian revelation calls for a deeper understanding of the laws of the social order. The Church has a duty to render a moral judgment on economic and social issues when the fundamental rights of the person and the salvation of souls are at stake. The social teaching of the Church proposes principles for making such judgments and guidelines for social action.

The Church must maintain an interest in the temporal common good of every human being because people are destined for God. What happens to people here affects their final goal. We must help all people on their journey to God, honoring and enabling their dignity here and their destiny hereafter.

The Church makes clear that the moral law opposes any behavior that enslaves human beings or buying and selling them as though they were merchandise. Social teachings make a connection between the mineral, vegetable, and animal resources of the earth and the moral responsibility to use them wisely for people today and generations to come.

"Man is himself the author, center, and goal of all economic and social life." (CCC 2459) God has intended that the goods of the earth should be available for every person in a just and loving manner. The value of work proceeds from the human person who is both the author of work and its beneficiary. When we work we share in the very processes of creation. When we unite our labors with Christ's intentions for us, our efforts can be redemptive because Christ wills it so.

For over a century the popes have been active in developing the Church's social teachings in the light of problems caused by the industrial revolution and the technological revolution, which is upon us now. Pope John XXIII taught that peace will come more easily when people are treated justly. Pope Paul VI argued that the rich nations of the world have a responsibility to help the poor ones. Pope John Paul II has said that the state has an essential obligation to assure that workers can enjoy the fruits of their labors. While the state has an obligation to protect human rights in the economic sector, the primary responsibility for this belongs to the institutions, groups, and associations that make up a society.

St. Rose of Lima said that when we serve the poor and the sick, we serve Jesus. We must not neglect our neighbor, because it is Jesus whom we serve.

1. What does the seventh commandment say about stealing?

"Theft is the usurpation of another's goods against the reasonable will of the owner.

"Every manner of taking and using another's property unjustly is contrary to the seventh commandment. The injustice committed requires reparation. Commutative justice requires the restitution of stolen goods." (CCC 2453-2454)

2. Why does the Church have social teachings?

"The Church makes a judgment about economic and social matters when the fundamental rights of the person or the salvation of souls requires it. She is concerned with the temporal common good of men because they are ordered to the sovereign Good, their ultimate end." (CCC 2458)

3. What is the human dimension in social teaching?

"Man himself is the author, center, and goal of all economic and social life. The decisive point of all social questions is that goods created by God for everyone should in fact reach everyone in accordance with justice and with the help of charity." (CCC 2459)

Response to objections

Whenever we deal with the Church's teachings, we should invoke the "principle of totality." This means we ought to look at the full picture of the Church's position on a given teaching and not just on a part of it. It is natural to be attracted to a particular aspect of a teaching because it suits our interest and passion for the moment. It is unwise to do this in such a way that another equally pertinent side of the teaching may be ignored, and this being done to the peril of the moral vision of the person.

The objection cited regarding the seventh commandment argues that issues of stealing, while legitimate, should cede to bigger and more pressing concerns raised by worldwide poverty, suffering, and injustice. We would concede immediately that matters of social concern are of enormous importance today. Popes since Leo XIII have spoken to the social conscience of the Church and all people of good will, urging them to hear the cry of the orphan, the widow and the alien and heal the symptoms and causes of their distress. That prophetic challenge needs constant proclamation and a concerted effort on the part of rich nations to embrace the poor ones in a worldwide strategy of solidarity and practical aid.

At the same time it would be foolhardy to ignore the everyday occurrences of plain stealing: white-collar crime, mugging, money laundering, cheating, embezzlement, shoplifting, overpricing, tax evasion, the vices of excessive campaign financing on the part of politicians, the wasting of taxpayers' money, armed robbery, various scams that bleed the income of innocent people — and all the other inventive arts of stealing that evil people have learned to invent.

It is praiseworthy to commit ourselves to bringing justice to the world. It is naïve to ignore the moral corruption that breeds everyday stealing in its myriad forms. Our baptismal call to holiness includes a commitment to honesty at personal levels as well as to a social conscience at the public stage. The stretching of our moral vision is a process that never stops as long as we breathe. It includes the personal and the communal, the private and the public, the short-range and the long-range aspects of all of life. Struggle for social justice by all means. And eliminate the scourge of stealing with equal passion.

For dialog 1. What do you think needs to be done to reduce and eliminate all forms of stealing: theft, cheating, burglary, mugging, breach of contracts, etc.? What virtues would make it possible to make everyone honest, trustworthy, and hardworking people?

2. What forms of generosity to the poor and helpless are regular practices in your family? What opportunities are available to you for volunteering at homeless shelters, food pantries, or similar charitable endeavors?

3. How do you see yourselves responding to the Church's social teachings? What political advocacy have you undertaken on behalf of the poor and helpless? How could you come to know the Church's social teachings more adequately?

Prayer Generous Father, you have placed us at the table of abundance, the goods of the earth. You have taught us that all these goods are meant for the benefit of every human being. You also give us the right to private property so our families can live in human dignity and have the stability we need for achieving proper goals here and in eternal life hereafter. At the same time you call our attention to the needs of the poor and helpless. They are our brothers and sisters and need our generosity and concern. Fill us with the courage and wisdom to keep their needs before us and do what we can to help them.

Glossary **Social Teachings of the Church** — Refers specifically to the papal teachings about social morality applied to a world where the industrial and technological revolutions raise issues about wealth, poverty, and human dignity. Beginning with Pope Leo XIII's *Rerum Novarum* to the present, these teachings form a body of developing guidance about social justice.

Universal Destination of the Goods of the Earth — This is a principle of social teachings that states that God has made the goods of creation for the benefit of every human being. People need these goods to maintain their human dignity, to provide for their families, and to achieve fulfilling goals on earth and eternal life hereafter.

"In our Gilded Age, the poorest of the poor are nearly invisible. Seven hundred million people live in the 42 so-called Highly Indebted Poor Countries, where a combination of extreme poverty and financial insolvency marks them for a special kind of despair and economic isolation."

Jeffrey Sachs,
Director of the Center for International Trade
and Development at Harvard University[2]

Endnotes

1. GS 88-89, Flannery, O.P., General Editor, *Vatican II* (Northport, NY: Costello Publishing, 1975).
2. *The Economist* magazine, August 14, 1999, p. 17.

Chapter 29

THE TRUTH WILL SET YOU FREE

CCC 2464-2513

"This above all, to thine own self be true,
And it must follow, as the night the day,
Thou canst not then be false to any man."

Shakespeare, *Hamlet*

Telling the Truth May Cause You Pain

A man named Dave, a listener of Dr. Laura Schlessinger's radio program, wrote her this story about his daughter, Michelle.

"My daughter was only days away from high school graduation when the speech and debate club took a trip to a contest. At the debate contest, the kids did some drinking. The debate coach found out the next morning and collected the kids, asking, 'Which of you were drinking?' Despite the fact that at least fifteen kids were involved, only Michelle and one other kid replied in the affirmative.

"The debate coach came down very hard on the two 'honest' students, going to the school administration and getting them kicked out of graduation, and nearly expelled without their high school diplomas. Michelle was class valedictorian, and her commencement speech was subsequently delivered by her best friend, who was threatened by the school administration, lest she should make any political statements about how two students who would not lie were treated.

"Michelle went on to college to earn a degree from Stanford with honors and distinction, a Master's from Oxford on a Marshall scholarship, and a Ph.D. from UNC Chapel Hill. She starts Yale Law School in the Fall and still has a tremendous aversion to lying.

"The 'cost' of that honesty back in 1989, has, I am sure, made Michelle even more determined that she will not have paid the price for nothing. Needless to say, I am very proud to be Michelle's father."[1]

Can We Know the Truth?

Some say... We cannot know the truth. We can only know opinions and verifiable facts. What we call truth is really subjective opinion, relative to that person's experience. We go further and assert that there is no objective truth to know.

We agree with the observation of Professor Alan Bloom in the book *The Closing of the American Mind:* "If there is one thing every college teacher in America can be certain of, it is that all, or nearly all of the students in his class will disbelieve, or think they disbelieve, in objective truth."[2]

Since we cannot know objective truth, all we can do is share our feelings and opinions. Much of what passes for truth is justification of our behavior or a rationalizing of what we would like to do. Skepticism is the only honest path to take in this situation.

Our patron saint is the philosopher Immanuel Kant. He taught that we cannot know things in themselves. We cannot know objective truth. All we can do is impose our mental categories on them, much as a baker imposes the forms of cookie cutters on unformed cookie dough. Kant realized his idea was radical.

He even called it a "Copernican Revolution in philosophy." Copernicus taught that the earth revolved around the sun, not the sun around the earth, as people had thought since the time of Ptolemy. Similarly Kant taught that truth is relative to the mind, not the mind to truth. The knower forms and determines what is true. Truth is subjective.

This is why we support ideologies and slogans and propaganda. We don't need to appeal to objective truth but rather deal with emotions and opinions. There is no right and true and proper because there are no objective standards. Objective truth is unattainable. It can't be taught. It can't be learned.

The Catechism teaches ... You shall not bear false witness against your neighbor.

The Bible teaches that God is the source of truth. Jesus Christ said, "I am the truth." (Jn 14:6) Jesus embodied truth and always told the truth. At the beginning of his Passion, Jesus was brought before Pilate where the issue of truth came to the fore. Pilate asked Jesus, "Are you a king?" (Jn 18:33) Jesus replied that his kingdom was a spiritual one, not a political realm.

A born politician always interested in power, Pilate pressed Jesus on the issue of kingship. So Christ's kingdom is spiritual. Does that mean he is king of such a realm? Jesus explained he is the king of truth. His role as king was to witness to the truth.

At the Last Supper Jesus had identified himself with truth. When Jesus spoke of truth, he included the truth of his teachings and his personal fidelity to God and others. Jesus personalized truth. Truth is attainable and it can be taught and learned. The mind can acquire truth both from revelation as well as using one's intelligence. Truth is truth whether it comes from God or from our brains.

A spiritual kingdom is based on truth. When Jesus witnessed truth, he showed how much he loved us. Truth in the mind is an idea. Truth in the heart is love. A spiritual life is possible for us because it flows from truth. This is why the Church always stresses doctrine — the truth of Christ's teaching — as well as valid philosophy that affirms that truth can be known.

Relativism in our modern culture claims there is no truth, only opinions that are more or less credible. Is it surprising then that so many people feel free to lie? Is it remarkable that many people, even Church members, downplay or ignore the Church's teachings? If doctrine is just another opinion among many in the "marketplace of ideas," then the truth of doctrine will be avoided. If we undermine the reality of truth, then we will sabotage the reality of the spiritual life. If we deny the possibility of knowing truth, then we will fail to enter Christ's spiritual kingdom, which is based on truth.

As Jesus gazed on Pilate, he saw a man trapped in pure pragmatism. He encountered a rule whose philosophy was, "To be personal is to be political." Pilate relied on compromise, power plays, ruthless action, pretense, vanity, show, and survival. He politicized his thinking to the point where his brain was virtually dead when faced with the possibility of truth. He could not believe people really lived by truth and would even die to defend it. Pilate would become one of history's best-remembered relativists.

Jesus reached out to him and offered him the hope of change. But all Pilate could do was to revert to form and mumble his cynical question, which the world has never forgotten.

"What is truth?" (Jn 18:38)

Christian martyrs know what truth means. They did not shed their blood for a lie. They surrendered their lives to stand up for truth. They showed themselves true in deeds, truthful in words. The last thing that would ever come to their minds would be duplicity, hypocrisy, or deceit. The records of the martyrs form an archive of truth whose text is written in letters of blood.

How do we sin against the truth? We have found many paths to lying: ruining the reputation of a neighbor by lies, rash judgment, detraction, perjury, calumny. Liars murder more than truth. Liars kill souls and even bodies. Hitler's book, *Mein Kampf*, proclaimed the value of lying. He argued that the Big Lie works better than small ones. Hitler's lies about the superiority of the Aryan race and the supposed danger posed by the Jews led to the Holocaust and the worst war in history. Lies violate the virtue of truthfulness. Every offense against truthfulness demands reparation.

The right to know the truth is not absolute. Charity and justice govern what may be communicated. People's safety, respect for privacy, and the common good are reasons for being silent or using discreet language about what should not be known. What is told to the priest in confession may never be revealed by the confessor under any pretext. The seal of confession is inviolable.

Similarly, professional secrets must be kept. Politicians, soldiers, doctors, lawyers, psychologists, and others in similar positions to receive confidences should preserve confidentiality. The trustworthiness of professional people is at stake, as well as the principle of keeping secrets confided under a seal of trust. In our personal relationships, where gossip arises or nosy people want to know more than they should, we should practice reserve and protect others from such intrusion on their personal lives.

The mass media has acquired enormous influence in shaping public opinion. Journalists and editorial writers and TV personalities, such as talk show hosts, should remember their responsibilities to justice, charity, and truth. As users and consumers of mass media, we should not mindlessly take in all we are fed. We must be actively engaged in looking for truth and use our critical faculties toward what we read and see. Parents need to protect their children from unhealthy and immoral influences and teach the young how to tell the difference between truth and lies, between fact and propaganda.

Truth works better than lies for the good of the family and society. Journalists and entertainers should get beyond the superficial need to shock, scandalize, and degrade by appealing to sex and violence. Just tell the truth and use imagination to build up the virtues that make for wholesome families and a healthy society. Politicians will lose the trust of people if they persist in half truths, evasiveness, and manipulation of people. Business leaders who want a loyal workforce will succeed more by being honest with employees than by bulldozing them with misinformation. Spouses will have better marriages when they insist on being truthful with each other.

The *Catechism* has an inspiring final section on the eighth commandment that deals with the connection between truth and beauty. Real art is truthful. True art invites us to contemplation of the beauty of God and the divine reflection in creation and human beings. Art expresses beauty in a language that is beyond words. In its best expression, art touches the depths of the human heart, exalts the soul, and opens the person to the mystery of God.

1. What is lying?

"Lying consists in saying what is false with the intention of deceiving one's neighbor.

"Respect for the reputation and honor of persons forbids all detraction and calumny in word or attitude.

"An offense committed against the truth requires reparation." (CCC 2508, 2507, 2509)

2. Should we preserve confidences?

" 'The sacramental seal is inviolable' (CIC, can. 983, 1). Professional secrets must be kept. Confidences prejudicial to another are not to be divulged." (CCC 2511)

3. What is the right of society regarding information?

"Society has a right to information based on truth, freedom, and justice. One should practice moderation and discipline in the use of social communications media." (CCC 2512)

Response to objections

Those who claim there is no objective truth and that it therefore cannot be known have an untenable position. We cite here the analysis of Peter Kreeft:

"All forms of skepticism of objective truth refute themselves.

'There is no truth.' Is *that* true?

'Truth is not objective.' Is that truth objective?

'Truth is not universal.' Except *that* truth?

'No one can know truth.' Except you, I suppose?

'Truth is uncertain.' Is *that* uncertain?

'All generalizations are false.' Including that one?

'You can't be dogmatic.' You say that very dogmatically.

'Don't impose your truth on me!' But you just imposed your truth on me!

'There are no absolutes.' Absolutely?

'Truth is only opinion.' So . . . that's only your opinion?"[3]

Telling the truth is the opposite of lying. The distinction between lying and telling the truth presupposes there is a truth that can be told. People have lied since the beginning of time. The real problem in our time is not that people are still lying — they are. The crucial issue today is that the so-called advanced minds and molders of thought argue there is no truth, or if there is, we cannot know it.

The result is that people have discovered all kinds of ways to justify lying because there is no truth to protect. Laborious distinctions in highly public cases of lying have reached ludicrous heights of putting fur and fuzz on the false testimony of public figures. There is even a film, *Liar, Liar*, which is based on the premise that a person cannot get through a normal day without lying. In other words, once the existence of objective truth is denied, lies occupy the playing field and their moral content is brushed away.

The casualty of shooting down truth is the loss of trust between people. The bonding of society is fragmented. The denial of truth is self-contradictory. But it is worse than that. It corrupts society and the person at the root. It breaks our covenant with Christ and God, our creator, and the Spirit, our divine teacher.

For dialog

1. What methods do you employ to assure an environment of truth telling among those you know and whom you can influence? Who is the most honest person you ever met? What was the secret of that person's trustworthiness?

2. When confronted with a lie, what do you do? When invited to share a confidence that should not be communicated how do you act? What would you do if you came across a confidence betrayed?

3. How do you help people be truthful? What can you do to train the young to evaluate TV programs, internet data, and other sources of information?

Prayer

Holy Spirit of truth, give us the gift of honesty. Show us how to tell the truth with simplicity of heart. Remind us that trust is the glue that holds people together. Help us meditate on Jesus who both taught the truth and embodied the truth in his life. Instill in us the moral courage that will make truth an act of integrity in our daily behavior.

Glossary

Relativism — Belief that one cannot know truth, only opinions.

Subjectivism — Similar to relativism. The subject is the individual who relies on oneself alone as the source of right and wrong, true and false, good and bad. This person does not subscribe to objective truths whether from divine revelation or from reason.

Truth — In the order of revelation, truth is found in Scripture, apostolic tradition, and the Magisterium of the Church — guided by the Spirit. In the human order truth can be acquired by the light of reason.

"Daytime talk shows and tabloid magazines flourish with lies and half truths. People love to hear controversy, and in many instances have lost any allegiance to the truth or any ability to search for and find the truth."

Rick Green, Southern Baptist Minister

Endnotes

1. Dr. Laura Schlessinger, *The 10 Commandments: The Significance of God's Laws in Everyday Life* (San Francisco: HarperCollins, 1999).
3. Allan Bloom, *Closing of the American Mind* (Touchstone, 1998).
4. Peter Kreeft, *Making Choices: Practical Wisdom for Everyday Moral Decision* (Servant, 1990).

Chapter 30

THE SEARCH FOR PURITY OF HEART

CCC 2514-2533

"A clean heart create for me, O God."

Psalm 51:12

King David's Heart

The Second Book of Samuel, 11:1-12:24, tells the story of King David's lust, its tragic consequences, and his subsequent repentance.

One warm and pleasant evening, King David went for a stroll on the roof of his palace. He saw a beautiful neighbor woman bathing and allowed himself to lust for her. He made inquiries about her, discovering her name was Bathsheba, the wife of Uriah, a soldier presently fighting at the front in Israel's war with the Ammonites.

David had her brought to him and they had sex together. Sometime later she sent him a message that she was pregnant by him. David summoned Uriah back from the war under the pretense of finding out the progress of the conflict. David praised the soldier, told him to take a furlough and spend time with his wife, thus hoping to cover-up his involvement in the pregnancy. But Uriah remained faithful to his pledge of temporary celibacy during active duty while a war was going on. He simply went to the palace gate and slept. He did not go home to sleep with Bathsheba.

David brought him to his quarters the next evening, plied him with food and wine and made him drunk, figuring his alcoholic state would weaken his will. But Uriah was unfazed. Once again he slept at the gate.

The next day David sent Uriah back to the war with a note to General Joab. "Place Uriah up front, where the fighting is fierce. Then pull back and have him struck down dead." (2 Sam 11:15) And so it was. Bathsheba mourned her husband. But once the mourning period was over, David sent for her. She became his wife and bore him a son.

Then the prophet Nathan went to David. He asked the king for a judgment on a certain case. In a nearby town there was a rich man and a poor one. The rich man had herds and flocks. The poor man had only one lamb whom he loved and raised like one of his children. Now the rich man had a guest. He would not kill one of his own lambs for a feast. Instead he took the poor man's lamb. What do you think of that? David grew angry. "As the Lord lives, the man who has done this merits death." (2 Sam 12:5)

Nathan said, "You are the man! God gave you a kingdom and wealth. Why did you let lust capture your mind and will? Why have you committed adultery with Bathsheba, tried to deceive Uriah and even make him drunk so that he would think he is the father? Why did you conspire to have him killed at a city wall?"

David said, "I have sinned against the Lord." (2 Sam 12:13)

The king repented of his sins. His prayer of repentance is preserved in Psalm 51. His story of how lust in the heart can lead to adultery, lies, abusing his authority by making a subordinate drunk and finally having him killed by sending him to the most dangerous part of a battle is a vivid morality story. If he had curbed the lust in his mind, heart, and will in the first place the other sins would not have occurred. He received the grace of repentance and learned from his sins. His story is both a cautionary narrative as well as a reminder that conversion is always possible no matter how deep the sin.

Are Bad Thoughts and Imaginings Immoral?

Some say... The only thoughts that mean anything are those that we decide to act upon. Our thoughts come and go all the time in an unending stream. By and large they are meaningless and have little to do with our daily acts. People who need to concentrate on a project are often distracted by this constant flow of ideas, most of which rarely have much positive impact on the issue at hand.

In the moral area, bad thoughts can arise with a certain frequency just as good ones do. Moralists try to convince us that if we decide to dwell on such evil ideas we have already begun to sin. But this cannot be so. They should be thought of as stray imaginings that come and go. It's only when we decide to act wrongly that we enter the arena of sin. A bad thought is not sinful. Only a bad act is.

Wicked thoughts are like phantoms. They have no existence. Only behavior is an existent fact. In a way we should consider the playful surge of our thoughts and imaginations as just that — restless children of our minds that race here and there, play hide and seek with our attention, but are relatively harmless regarding our behavior.

Even when these thoughts are lustful and perhaps exert a greater pull on our concentration, this makes no difference. They are just unreal and insubstantial figments of our mind. If these images are followed by lustful behavior, it is the act that is wrong, not the thought.

St. Teresa of Ávila wrote of the restless nature of her thoughts and imaginations. She called them the "monkeys of my mind." She counseled others who noticed these distracting images simply to ignore them and get on with the business of meditation. Most spiritual writers follow her lead and sometimes provide techniques for distraction-avoidance. It seems to us that they agree with our position that thoughts and imaginings are not sinful. Only evil acts are.

The Catechism teaches ...

You shall not covet your neighbor's wife.

The sixth commandment deals with external acts of fidelity and infidelity: chastity and fidelity to one's marital partner, adultery, fornication, and other allied sins.

The ninth commandment looks to the internal attitudes and intentions of the human mind and heart in areas of purity and lust.

The state of the human heart determines the morality of the person. Jesus taught that "Out of the heart come evil thoughts, murder, adultery, fornication. . ." (Mt 15:19) The sixth beatitude emphasizes the need for a pure heart for personal happiness. "Blessed are the pure in heart, for they shall see God." (Mt 5:8)

God's holiness demands that our minds and wills should excel in charity, chastity, and the love of truth that includes the content of faith. There is an essential connection between purity of heart, body, and faith. Those enslaved by a lustful heart and impure behavior will find it hard to accept the truths of faith. This is the wisdom contained in the conversation between a penitent and a confessor: "Father, I'm having problems of faith." "What is her name, my son?" There is often a moral cause for a doctrinal doubt. Sin in the heart can beget disbelief in the mind.

The modern struggle for purity. The history of Catholic doctrine associates the word "concupiscence" with the effort to be pure. Concupiscence simply means intense and passionate desire. Theology has taken the term to mean the rebellion of the sexual passions against the dictates of right reason and the sixth and ninth commandments of God. St. Paul led the way by speaking of it as the war between flesh and spirit.

This is not to say the flesh is intrinsically bad or that the passions are evil in themselves. It basically means that our minds and wills, informed by faith and strengthened by grace must keep the passions under control. We must redirect these potentially self-destructive energies to more positive and virtuous goals.

Baptism purifies us from all our sins, but the effects of original sin remain. Our minds find it hard to know the truth. Our wills are weak. Our passions are strong. This is why we must pray for the gift and virtue of purity that helps us love God with an undivided heart and treat others with reverence for their personhood, never treating them as objects, always as persons.

God's grace will give us a purity of intention by which we see clearly what God has planned for us and take the means to achieve the goal which God intends for us. We must learn to pray for purity and see it as a gift just as St. Augustine did. "I thought that continence arose from one's own powers, which I did not recognize in myself. I was foolish enough not to know . . . that no one can be continent unless you grant it. For you would surely have granted it if my inner groaning had reached your ears and I with firm faith had cast my cares upon you."[1]

Modesty. It has always been known that modesty is needed to be pure. Modesty is a form of the virtue of temperance or self-restraint. This is the very opposite of the worldly axiom, "Let it all hang out." The modest person refuses to reveal what should be hidden. The current fashions tease and torment and seduce, the very opposite of what a modest dress code would be like. Modesty also includes how we look at one another with our eyes, how we touch one another, how we act.

Modesty protects the mystery of the human person so that we do not exploit one another. Such an attitude introduces patience and reserve in our approach to one another. There is neither an unbecoming stripping of ourselves nor of the other. It becomes mutually understood that we are committed to the conditions of intimacy that are laid down by our very natures due to God's natural law implanted in our hearts as well as the principles of sexual activity laid out in revelation — in other words, the absolute connection between sexual behavior and the marital state.

The ideal of modesty is sorely challenged in a culture that has become so sexualized it is taken for granted that this is the way it should be. The thousands of sexual stimulants bombarding everyone each day from the ads in the papers and magazines, the visuals on TV, in the movies, and the internet assail the spiritual and moral sensibilities of every living person. This environment of indecency challenges all men and women both of faith and those of good will to choose modesty and to undertake the purification of a culture gone mad.

The permissive culture is based on a false premise of human freedom. It says we are free to do what we want. It should say we are free only to do what we should. We must not be discouraged. The gospel was first preached to a permissive culture, and it won the day. The gospel can renew and purify our decadent culture and remove what increases the attraction of sin. We must reassert the gospel by word and witness so that we may elevate the morality of our culture and take the potential virtues in the human heart and make them blossom by restoring them to Christ.

1. What does the ninth commandment require?

"The ninth commandment warns against lust or carnal concupiscence." (CCC 2529)

2. How shall we struggle against carnal lust?

"The struggle against carnal lust involves purifying the heart and practicing temperance." (CCC 2530)

3. What does purity of heart need?

"Purification of the heart demands prayer, the practice of chastity, purity of intention and of vision.

"Purity of heart requires the modesty which is patience, decency, and discretion. Modesty protects the intimate center of the person." (CCC 2532-2533)

Response to objections

Jesus taught, "You have heard it was said, 'You shall not commit adultery.' But I say to you, everyone who looks at a woman with lust has already committed adultery with her in his heart." (Mt 5:27-28)

Ideas have consequences. That is why it is important to act only on good ideas not bad ones — and why it is necessary not to act on immoral ideas.

The evil that is conceived in the heart becomes evil when it is retained, dwelt upon, and consented to even before any act has occurred. It is true that many such thoughts can enter our awareness, particularly today with the barrage of sexual images coming from the media and other parts of the culture. The image or thought in itself does not become evil for us until we willingly embrace it. Just being bothered by evil thoughts is not sinful, so long as we resist indulging in them and letting them influence our attitude and behavior.

The growth of and assent to evil thoughts and imaginings is already sinful because it shapes our character and attitudes which in turn dispose us to wicked behavior. Actions do not spring out of nowhere. Human acts are the results of human ideas and images.

If my thought says, "Raise your right hand and salute the flag," that is what my hand will do. If my will commands me to get out of my chair, then that is what I will do. If my head is full of lustful thoughts and my will consents to acting them out, some kind of illicit sexual behavior is likely to occur. But the sin is already in the soul before the body acts on it, thus compounding the evil.

Because we have darkened minds and weakened wills due to the damage from original sin, we will frequently find ourselves doing what we don't want to do and not doing what we want to do. This inner conflict was noticed by St. Paul in himself. "For I do not do the good I want, but I do the evil I do not want. (Rom 7:19)

This enduring moral battle between our inner life and public behavior both highlights our point about the connection between thoughts and acts, as well as the spiritual combat we are called to engage in so that there will be a proper integration between mind, imagination, and behavior.

Spiritual writers and directors urge us to confront our sinfulness both internally (in our minds, wills, and imaginations) and externally in our acts. They give us great hope for living virtuously by drawing on the saving graces of Christ given to us in the sacraments and in prayer and in the saving illumination that comes to us from Christian doctrine. Faced with this moral challenge, St. Paul seemed to throw up his hands in despair when he said, "Miserable one that I am! Who will deliver me from this mortal body? Thanks be to God through Jesus Christ our Lord." (Rom 7:24-25) In Christ he found the solution and salvation.

Therefore, our moral and spiritual growth will include the purification of our souls as well as our external acts, both by reliance on Christ's graces and the acts of virtue to which his graces lead us. Bad thoughts and imaginings can be immoral, but they can be changed and we can be transformed more deeply into Christ.

For dialog

1. How is modesty practiced in your household? What expectations do you have about clothing, music, language, TV, movies, and the Internet? What success stories from other families have been helpful to you?

2. If you were able to create a neighborhood or other communal environment that supports your Catholic family values, what would you require? What help in this matter do you expect from your parish family? How can the Church be your partner in producing a chaste culture?

3. What is the greatest obstacle you see that makes it difficult to be chaste today? What is the relationship between chastity and Marriage?

Prayer

Jesus most pure, bring to me, my family and friends the gift of chastity and modesty. Help us to resist the allurements of lust that come to us from so many parts of the culture. Help us also to overcome the rebellion of our inner passions. Draw us to meditate on your example, that of your Blessed Mother, and all the saints. Open us to realize that your divine assistance is essential for our self-conquest.

Glossary

Chastity — Bodily chastity means abstaining from sex outside of Marriage. For spouses it means no sex with anyone else. Chastity of heart means overcoming sexual lust for anyone, because lust degrades, dehumanizes, and exploits the other for one's own selfish pleasure. Married and unmarried people (priestly and religious celibates, singles, widows, and widowers) should have chastity of heart.

"In all these things we conquer overwhelmingly through him who loved us."

Rom 8:37

Endnote

1. Augustine, *Confessions* 6, 11, 20.

Chapter 31

THE LOVE OF MONEY IS
THE ROOT OF ALL EVIL

CCC 2534-2557

"Whether a man is rich or poor, observe his reaction to his possessions and you have a revealing index to his character."

Oswald Sanders

The Real Philadelphia Story

The young Katharine Drexel was one of the richest and most influential women of her time. Born in Philadelphia right after the Civil War, Katharine was the daughter of a wealthy international banker. The family firm had grown into Wall Street's powerhouse, Drexel, Burnham, Lambert. Her parents taught Katharine to be generous with her money. Mr. Drexel trained his daughter to realize money is meant to be shared with others.

Katharine experienced a personal conversion during a vacation to the western United States. She saw Native Americans mistreated and living in extreme poverty. She witnessed the misery of African-Americans dehumanized by racism. She became a major donor to the missions in the American south and west.

Her greatest gift was herself. In 1887, she met with Pope Leo XIII. She told him about the plight of the Indian and Negro peoples. She asked him if there was a religious order who worked with them. She wanted to support them. The pope responded, "Why don't you become a missionary yourself?"

At the age of thirty, following the pope's advice, she entered the Sisters of Mercy. Two years later, the heiress of the Drexel fortune founded her own religious order, the Sisters of the Blessed Sacrament. Her sisters took the vows of poverty, chastity, and obedience — and a vow "to be the mother and servant of the Indian and Negro races."

Mother Katharine Drexel used the income from her father's trust — $350,000 a year in the 1900s — to build over one hundred schools in the rural west and south. She also established Xavier University in New Orleans, the only Catholic black college in the United States. She struggled for civil rights, taking on the Ku Klux Klan and financing some of the NAACP's investigations into exploitation of black workers. At the time of her death in 1995, Mother Katharine Drexel had given more than $21 million to help found churches, schools and hospitals across the United States.

Canonized in the Jubilee Year 2000, Katharine Drexel lived the true meaning and virtue of the tenth commandment, which is heartfelt generosity — as contrasted to those who use money for greedy purposes. She put her money and her life where her heart was.

What Is the Best Way to Help the Poor?

Some say... The best way to help the poor is to increase wealth by promoting economic and technical growth. This is the "development model" that works so well for the industrial and technological nations and will be the hope for the poorer nations as well. This causes a rising tide of prosperity. When the tide rises, all the boats rise at once.

To use yet another image, we should make the pie bigger so there is more to go around for everyone. Prosperity will trickle down from the rich and benefit the poor. When there is more for everyone, everyone will have more.

Generosity and charity to the poor is a temporary solution. The structural and lasting solution is economic and technical development. Money and technology are the principal source of development. It is not the sphere of religion whose competency does not lie in these areas.

It is regrettable that greed, avarice, and exploitation will often accompany economic development. This we never approve of and heartily condemn. But we do not thereby believe that development should not happen. We argue that the tenth commandment, which forbids greed, will best be lived out in a real world by supporting the development model.

Some might say it is better to "be" more than to "have" more. But it is our experience that being more results from having more. There is not much human dignity in being dirt poor. So the most productive answer to the vision of the tenth commandment is developing all peoples to their full technological, economic, and political potential.

The Catechism *teaches* ...

You shall not covet your neighbor's house or fields nor anything that belongs to him.

Every human being faces the choice either to be greedy or to have a generous heart. Money is not the root of all evils. "The *love* of money is the root of all evils." (I Tm 6:10; emphasis added) The seventh commandment deals with the external acts of stealing and envy and injustice. The tenth commandment treats of the inner attitudes of greed and envy on the one hand and of generosity and giving on the other.

Our sinful inclinations lead us to envy what others have and to give into an unrestrained desire to amass material goods. We are born with a legitimate desire to obtain what we need to survive and take care of our families. But here we deal with a disordered expansion of such a desire. It has gotten out of hand. The greedy person will violate all laws of reason or justice to get money or property. Such a person will then sin further to keep what has been gained and may use money and possessions to commit other kinds of sins.

The *Catechism* establishes a close connection between greed and envy. Envy is an act of sadness at the sight of others' goods and can result in a disordered desire to acquire them for oneself, even if unjust means are necessary to do so. It is a tightening of the heart and a refusal of love. Baptized people should counter envy with a spirit of detachment and greed with a habit of generosity.

The tenth commandment needs the light of the first beatitude about poverty of spirit for its proper practice. The poor in spirit have learned that the ultimate and most worthy end of human desire should be God. The first beatitude calls us to be poor in spirit and preserves us from the dangers of riches, worldly honor, and useless vanity.

1. What is forbidden by the tenth commandment?

"The tenth commandment forbids avarice arising from a passion for riches and their attendant power." (CCC 2552)

2. What is envy?

"Envy is sadness at the sight of another's goods and the immoderate desire to have them for oneself. It is a capital sin.

"The baptized person combats envy through good-will, humility, and abandonment to the providence of God." (CCC 2553-2554)

3. What should be our attitude to wealth?

"Detachment from riches is necessary for entering the Kingdom of heaven." (CCC 2556)

Response to objections

The best way to help the poor is to begin with the sacred dignity and image of God found in every human person. To this vision should be added the kind of conscience formation that will uphold the beliefs, attitudes, and practices that make it possible. Having more is never enough. We should always begin with the principle of *being* more.

Development without a soul creates moral and spiritual poverty. It actually leads to the greed and avarice condemned by the tenth commandment. An excess of affluence is just as bad as an excess of poverty. When faith and God's plan for human dignity are central to our thinking and behavior, then the processes of economic, technological, and political development take their proper place.

E. F. Schumacher has this to say about the problems generated by greed and envy:

"I suggest that the foundations of peace cannot be laid by universal prosperity, in the modern sense, because such prosperity, if attainable at all, is attainable only by cultivating such drives as greed and envy, which destroy intelligence, happiness, serenity, the peaceableness of man. It could well be that rich people treasure peace more highly than poor people, but only if they feel utterly secure — and this is a contradiction in terms. Their wealth depends on making inordinately large demands on limited world resources and thus puts them on an unavoidable collision course — not primarily with the poor (who are weak and defenseless) but with other rich people.

"No one is really working for peace unless he is working primarily for the restoration of wisdom."[1]

In our study of the commandments, we have stressed repeatedly that they hold up for us a virtue to acquire as well as a vice to avoid. All of us have the opportunity to learn a healthy freedom regarding material goods. When there is a generous spirit of sharing, there is a corresponding decline in envy. When a giving attitude prevails, then the people cease to think about taking. When we find true enjoyment in one another, the hunger for things is less frantic. The consumer culture will keep breeding greed, but a Christian ethic of sharing and giving is a powerful defense against this and a positive contribution to society.

For dialog

1. If envy were out of control in your home, what would you do to turn the situation around? What family rules do you have to contain a greedy and avaricious attitude? How do you cope with our consumer culture?

2. What experiences have you had of people that were ruined by a gross

attachment to material possessions? What people do you admire for their simple lifestyle? How did they achieve it?

3. How successful are you in giving of your time, talent, and treasure to others in need? How do you think people come to know the "joy" of giving? What did St. Francis mean when he said, "It is in giving that we receive"?

Prayer

Generous God, you have poured your abundance into creation for our benefit. You have given each of us the potential for happiness so long as we use your gifts for the purpose you had in mind. Help us to put aside all envy and greed and replace these attitudes with those of generosity and selfless giving. Save us from the materialism of our culture and raise us on the food of higher virtues. Teach us to practice the maxim that it is in giving that we receive.

Glossary

Covetousness — Another name for greed. Usually refers to a selfish and unrestrained desire and effort to acquire material wealth and the power that comes with it.

Love of Money — Money alone does not corrupt us. It is the "love of money" that generates envy and greed that leads to power and domination over others.

"God divided the hands into fingers so that the money could slip through."
Martin Luther

Endnote

1. E.F. Schumacher, *Small Is Beautiful: Economics as if People Mattered* (NY: Harper-Collins, 1989).

Chapter 32

PRAYER FEEDS THE SOUL
CCC 2558-2758

"I will bless the Lord at all times. His praise will be ever on my lips."
Psalm 34:1

The Hour That Makes My Day

"Just before my ordination the thought struck me, 'Why not make an hour of adoration in the presence of the Blessed Sacrament every day?' I began that practice the following day and have continued it for over sixty years.

"The purpose of the Holy Hour is to encourage deep personal union with Christ. The holy and glorious God is constantly inviting us to come to him, to converse with him, to ask for such things as we need, and to experience what a blessing it is to give self entirely to Christ.

"Sensitive love or human love tends to decline with time, but divine love does not. The first is concerned with the body that becomes less and less responsive to stimulation, but in the order of grace, the responsiveness of the divine to tiny human acts of love intensifies.

"Neither theological knowledge nor social action alone is enough to keep us in love with Christ unless both are preceded by a personal encounter with him.

"I have found that it takes some time to catch fire in prayer. This has been one of the advantages of the Holy Hour. It is not so brief as to prevent the soul from collecting itself and shaking off the distractions of the world.

"Sitting before the Presence is like a body exposing itself to the sun to absorb its rays. In those moments one does not so much pour out written prayers, but listening takes its place. We do not say, 'Listen Lord, for thy servant speaks,' but 'Speak Lord, for thy servant listens.'

"The Holy Hour became a teacher for me. Although before we love anyone we must have a knowledge of that person, nevertheless, *after* we know, it is love that intensifies knowledge.

The Holy Hour kept my feet from wandering too far. Being tethered to the tabernacle, one's rope for finding other pastures is not so long. The dim tabernacle lamp, however pale and faint, had some mysterious luminosity to darken the brightness of 'bright lights.'

"The Holy Hour became like an oxygen tank to revive the breath of the Holy Spirit in the midst of the atmosphere of the world."[1]

Doesn't Prayer Work Best When We Feel Like Praying?

Some say... In most people's experience prayer seems to work best when the urge to pray comes upon them. This is most evident of course in times of trouble. When a spouse or a child suddenly becomes ill, we are spontaneously moved to pray and ask others for prayer. All news reports of tragedies such as earthquakes or hurricanes normally include items about people praying for safety for loved ones.

The rash of killings in school and church settings are followed by stories about people gathering in prayer to find inner support in the face of such senseless violence.

World War II popularized the saying, "There are no atheists in foxholes." The imminent threat of death caused countless soldiers to dig deep in their hearts and beg God for protection.

The reason why prayer appears to be most effective in these limited situations is that our capacity to focus our full attention on God is clearly much easier. When facing life-and-death events, all transitory interests fade away.

Even atheists are imagined as strangely groping with a way to pray as the fabled lines are applied to them, "O God, if there be a God, please help me."

Experience shows that we pray best when we are inclined to pray. It definitely helps to have an emotional push in order to pray. The feeling that we need to pray will usually motivate us to pray.

It does not seem very practical to call people to pray when they have no immediate desire to do so. That simply results in a formalistic attempt at prayer that neither satisfies the person nor contains much influence on God. There ought to be an interior fervor to accompany the prayer and this does not happen very often. It is better to wait until a situation arises which naturally attracts one to pray. When the heart is on fire, the soul will pray.

The Catechism teaches ...

God calls us to prayer. Always. We should "pray always." (1 Thess 5:17)

What is prayer?

In prayer we raise our minds and hearts to God and ask for the good things we need.

Our prayer is Trinitarian. The One God calls us to prayer. The Father gives us renewed life in our prayer. The Son advances our salvation. The Spirit increases our holiness.

Heart prayer occurs where we make our decisions that direct our futures. This prayer is beyond our psychic drives, hence pious emotions and feelings are not the same thing as heart prayer. Emotion is useful, but we must pray even when we don't feel like it. The heart beats whether we are feeling emotional or are just washed out. Heart prayer arises at the center where we experience God's truth. Finally, heart prayer is the holy ground where we encounter God.

Our prayer should arise from the heart. The word "heart" appears one thousand times in the Bible. What does this mean? The *Catechism* lists seven qualities of heart prayer. It happens where I live in the deepest part of myself. It is beyond reason, though not opposed to it. Prayer is more than thinking deep and inspiring thoughts. Such prayer is known by the Spirit whose "ear" rests next to my heart.

Scripture is filled with stories of prayer. The *Catechism* calls this the "Revelation of Prayer." God starts prayer by calling each of us to a conversation with him. We all know that God called Abraham to have faith and the patriarch responded with humble belief and trust. God called Moses to be a savior of Israel and Moses thus led his people to freedom. God called David to write the greatest prayers ever written, the Psalms, which are sung every day all over the world. God called Mary to say "yes" to having the divine child who would save the world. Her "yes" was the most important prayer response ever made.

Prayer can be seen in the whole history of salvation. It is always an event in which God calls and the person responds — and even receives the grace needed to respond. Prayer is a uniquely divine-human event, with the divine graces calling us and helping us to answer.

Jesus gave us the Holy Spirit to teach the Church and its members what Jesus wanted us to know, remember, and practice. The Spirit is our chief prayer teacher. From the Spirit we learn how to praise God for every single blessing we have. The Spirit moves us to ask God for what we need, not because God doesn't know our needs, but because we need to express and realize what is necessary for our lives. The Spirit creates a lifeline between us and Mary and the saints, who have a powerful place of intercession in the heavenly court. The prayer of intercession puts constantly on our lips the words "Pray for us."

There is never a moment in which we are not the beneficiary of divine gifts — our life, family, friends, food, material benefits, etc. Hence our mouths should always be filled with "Thank You! Thank You! Thank You!" All we own we owe to God. A grateful heart is a prayerful heart. Because God blesses our hearts, they have the intrinsic skill needed to bless God in return.

The Tradition of Prayer. The Spirit manifested the Church at Pentecost and continues to sustain and nourish the Church, especially the Church's prayer life. Our prayer will be authentic when it is fed from the richest possible sources: Scripture, the Church's liturgy, and the practice of the virtues of faith, hope, and love. When trained by these sources we quickly learn that prayer is primarily addressed to the Father, from whom all blessings flow.

Various schools of spirituality have arisen throughout Church history that have stayed in constant and productive touch with the Church's living tradition of prayer. These schools offer us incomparable guidance for our spiritual life. To cite a few of these approaches, we mention the *lectio divina* (the divine reading — meditative reading of the liturgical texts and Scripture) of the Benedictine and Trappist tradition, the contemplative wisdom of the Carmelite school, and the Jesuit Exercises of St. Ignatius.

But no school can replace the family, which is the domestic church and the first place we learn to pray.

The Life of Prayer. In the name of God, the Church calls us to prayer every day. We should not wait until we feel the "urge" to pray. It matters little what we feel. It's the call that counts and that is given to us always. The "ear" of the Spirit is always next to our heart waiting to hear our cry. The Church trains us in prayer by instructing us to begin and end our days with personal prayers. The Church invites us also to daily Eucharist and the Liturgy of the Hours — especially Morning and Evening Prayer. For this latter prayer, consider using "The Prayer of Christians," which contains the morning and evening Liturgy of the Hours.

When our prayer flows from the liturgy (including the feasts of the liturgical year), we are put in touch with the whole Body of Christ. Our minds and hearts are shaped by the universal prayer of Christ praying in the heart of the Church. "Pray in us, Jesus, as head of the Church. Pray for us as our priest. We adore you as our God." The daily training and practice we receive from liturgical prayer establishes the rock upon which our meditative prayer can rest securely. In liturgical prayer we learn directly from the Holy Spirit how to pray and why we must never tire of praying.

The Three Expressions of Prayer. The three ways to pray may be captured in this prayer: "May the Lord be in my mind (meditation), on my lips (vocal prayer), and in my heart (contemplation)." These three forms of prayer always are connected to the "heart prayer" mentioned above.

• Vocal Prayer — Lips. It is not unusual that prayer should be associated with something physical, such as our voices. After all, the Word became flesh to speak to us. Our words "become flesh" in prayer. Jesus prayed out loud in the Temple, the Upper Room, at Gethsemane, and on the Cross. If Jesus did it, so can we. We are body and spirit. We need to translate our inner feelings and thoughts externally. Nonetheless, all vocal prayer should be accompanied by the presence of our heart, so that our words are more than mere idle chatter.

• Meditation — Mind. The mind needs to understand what God wants of us. This is not easy to do. Books help us, especially the Bible, the writings of the Fathers, and the great masters of the spiritual life. We can also learn from the "books" of creation and history. Meditative writings help us to pass from our thoughts to the reality of our lives. They train us to be reflective in an atmosphere of grace. There are many meditation methods. A method is a means to an end, which is an encounter with Jesus. Let the Spirit guide you along this path. Meditation mobilizes thoughts, imaginations, feelings, and desires to one purpose — meeting Christ.

• Contemplation — Heart. In an excellent section on this topic (CCC 2709-2719), the *Catechism* offers the following suggestions for contemplation prayers.

(1) Take time to be alone with Christ. Choose a regular time every day for this. Gather up your whole self to enter the presence of Jesus who awaits you. Pray with the humble childlikeness of a forgiven sinner, aided by the Spirit. Recall that contemplative prayer is always a gift that we should accept with humility and a recognition of our poverty.

(2) Surrender to the "intensity" of this prayer so that you will be grounded in love. Gaze with faith upon Jesus. You will learn that Christ in turn gazes on you with affection and with a look that is purifying. Listen to God's word with the obedience of faith (Rom 16:26). Sink from this divine word into the silence of God. Learn that your contact with the mystery of Christ in contemplation enriches your encounter with Jesus in the Eucharist. All prayer must cope with distraction and dryness. It will not always be easy. Hence, be ready to abide in the "night of faith" of Jesus at Gethsemane, the tomb, and the Easter vigil for the sake of the Church.

1. What is the "Revelation" of prayer?

"God tirelessly calls each person to this mysterious encounter with Himself. Prayer unfolds throughout the whole history of salvation as a reciprocal call between God and man." (CCC 2591)

2. What is the Holy Spirit's role in prayer?

"The Holy Spirit who teaches the Church and recalls to her all that Jesus said also instructs her in the life of prayer, inspiring new expressions of the same basic forms of prayer: blessing, petition, intercession, thanksgiving, and praise." (CCC 2644)

"By a living transmission — Tradition — the Holy Spirit in the Church teaches the children of God to pray." (CCC 2661)

3. How often should we pray?

The Church must "'pray constantly' (1 Thess 5:17) It is always possible to pray. It is even a vital necessity. Prayer and the Christian life are inseparable." (CCC 2757)

Response to objections

St. Paul teaches that we should "pray always." (1 Thess 5:17)

To argue that we should pray only when we feel like it is like saying we should breathe only when the urge to do so moves us. Prayer is the life blood of the soul, just as breathing is for the body.

To claim that praying is effective only when we experience hard times is like arguing that love should be reserved for times of crisis alone.

Like love, prayer is the expression of a relationship. Successful relationships need constant attention and care. So also does prayer. Prayer is an act of love for God. If we let days and weeks and years go by without praying, how can we say we love God?

To reserve prayer for occasions when our emotions stir us is to build our relationship with God on the shifting sands of feelings. Feelings come and go, but a real relationship should last all the time. If we show affection for friends only when in the mood to do so, we will not have any friends. People expect us to be steady in our commitment to them.

God invites us to be firm in our love for him. Of course God never stops loving us. But God cannot force us to love him. Regular prayer is a sign that we do so. We do not pray to pacify God. We pray to receive the love that will keep us from all evil and fill us with the energies that will make us perfectly human — and like unto God.

When St. Paul advises us to pray always, he is asking us to never stop finding ways to love God. Love is a virtue. A virtue is a habit. A habit can only be acquired by repeated, small acts until the behavior becomes second nature to us. A habit grooves the body as well as the soul. Those who have the habit of daily exercise will maintain the behavior to the point where the failure to do so will make us miss it. The body will "complain" and itch us to get out and walk — or whatever we have been doing.

The same is true with the habit of prayer. Once the virtue is grooved into our souls, we will do it easily and miss it if we fail to keep it up.

No, we should not just pray when we feel like it.

We should pray always.

For dialog

1. What have you been doing to deepen your prayer life? How do you balance and integrate meditation with spoken and communal prayer? Why is it important to pray every day at regular times? What is the connection between liturgical prayer and your personal and private prayer?

2. How could you create a meditation space where silence makes it possible for some daily meditation? What are some books and articles you have read which motivate you to pray? What do you find is the best time to pray?

3. Who are people you admire for their prayer lives? What could you learn from them? What are some prayers God has answered for you? How do the liturgy and Scripture help you to pray?

Prayer

Father, you call us to prayer constantly. You also provide us with the graces to respond. Help us to be aware of your invitations to pray and of the presence of the Holy Spirit who helps us meet you in prayer. May we learn that prayer is our lifeline to you and the food of our souls. We know the Spirit places his "ear" to our hearts to hear our response. In your kindness prompt us to join you in this communion of love, which is the act of prayer.

Glossary

Prayer — The raising of one's mind and heart to God or the requesting of good things from God.

"I always begin my prayer in silence, for it is in the silence of the heart that God speaks. God is the friend of silence — we need to listen to God because it's not what we say but what He says to us and through us that matters.

"Prayer feeds the soul — as blood is to the body so prayer is to the soul.

"Prayer brings you closer to God. It gives you a clean and pure heart. A clean heart can see God, speak to god, and can see the love of God in others."[2]

Mother Teresa

Endnotes

1. Fulton J. Sheen, *Treasure in Clay: The Autobriography of Fulton J. Sheen* (Ignatius Press, 1993).
2. Mother Teresa, *A Simple Path* (Ballantine, 1995).

Chapter 33

PRAYING THE OUR FATHER
CCC 2803-2865

"For me, prayer is a surge of the heart; it is a simple look toward heaven, it is a cry of recognition and of love, embracing both trial and joy."

St. Thérèse of Lisieux

Prayer Makes the Soul One With God

"If we do what we can and ask in truth for mercy and grace, then all we lack we shall find in him.

"I am sure that no one can ask for mercy and grace with his whole heart, unless mercy and grace have already been given him.

"We follow God and he draws us to himself by love. For I saw and understood that his great overflowing goodness fulfills all our gifts.

"Prayer makes the soul one with God.

"The soul is immediately at one with God, when it is truly at peace in itself.

"God is our sure rock, and he shall be our whole joy and make us as changeless as he is, when we reach heaven.

"When we come to receive the reward that grace has won for us, then we shall thank and bless our Lord, forever rejoicing that we were called upon to suffer.

"I saw full surely that wherever our Lord appears, peace reigns and anger has no place. For I saw no anger in God either in the short or long term.

"Truth sees God, wisdom beholds God and from these two comes a third, a holy and wondering delight in God which is love. Where there is truth and wisdom there is also true love, springing from them both.

"Flee to God and we shall be comforted. Touch him and we shall be made clean. Cling to him and we shall be safe and sound from all kinds of danger. For our courteous Lord wills that we should be as at home with him as the heart may think or the soul desire."[1]

What Kind of Needs Should We Pray For?

Some say... It would seem that people can be persuaded to pray when they have immediate material and physical needs to satisfy. Even Jesus recommends in the Our Father that we say, "Give us this day our daily bread."

When a man has an empty stomach he wants food. In any pyramid of needs, it appears we should start with survival. People are more likely to pray for food in the kitchen and some money in the pocket before they begin to pray for heavenly and spiritual benefits.

Virtually all prayers that people ask for concern safety and health. This demonstrates that human need at the material and physical level deserves to have the priority in prayer. People that are anxious about family stability and personal security will direct their prayers to these concerns before anything else.

Take a walk through a hospital and the plea you will hear is a prayer for healing. Stop at a shelter for the homeless and you will hear the cry of the poor for a clean bed and a bowl of soup. Eavesdrop at a welfare office and you will hear people beg for enough money to pay this month's rent. Human need is what moves people to pray for life's necessities.

When a crazed gunman invades a school cafeteria, the prayer from the panic-stricken students is for mercy and safety from harm. Someone being mugged will pray that the robber spares his or her life. "Just take the money but leave me alone."

Prayer needs begin at these fundamental levels. When bombs fall parents pray to God to spare their children. When ticks and mosquitoes bear lyme disease and encephalitis, people worriedly check their bodies and pray that the poison has not entered their systems.

There is doubtless a time when we should pray for heavenly gifts, such as forgiveness of sins and a place in eternal life. But our inclination is to pray for more down-to-earth needs.

The Catechism teaches ... Certainly Christ teaches that we should pray for our human needs. But he places all prayer in a context of the purpose of our lives, which is salvation from sins and life in the Holy Spirit and our ultimate destination, which is heaven. This is made most evident in the seven petitions of the Our Father.

The gospels show Jesus praying many times, both in public as well as alone all night on a mountain. Christ's witness of prayer so impressed the apostles that they asked him to teach them how to pray. Christ replied by teaching them the Our Father. The *Catechism* devotes its final section to a meditation on the seven petitions of the Our Father. Here we look at the highlights of the *Catechism's* treatment of the Lord's Prayer.

Our Father. Jesus began with the words, "Our Father." Jesus tells us that he wants us to meet his Father and to know what he is like. By his saving work in the paschal mystery of his death and Resurrection, Jesus can bring us to the Father as an adopted son and daughter. That is why we are able to say "Our" because we have become the Father's children in the adoption of grace. We are in communion with Jesus and the Church and thus have drawn away from any individualism that isolates us from others. We are indeed unique persons, but always in communion with one another and the members of the Trinity.

Hallowed Be Thy Name. We first heard the name of God when it was revealed to Moses at the burning bush. God said, "I AM." God therefore was not a thing, not the moon worshiped by the Babylonians, nor the sun adored by the Egyptians, nor a star worshiped by the Assyrians. God is a person who can know and love us and save us from our sins and follies. Philosophy can know God from reason, but such a god is hardly more than an idea, an abstraction that leaves us cold. God revealed himself as a person to Moses and the prophets.

Then Jesus came and showed us that God is a Father who has begotten a Son, both of whom sent us the Spirit. The Name of God is Trinity, a loving community of persons — loving each other and loving us with infinite, compassionate, and forgiving affection. God's name is holy because the Father is divine and beyond us, yet through love as near to us as our hearts. The infinite God is both "mighty Father" and intimate, an affectionate Hebrew term for "daddy" — Abba.

Thy Kingdom Come. Jesus preached the kingdom of God during his ministry in Galilee and Judea. Jesus said that his gospel and his very self embodied this kingdom, already present, yet still to come in us and the Church in all its fullness. The kingdom exists, but we pray that the kingdom will take possession of us so that we may live and witness it in the world.

What is this kingdom? It is the appearance of God's rule in the world, a rule that establishes love, justice, and mercy. It is a divine, transcendent, supernatural kingdom that by the Father's power penetrates the world through the Church and its members. This kingdom is only partially realized on earth. We will experience its fullness in heaven.

Though it sounds like a political term, the reality of the kingdom is never the same as a state, a government, or a social arrangement. True, it has the quality of a dream, of an ideal human system that leads some thinkers to imagine a "utopia" on earth. But the kingdom is resolutely a divine reality that does indeed have an impact on politics and society, though it is meant to move us all beyond the present age to the world to come.

We beg the Father to make his kingdom come more effectively in our lives, our Church, and the world. We are basically praying for Christ's love, justice, and mercy to take hold of all of us more deeply.

Thy Will Be Done. The human heart is the fundamental battleground in the world. All external conflicts are reflections on this interior war we experience within ourselves. Reduced to its simplest components, this war is between God's will and ours. Our song is usually, "I'll do it my way." That was the fatal lyric of Adam and Eve — as well as of the devil and his fallen angels. God declares his will. We are faced with the choice of his will or ours. We can choose the obedience of faith or the disobedience of pride. We should say this prayer often and with great fervor, "Thy will be done."

Why do we act otherwise? Why is it hard to follow God's will? We are born in the state of original sin, the result of the disobedience of our first parents. By Baptism we are delivered from this state and restored to original holiness and justice. Christ's saving act on the Cross and in the Resurrection made this possible.

But we retain what St. Thomas Aquinas calls the "wounds" of original sin. They are: (1) Ignorance in the mind, which makes it hard to know the truth or even to believe knowledge of truth is possible; (2) malice in the heart, a movement that replaces the heart's instinctive wish to love with a spiteful approach to others; (3) emotionalism, which should be at the service of reason, but is rebellious, advocating an independence of the passions; and (4) weakness in the will, which ought to be submitting to God's will, but tends to prefer one's own wishes to those of God.

Our problematic wills cause us the most trouble and activate the other three wounds to push us away from God. It's no mistake that abortionists use the expression "pro-choice," a celebration of a sinful will. We should reverse this misuse of the will by praying with all our hearts that God's will be done.

Give Us This Day Our Daily Bread. St. Augustine says we pray, not to let God know our needs, but to remind ourselves of our needs. After all, God does know what we need, but until we are aware of what those needs are, God cannot give us what we don't think we should have. God never forces himself on us. He respects our freedom and urges us to use it productively.

Above all, the Eucharist is our daily bread. The Eucharist is the summit and source of our holiness and salvation. Every spiritual gift that we need is contained in the Eucharist. Just as we need physical food for daily nourishment, so we need supernatural food to minister to the hunger of our souls.

We should not be too proud to beg. We ought not be like the biblical man who said he was too weak to dig and too ashamed to beg. There is dignity in begging for graces we cannot obtain unless we ask for them. The fictional woman Auntie Mame, said "Life is a banquet and all you fools are starving!" What she said about worldly pleasures is also true of spiritual ones. Why starve when our Father has an armload of Bread for us, if only we would ask?

Forgive Us Our Trespasses As We Forgive Those Who Trespass Against Us. The best way to obtain mercy is to be merciful. The measure of forgiveness that we hope will come our way is proportionate to our willingness to forgive others. Failure to forgive others is one of the greatest of all human problems. Holding grudges against others is as common as the air we breathe. Families, neighborhoods, and countries are routinely torn apart by failures to forgive.

Read and meditate on Psalm 37: Fret not. Be still before the Lord. Wait in patience. Calm your anger and forget your rage. God does not accept the sacrifices of the sowers of disunity. We celebrate the Eucharist of forgiveness. We must practice it too. God practices fore-giveness, not after-giveness. Forgiveness causes repentance and makes reconciliation possible. After-giveness is too pompous because it means we withhold our forgiveness until the other grovels and apologizes before us. We want to humiliate, not forgive. We want to exact our pound of flesh before we give mercy.

By offering forgiveness, we receive the forgiveness we need and open others' hearts to the repentance that leads to reconciliation.

Lead Us Not Into Temptation. Temptations help us see what our moral weaknesses are and motivate us to correct our character flaws. The Holy Spirit helps us distinguish between challenges that develop our moral character and temptations that lead us into sin. Our response to temptation is a decision of the heart. Jesus endured temptations in the desert at the beginning of his public ministry and at Gethsemane at the end of his ministry. Jesus resisted temptations, exposed the lies of the tempter, and submitted to the Father's will instead.

No temptations need overcome us. "God is faithful and will not let you be tried beyond your strength; but with the trial he will also provide a way out, so you may be able to bear it" (1 Cor 10:13). A life of prayer is essential for overcoming temptations. A solid spiritual life is the best guarantee for having the strength to resist temptations to sin.

But Deliver Us From Evil. We live in a world where good and evil live side by side. We cannot escape the presence of evil around us. But we can be delivered from its power to corrupt and damn us. We pray to God for the practical application of the salvation we receive and experience as members of the Church, participants in the sacraments, and practitioners of the virtues. We are always in the process of being saved, which is another way of saying we need a lifelong purification from sin and its effects as well as growth in union with Christ and the practice of virtues. A saint is a sinner making progress toward holiness.

The *Catechism* in this section highlights the reality of Satan as a source of evil temptations. This is to say that evil is more than an abstraction; it is embodied in a person. Satan was a "murderer from the beginning. . . . When he tells a lie, he speaks in character, because he is a liar and the father of lies." (Jn 8:44) We are engaged in a spiritual warfare. We struggle against the principalities and powers of evil.

But we do not fight alone. Christ fights with us. The Spirit and the Church are our helpers. We must remember that God is more powerful than evil. Grace is stronger than sin. Hence there is no reason for pessimism or defeatism. We have won the victory over evil through the work of Christ. With him, in him, and through him we shall prevail. Christian tradition, with a surge of gratitude for this teaching on prayer, has added, "for the kingdom, the power, and the glory are yours now and forever." This exclamation of praise is found in many passages of the Book of Revelation, one text of which we cite here:

Doxology
"Worthy is the Lamb that was slain
to receive power and riches,
wisdom and strength,
honor and glory and blessing" (Rev 5:11).

1. What does the Lord's Prayer summarize?
" 'The Lord's Prayer is truly the summary of the whole gospel' [Tertullian, *De Orat.* 1: PL 1, 1251-1255]." (CCC 2774)
"[It] is the quintessential prayer of the Church." (CCC 2776)

2. Why can we call God "Father"?
"We can invoke God as 'Father' because the Son of God made man has revealed him to us. . . .
"The Lord's Prayer brings us into communion with the Father and with his Son, Jesus Christ." (CCC 2798-2799)

3. What are the purposes of the seven petitions of the Lord's Prayer?
"In the Our Father, the object of the first three petitions is the glory of the Father: the sanctification of his name, the coming of the kingdom, and the fulfillment of his will. The four others present our wants to him: they ask that our lives to be nourished, healed of sin, and made victorious in the struggle of good over evil." (CCC 2857)

Response to objections

All prayer should be undertaken with our final purpose and future destiny in mind. That is why the first three petitions of the Our Father lift our hearts to God whose kingdom is our ultimate home and whose will guides us there. God always answers any prayer that is directed to the goal of our existence, which is union with him in eternal life.

God will respond favorably to any prayer we make for our material and physical needs so long as they are consistent with the reason for our existence and assist us to reach our heavenly goal. If we think God has not answered a given prayer, we should reflect on our desires and consider whether or not what we want will bring us closer to God.

It has often been said that God answers every prayer. Sometimes he says "No." This is because his wisdom tells him that what we desire will hold us back from progress in our pilgrimage to eternal life. God's denial of our petition may also mean that what we want would impede our personal spiritual and human growth and development — or that of those for whom we pray.

God's response to us always arises from his love and affection from us. He knows what we need to make progress in happiness, virtue, and grace. God will never give us what could dehumanize us or reduce the authentic joy that we seek.

Our insight into ourselves is no easy matter. It takes time and experience to realize what our basic spiritual needs really are. We have noted that God knows beforehand what we need. Our prayers are devices by which we grow in awareness of what we require. As we gain spiritual maturity, we begin to conform our wills to the divine will. Gradually our prayers are identified with what God would love to give us because we are now intuitively in touch with the loving will of the Lord.

Every saint echoes the plain and simple truth, "Thy will be done." That is our goal. It is simple to say, but hard to achieve. When we have experientially learned how to do this, with God's grace, then we have arrived at what petitionary prayer is all about.

For dialog

1. What prayers have you memorized? Which ones should still be added to your memory? What is the value of a memorized prayer? Why is it important to know and probe the meaning of memorized prayers?

2. What are some prayer stories from your family you would like to share with others? What prayer stories from other families have you heard which have inspired you? What has been your experience in surrendering yourself to God's will? How persistent have you been in prayer

especially when it seems that God seems to be saying "No" too often?

3. What has convinced you to believe in the power of prayer? Why do you think some people stop praying? What are examples of prayer converting people who otherwise would have seemed impossible cases?

Prayer

Lord Jesus, thank you for giving us the Our Father to show us both how to pray and what to pray for. Each time we say the Our Father, be with us to say the words from our hearts and with the same attitude you brought to the prayer. Show us how to avoid being mechanical in our praying. Fill us with the patience and peace that makes profound praying so settling for our souls and so beneficial for those for whom we pray.

Glossary

Hallowed — Old English word for holy. In the Our Father we sound as if we are saying that God's name should become holy. But God's name is already holy. Our petition both reminds us of God's holiness and our responsibility to reverence the holiness of God.

Trespass — Our sins, especially those sins of failure to forgive. We ask for forgiveness of our sins in the measure of our willingness to forgive others' offenses against us.

"Hold thou thy Cross before my closing eyes;
Shine through the gloom and point me to the skies;
Heaven's morning breaks, and earth's vain shadows flee;
In life, in death, O Lord, abide with me."

H. F. Lyte

Endnote

1. Mother Julian of Norwich, *Enfolded in Love.*

Appendix

Prayers Every Catholic Should Know

The Sign of the Cross

In the name of the Father, and of the Son, and of the Holy Spirit. Amen.

Our Father (Lord's Prayer)

Our Father who art in heaven, hallowed be thy name; thy kingdom come; thy will be done on earth as it is in heaven. Give us this day our daily bread; and forgive us our trespasses as we forgive those who trespass against us; and lead us not into temptation, but deliver us from evil. (For thine is the kingdom and the power and the glory forever.) Amen.

Hail Mary

Hail Mary, full of grace. The Lord is with you. Blessed are you among women, and blessed is the fruit of your womb, Jesus. Holy Mary, Mother of God, pray for us sinners, now and at the hour of our death. Amen.

Prayer of Praise

Glory be to the Father, and to the Son, and to the Holy Spirit: as it was in the beginning, is now, and will be forever. Amen.

Prayer to the Holy Spirit

Come Holy Spirit, fill the hearts of your faithful, and enkindle in them the fire of your love. Send forth your Spirit and they shall be created, and you shall renew the face of the earth.

O God, who instructed the hearts of the faithful by the light of your divine Spirit, grant us by that same Spirit to be truly wise and to rejoice in your holy consolation through the same Christ, our Lord. Amen.

Act of Contrition

O my God, I am heartily sorry for having offended Thee, and I detest all my sins because of Thy just punishments. But most of all because they offend Thee, my God, who art all good and deserving of all my love. I firmly resolve, with the help of thy grace, to confess my sins, to do penance, and to amend my life. Amen.

Apostles' Creed

I believe in God the Father Almighty, Creator of heaven and earth; and in Jesus Christ, his only Son, our Lord. He was conceived by the power of the Holy Spirit, and born of the Virgin Mary. He suffered under Pontius Pilate, was crucified, died, and was buried. He descended to the dead. On the third day he arose again. He ascended into heaven, and is seated at the right hand of the Father. He will come again to judge the living and the dead. I believe in the Holy Spirit, the holy Catholic Church, the Communion of Saints, the forgiveness of sins, the resurrection of the body, and life everlasting. Amen.

Act of Faith

O my God, I firmly believe that you are one God in three divine persons, Father, Son, and Holy Spirit; I believe that your Divine Son became man and died for our sins, and that he will come to judge the living and the dead. I believe these and all the truths that the holy Catholic Church teaches, because you revealed them, who can neither deceive nor be deceived. Amen.

Act of Hope

O my God, relying on your infinite goodness and promises, I hope to obtain pardon of my sins, the help of your grace, and life everlasting, through the merits of Jesus Christ, my Lord and Redeemer. Amen.

Act of Love

O my God, I love you above all things, with my whole heart and soul, because you are all good and worthy of all love. I love my neighbor as myself for the love of you. I forgive all who have injured me, and I ask pardon of all whom I have injured. Amen.

The Rosary

The rosary is an important prayer in Catholic Tradition. It involves vocal prayers (Apostles' Creed, Our Father, Hail Mary, Prayer of Praise), meditative prayer (on the mysteries of the rosary), and usually the use of rosary beads as a person or a group of people say the rosary.

Mysteries of the Rosary

Joyful Mysteries — events surrounding the birth and early life of Jesus
Annunciation
Visitation
Birth of Jesus
Presentation in the Temple
Finding the Child Jesus in the Temple

Sorrowful Mysteries — events surrounding the passion and death of Jesus
    Agony in the Garden
    Scourging at the Pillar
    Crowning with Thorns
    Jesus Carries His Cross
    Death of Jesus on the Cross

Glorious Mysteries — events and faith of the early Church's experience
    Resurrection of Jesus from the Tomb
    Ascension into Heaven
    Descent of the Holy Spirit upon the Apostles
    Assumption of Mary into Heaven
    Coronation of Mary as Queen of Heaven and Earth

Seven Sacraments in the Catholic Church

Baptism
Confirmation
Eucharist (Communion)
Reconciliation (Penance, Confession)
Marriage
Holy Orders
Anointing of the Sick (formerly called Extreme Unction)

Seven Capital Sins

    Pride
    Covetousness
    Lust
    Anger
    Gluttony
    Envy
    Sloth

Order of Mass

    Gathering and Entrance Procession
    Greeting
    Opening Prayer
    Prayer of Praise
    Penitential Rite

Liturgy of the Word
First Reading (usually from the Old Testament)
Psalm Response
Second Reading (usually from an epistle in the New Testament)
Gospel
Homily
Creed
Prayer of the Faithful

Liturgy of the Eucharist
Preparation and Offering of the Gifts of Bread and Wine
Preface Prayer of Praise and Thanksgiving
Eucharistic Prayer (including words of consecration and concluding with the community's great AMEN)
Communion Rite: Lord's Prayer, Sign of Peace, Communion, Meditation
Concluding Prayer
Blessing
Dismissal

Rite of Reconciliation for Individuals
(Penance, Confession)

Greeting from the Priest
Sign of the Cross
Scripture Passage
Confession of Sin
Here, honestly confess the sins that have been part of your life. All serious matter should be included, as well as less serious things that are troublesome in your life with the Lord.
Advice and Spiritual Counseling
Penance
The prayer or good work that you will be asked to take on is a sign of your sincere repentance.
Prayer of Sorrow or Contrition
Absolution
The Priest places his hands on your head (or extends his right hand toward you) and prays these words of forgiveness:

"God, the Father of mercies, through the death and resurrection of his Son has reconciled the world to himself and sent the Holy Spirit among us for the forgiveness of sins; through the ministry of the Church may God give you pardon and peace, and I absolve you from your sins in the name of the Father, and of the Son, and of the Holy Spirit."

Prayer of Praise, such as:
> Priest: Give thanks to the Lord, for he is good.
> Response: His mercy endures forever.
> Dismissal, such as:
> The Lord has freed you from your sins. Go in peace.

Responsibilities for Catholics

The Great Commandment

"You shall love the Lord your God with all your heart, with all your soul, and with all your mind. You shall love your neighbor as yourself." (Mt 22:37-39)

The Ten Commandments

(cf. Ex 20; Chapter 15 of Invitation)

1. I am the Lord your God. You shall honor no other god but me.
2. You shall not misuse the name of the Lord, your God.
3. You shall keep holy the Sabbath.
4. You shall honor your father and mother.
5. You shall not kill.
6. You shall not commit adultery.
7. You shall not steal.
8. You shall not bear false witness against your neighbor.
9. You shall not covet your neighbor's wife.
10. You shall not covet your neighbor's goods.

The Beatitudes

(cf. Mt 5)

1. Blessed are the poor in spirit; the reign of God is theirs.
2. Blessed are the sorrowing; they shall be consoled.
3. Blessed are the lowly; they shall inherit the land.
4. Blessed are they who hunger and thirst for holiness; they shall have their fill.
5. Blessed are they who show mercy; mercy shall be theirs.
6. Blessed are the single-hearted; they shall see God.
7. Blessed are the peacemakers; they shall be called sons of God.
8. Blessed are those persecuted for holiness sake; the reign of God is theirs.

Spiritual Works of Mercy

> To admonish the sinner
> To instruct the ignorant
> To counsel the doubtful

To comfort the sorrowful
To bear wrongs patiently
To forgive all injuries
To pray for the living and the dead

Corporal Works of Mercy
To feed the hungry
To give drink to the thirsty
To clothe the naked
To visit the imprisoned
To shelter the homeless
To visit the sick
To bury the dead

Laws of the Church
Read the *Catechism* 2041 to 2043.

Holy Days of Obligation *(in the United States)*
January 1 — Solemnity of Mary, Mother of God
Ascension Thursday — 40 Days after Easter
August 15 — Feast of the Assumption
November 1 — All Saints' Day
December 8 — Feast of the Immaculate Conception
December 25 — Christmas Day

Regulations for Fast and Abstinence
Fasting means giving up food, or some kinds of food, for a specified period of time. In Church regulations, abstinence means giving up meat for certain times. (For many years, abstinence was required of Catholics every Friday, as a communal way of observing Friday as a day for special penance. Catholics are no longer required to abstain from meat each Friday, although they are expected to exercise some form of penance on that day, in remembrance of Jesus' death for us.) Catholics are expected to fast from food and liquids (other than water and medicine) for one hour before receiving Holy Communion.

Certain days are also set aside as days of fast and abstinence for Catholics, when adults are expected to eat only minimum amounts of food, no meat, and nothing between meals at all. In the United States, Ash Wednesday and Good Friday are such days of fast and abstinence.

Index

List of Abbreviations

Acts	Acts of the Apostles, New Testament
Col	St. Paul's letter to the Colossians, New Testament
Cor	First and second letters of St. Paul to the Corinthians, New Testament
CPG	Solemn Profession of Faith: Credo of the People of God
DS	Denzinger-Schönmetzer, *Enchiridion Symbolorum et Definitionum*, handbook on the decrees and enactments of the councils written in 1854.
Dt	Deuteronomy, Old Testament
DV	*Dei Verbum*, Divine Revelation, Vatican II document.
Eph	St. Paul's letter to the Ephesians, New Testament
Ex	Exodus, Old Testament
GCD	General Catechetical Directory
Gn	Genesis, Old Testament
GS	*Gaudium et Spes*, The Church in the Modern World, Vatican II document
Heb	Letter to the Hebrews, once thought to be authored by St. Paul, New Testament
John	Gospel according to John, New Testament
LG	*Lumen Gentium*, The Light of the World, Vatican II document
LH	Liturgy of the Hours
MC	*Marialis cultus*, Devotion to the Blessed Virgin Mary, Pope Paul VI
Mt	Gospel according to Matthew, New Testament
OR	Office of Readings
Pt	First and second epistles (letters) from Peter, New Testament
Rom	St. Paul's letter to the Romans, New Testament
RSV	Revised Standard Version (of the Bible)
SC	*Sacrosanctum Concilium*, Sacred Liturgy, Vatican II document.
STh	*Summa Theologica*, St. Thomas Aquinas' explanation of Christian beliefs, 1267.
Tim	St. Paul's letter to Timothy, New Testament

Our Sunday Visitor

*Your Source for Discovering
the Riches of the Catholic Faith*

Our Sunday Visitor has an extensive line of materials for young children, teens, and adults. Our books, Bibles, booklets, CD-ROMs, audiocassettes, and videos are available in bookstores worldwide.

To receive a FREE full-line catalog, or for more information, call **Our Sunday Visitor** at **1-800-348-2440**. Or write: **Our Sunday Visitor**, 200 Noll Plaza, Huntington, IN 46750.

❏ Please send me a catalog.

Please send me material on:

❏ Apologetics/Catechetics   ❏ Reference works
❏ Prayer books   ❏ Heritage and the saints
❏ The family   ❏ The parish

Name _____

Address _____

City _____ ST _____ Zip_____

Telephone (_____)_____

AO3BBABP

❏ Please send a friend a catalog.

Please send a friend material on:

❏ Apologetics/Catechetics   ❏ Reference works
❏ Prayer books   ❏ Heritage and the saints
❏ The family   ❏ The parish

Name _____

Address _____

City _____ ST _____ Zip_____

Telephone (_____)_____

AO3BBABP

OUR SUNDAY VISITOR BOOKS	**Our Sunday Visitor** 200 Noll Plaza Huntington, IN 46750 **1-800-348-2440** E-mail us at: osvbooks@osv.com Visit us on the Web: http://www.osv.com

Your source for discovering the riches of the Catholic Faith